Ted Annemann

ANNEMANN'S CARD MAGIC

An Unabridged Republication of the Two Volumes
Edited by John J. Crimmins, Jr.

TED ANNEMANN'S
FULL DECK OF IMPROMPTU CARD TRICKS
and
ANNEMANN'S MIRACLES OF CARD MAGIC

With 48 Illustrations by
NELSON HAHNE

DOVER PUBLICATIONS, INC., NEW YORK

*"It's a fact that if you want to be a profes-
sional success, or amateur personality, you've
got to make people say, 'That's Joe Doakes,
he's a great entertainer!'—not, 'I know a
magician; his name is Doakes.' And if you
think I'm kidding, read up on the life of
Houdini, and Barnum."*

Gabbatha!

THEO. ANNEMANN

Note:

*Ted Annemann's Full Deck of Impromptu
Card Tricks* begins on page iii.
Annemann's Miracles of Card Magic begins
on page 79.

Published in Canada by General Publishing Company,
Ltd., 30 Lesmill Road, Don Mills, Toronto, Ontario.
Published in the United Kingdom by Constable and
Company, Ltd.

Annemann's Card Magic, first published by Dover Publications, Inc., in 1977, is an unabridged and slightly
corrected republication of the following two works, both
originally selected from *The Jinx* magazine and edited
by John J. Crimmins, Jr., and published by Max Holden
in New York in the years indicated:
Ted Annemann's Full Deck of Impromptu Card Tricks,
1943.
Annemann's Miracles of Card Magic, 1948.

International Standard Book Number: 0-486-23522-X
Library of Congress Catalog Card Number: 77-075234

Manufactured in the United States of America
Dover Publications, Inc.
180 Varick Street
New York, N.Y. 10014

TED ANNEMANN'S FULL DECK OF IMPROMPTU CARD TRICKS

A Few Words . . . .

Card effects, such as the ones which follow, are to be welcomed at any time for that impromptu type of "do something" trick which every perpetrator of magic is called upon to do —generally at off moments when the favorite gimmick is in another suit. Just learn a few of them and you'll be ready at the drop of a hat to pick up your host's deck and maintain your reputation.

These 52 tricks were favorites with Ted Annemann and the majority bear the earmarks of his genius for substituting subtlety where difficult sleights would ordinarily have been called for. Among the effects are contributions by such famous card men as Dai Vernon, Dr. Daley, Jean Hugard, Al Baker, Audley Walsh, Stewart Judah, and many others. All the tricks bear Annemann's endorsement as well as the acclaim of the readers of the early issues of THE JINX Magazine, now out of print.

We know you'll enjoy doing these tricks, as each one has been streamlined to obtain the maximum of effect with the minimum of effort. We feel sure, too, that you will prize this collection of 52 impromptu card tricks and that this book will prove to be one of the most popular books in your library.

MAX HOLDEN

J. J. CRIMMINS, JR.

CONTENTS

Extemporaneous Magic

THE CARD ON THE CEILING
TED ANNEMANN

For those who might like to try this card effect (which is one of the most effective of all card tricks) I can give a most practical bit of information. Get a small, sample size salve tin with cover. Into it put some Woolco Paste, obtainable in nice large jars from Woolworth stores—for a dime.* Be sure that it doesn't come to the top of the tin. Just carry this around for the time when you'll need it. Opportunity arising, remove the top, transfer it to the bottom and keep in your right trouser pocket. With the tin not too full, the paste won't start sticking up things.

Use any deck—have the card selected and replaced. Get it to the top and ask if anyone has a suggestion as to how you might find it. The stall serves you well. Your right hand drops to your pocket and the second finger gets a dab of paste which is then applied to the back of the top card. Now, remark that you have an idea (it will be more bizarre than any offered). Give the deck a last minute dovetail shuffle leaving the sticky card on the top. Hold in right hand with second finger and thumb at the ends. Throw flatwise to ceiling with a little twist to the right as you let it go. The circular or rotary motion of pack is what assures a nice flat contact—the deck falls and the card is there for all to see and remark about until the janitor or house boy gets a ladder. This particular paste works better than soap, etc., and all those things which have been written about before. And for the first time I think I've brought out the partial spin of the deck which makes this effect a sure thing.

It will save you a lot of time and trouble in getting the knack of the throw if, when you practice, you tie the deck each way several times with thread.

*Unchanged from 1943 edition. Almost any strong paste can be used.

THE UNDERCOVER MYSTERY

TED ANNEMANN

This effect has all the elements of the type of trick which will be long remembered by your audience. It is ideal for an impromptu "quickie" in a bar, cafe or anywhere that a tray is available.

Effect: Borrow a deck of cards and have two selected. Now ask for a tray and drop it, bottom up, on the floor. Ask for the name of one of the selected cards and drop the deck onto the tray causing this first selected card to reverse itself on the top of the deck. Drop the deck a second and third time, but the second selected card refuses to make an appearance. However, as a finale, someone lifts up the tray and finds the second card face up on the floor beneath the tray.

Method: First have two cards chosen and returned to the deck. It is now necessary to get one of them to the top and the other to the bottom of the deck. Probably the easiest is to have both cards returned to the deck together, then insert the

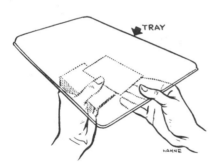

little finger and make the pass. Remember which is on top and which is on the bottom. Now hold the deck in your left hand by the side with the thumb at the face of the deck and the fingers across the top. Have the deck well into the thumb and first finger crotch. Ask for the tray and take it up side down with the right hand, fingers underneath and thumb on the upper (bottom) side. Step back a little, as if looking for a good spot on the floor. At the same time bring the hands together so that the tray covers the left hand which turns the deck face up. The left thumb now slides off the face card and it is grasped by the right fingers on the under side of the tray.

Apparently finding a good spot, drop the tray down flat from a standing position letting the card go with it. If you just let it go you have nothing to worry about. And it is a very disarming bit of business. Exlain at this point that you use a metal tray because it will work only on metal and not on a wooden floor or surface. Ask the person whose card is still on top of the deck to name it. Drop the deck onto the tray and the named card flips face up. This is merely the age old trick of sliding the top card sidewise about half an inch so that the air will flip it face up as the deck drops. Many know it but it is a build up for the finish. Pick up the cards and ask the name of the second card. Drop the deck again but this time nothing happens. Try it once again and then hand the deck to the spectator and ask him to take out his card. He can't find it and, as a climax, you have him lift up the tray and his card is looking right up at him.

No one even remembers that you put the tray down and I've had them swear they put it down themselves. And the wise ones who know the air current flip over are given something to think about when the finish comes.

THE WALK AROUND DISCOVERY

TED ANNEMANN

Whether or not this effect will be accepted as a "freak" trick as was my idea of finding a card by music, in "Sh-h-h--! It's a Secret," I don't know. However, I do know that this brain storm has garnered much applause, and not a little talk when performed in front of goodly sized groups of people.

It consists only of effect and little else, but to date it has not failed to get a laugh when the "walk-around" begins. It is so unlooked for, and so unexpected, that it evidently appears funny that one should try and find a card in that manner. But, as those who make a living before the public know, the out of the ordinary effects are those that are remembered longest, and build up reputations for the performers first to do them.

Effect: From the viewpoint of the audience, a card is selected, returned as usual, but then the deck is placed face down on the floor and spread around over the area of about one square yard. Now the performer starts WALKING AROUND IN A CIRCLE ON TOP OF THE CARDS! He asks that the selector concentrate upon his chosen card and imagine the performer walking over it, coming closer and closer to it with each circle he makes. Suddenly the performer stops. Saying that he is quite sure the chosen card is under his right foot as it stands, he kneels on his left knee, lifts his right foot a bit and removes from beneath, a card which he keeps face down and places it, still face down, to one side. The cards on the floor are picked up and the spectator who selected one is asked to name it aloud. Turning the oddly located card over, the performer shows it to be the actual one originally selected!

Method: So that's my story, and I'll stick by it. Use any ordinary deck. Just before starting in to work, put a piece of magician's wax, or better still, a piece of diachylon (lead plaster) wax, about the size of a pea, about an inch from the instep towards the toe on the sole of your right shoe. When this is stepped on, it flattens out to about the size of a quarter. And don't worry about walking on it. It may pick up dirt and dust, but it will be ready when you need it. Have the deck shuffled and a card removed. Take the deck back as you hand the spectator a pencil to mark the card. Then have the card replaced, and in your own way get the pasteboard to the top of the deck. After a riffle shuffle or two, leaving the top card in place, put the deck

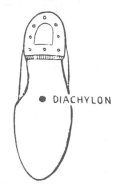

DIACHYLON

on the floor with your right hand, and spread it rather evenly toward the right in a long, straight spread, Now move towards the spread a bit, and turn your body slightly to the left. Your right foot comes directly on top of the right hand end card, you figuring to get the wax on about the center of the card's back. By doing this, part of the card will be sticking out under instep. As your foot covers the card, your right and left hands, scatter the row of cards in each direction, until they cover about a good square yard of space. Thus, no one ever sees you deliberately put your foot on the deck, or obviously steal away a card. Now walk over the cards in a circle, and watch the reaction of the audience.

You go through the business of telling the spectator to think very hard of his card and that you will try to stop near it. Let your audience know, in this case, about what you are doing. Suddenly it occurs to you to stop, or so it seems to the watchers. You state that you are sure the card is beneath your foot. Now kneel on the left knee, raise your right foot at the heel, and your left hand goes under your instep on the protruding end of the card and presses it to the floor as your foot is removed. Thus, it is not seen that the card is, or has been attached to your foot. Hand it face down to someone or put it face down. to one side. Before standing, scrape the cards together if you wish, or leave them for your assistant. Then have the card named, show it, and return it to the selector. As I said in the beginning, you'll actually have to try it before you will be completely convinced of its value.

LOCATRIX

TED ANNEMANN

A simple method of location is that which follows. The basic principle together with the disclosure make an exceptionally clean stunt, and while the principle is not new it has been enlarged upon to the point where it will confuse even those who are acquainted with or have used the old, single key card idea.

Effect: The deck is handed to a spectator while the performer turns his back. He requests that the person deal the cards face down into a pile, singly and silently, and to stop dealing at any time that he pleases. At such a time, he is told to look at the top card of either the pile he is holding or the pile on the table, then to place the two packets of cards together and cut the assembled deck a couple of times.

Turning around for the first time, the performer takes the cards, glances through them, and finally says that it may be easier to locate the card while the pack is behind his back. Putting the cards behind his back for a moment, he remarks that he has it at last, and the deck is brought around and placed face down on the table. The spectator names the pasteboard he orginally noted, and the performer discloses it correctly and without a chance of failure.

Method: While this is not a sensational trick, you will find it one of those nice impromptu effects that is easy to remember and to present at a moment's notice. The top and bottom cards are noted and remembered as keys before the deck is handed out. It will be seen from the above directions, which are given very carelessly, that the spectator receives the impression he does just about what he pleases. He stops dealing when he desires, looks at the card on the top of either heap, puts it back on either heap, and places the two piles together and cuts. And there is no chance that he may do the wrong thing as far as the performer is concerned.

On running through the pack, the performer looks only for the card to the RIGHT or under each of the remembered key cards. One of these is the noted card without fail. Both are brought to the top of the deck and, remembering the top one, the performer states that it may be easier to locate the card behind his back. The deck is placed behind his back for a moment and the top card is pushed, face up, into the center of the deck. The hands are brought to the front again and the deck is laid face down on the table as the spectator names his card. The performer formally discloses it, either by turning over the top card or by spreading the deck on the table to reveal the face up pasteboard in the center of the spread.

AUDLEY WALSH COINCIDENCE

Effect: Have a deck in hand for following these para-graphs to make it much easier. In effect, the performer gen-uinely shuffles a borrowed deck and fans them face down. One after the other, four people (two alternately, or even one) sel-ect any card freely by pulling it only half out of the fan. These are openly shifted to the bottom of the deck which is handed a watcher who puts these four bottom cards face down on the table in a row. As yet no one has seen their faces. The spect-ator is asked to run through the deck and remove the four Aces so that you may show him a great coincidence! The Aces are gone and found on the table! That's the coincidence! Taking the deck you ask one person to give you the Aces one at a time in his favorite order, and you place each one at different spots in the deck face down. Giving the pack a shuffle or two, you deal four hands of poker and turning them over, you have the four Aces. This makes a nice, quick bit of work and there is nothing difficult at all.

Presentation: Have the four Aces on the bottom of the deck to start. Dovetail shuffle and keep them there. Now fan the deck and have four cards pulled out a little more than half way. Close the deck with these cards protruding at front. The left thumb and second finger hold the sides of the deck at the front end from below with the first finger curled up against the bottom. With the right second finger tap the front edges of the protruding cards to make them even and sticking out about an inch and a half. The right thumb and

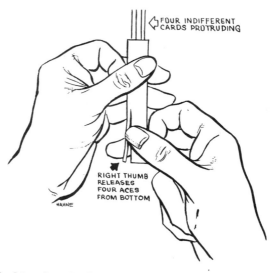

FOUR INDIFFERENT CARDS PROTRUDING

RIGHT THUMB RELEASES FOUR ACES FROM BOTTOM

HAHNE

second finger now holds the deck at the sides near the rear end and as you remark about the freedom of choice and the coincidence you want to show them, the right thumb counts off four or more cards from the bottom. The right hand raises the pack just a trifle and this group is held by the left thumb and the second finger at the front end. This hand immediately moves forward with the packet under the protruding cards and the thumb and second finger grasp the front edges of the protruding four. Now the right hand pulls the deck from these cards held by the left hand and drops it on top.

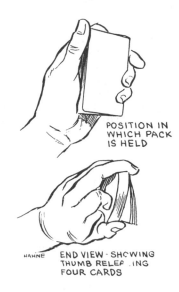

POSITION IN WHICH PACK IS HELD

HAHNE END VIEW - SHOWING THUMB RELEASING FOUR CARDS

The illusion of it all is quite perfect. Onlookers only see you square and pull out the four chosen cards, putting them on the bottom of the pack.

The spectator now takes the deck and puts the four bottom cards face down on the table in a row. He looks through the deck for the Aces, at your request, and then is told to turn over the tabled cards, taking the deck you hold it face down in your left hand with the left thumb at the upper left corner, so that it may riffle the corner downward. The pack is really held tightly between the base of the thumb on one side and the fingers on the other. Ask for the Aces singly and in any order. The left thumb riffles down three cards and taking the first Ace face down you carelessly insert it about half way at this point, but sticking out a little to the left also. This covers the thumb completely which riffles three more cards while the second Ace is handed to you. Stick this in the pack apparently at random and continue letting three cards go by your thumb for the third Ace and again for the last Ace. Put the Aces in carelessly so that they stick out at angles and at different lengths and it is very convincing.

Now dovetail shuffle leaving the top 16 cards in place, make a false cut if possible, and deal out four poker hands. You must get the Aces because you put them in the proper places. This is an extremely neat table routine for clubs. In the first part be certain that your audience appreciates the fact that the selection is perfectly free and not forced. If you remark at the outset that four different cards are needed in order to show a strange coincidence, no one will ever suspect what is going to happen. In the second part do the bit of thumb riffling each time as the spectator is picking up an Ace and you are watching him.

UP AND DOWN

DAI VERNON

While this trick is not wholly original, the method of handling makes it a self contained mystery, and does away with the older way of dealing the cards into table piles, a procedure that is quite boring and mechanical looking.

Effect and Routine: From any deck the performer deals 20 cards and the Joker. While a spectator shuffles the 20 cards, the performer runs through the rest of the deck and removes two cards which he places face down in front of two of his audience. He now hands the Joker to one spectator who inserts it anywhere in his packet of 20 cards, then fans through the packet and notes the card in back of, or to the LEFT of the Joker. He closes the cards and hands them to the second spectator who fans through them and notes the card in front of, or to the RIGHT of the Joker. He closes the fan of cards and cuts them a time or two.

Taking the packet, the performer holds the cards with faces towards the first person and says he will run through, putting one up and one down, and the spectator is to note whether or not his card goes in the UP bunch or the DOWN bunch. The cards are held in the left hand with their backs towards the performer as he separates the cards as follows: The right hand takes the top card from the back of the packet, calling it UP. The next card is taken by the right hand in front of the first card, but DOWN about half way so that it covers the lower half of the first card. The next card goes in front also but is an UP card and thus squares with the first card. The fourth card is DOWN, squaring with the second card. Continue this maneuver throughout the packet, and at the finish, just pull out the bottom interlacing bunch and drop them on top of the face down upper group. Regardless of whether the spectator sees his card or not, or where, that part is just a blind. Now repeat the same thing with the second person. This idea does away with all dealing of cards on a table.

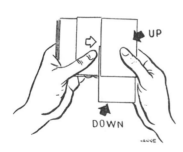

At the finish of the second time through, fan the deck face toward someone and have him remove the Joker from wherever it is. All through the effect you emphasize that you never see the faces of the cards. When the Joker is taken out, cut the deck at that spot. Count off the top ten cards (don't disarrange them) saying that you will divide the packet in half, and put them, face down, in front of the first person. Put the remaining ten cards in front of the second person. Now state that before any selections were made, you placed a single card face down in front of each person and that these are "prophecy" cards and will indicate where the selected cards are to be found. Turn over the first of these "prophecy" cards—it's a 5 spot! Openly count down in the first man's packet and hold the fifth card face down. He names his selection, you turn up the card you are holding and it is correct! Turn over the second man's "prophecy" card. It is a 6 spot! Count down and hold the sixth card in his packet. He names it and you are correct again!

You should like this feat because it's clean and neat, working automatically. Just put down a 5 and 6 spot for the two prophecies. Follow through as described and everything is bound to work.

WISE GUY CATCH
S. WIMBROUGH

Effect: Hand a man a deck of cards. He stands in front of the audience and holds them face down behind his back. You tell him to remove any card from within the deck, keep his eyes tightly closed, and while thus incapacitated bring the card around, still with its back to the audience, touch it to his forehead for a second and then put it safely into his back pocket.

He can't (and doesn't) know what it is. You can't possibly read his mind because of that. And yet, after he opens his eyes, you tell him to pick out any person in the front row of those watching and ask him to name a card. THAT PERSON NAMES THE CARD HE HAS IN HIS POCKET!

Method: Aptly named, this effect is one of those ideas to be kept in the mind for the wise guy who always seems to pop up. Just before handing the deck to this ever present type of obnoxious personality, simply reverse the top and bottom cards. Following your directions as given above he provides the whole audience (let alone the front row) with the name of the card he has chosen, for upon putting it to his forehead (while his eyes are closed) IT IS FACING THE AUDIENCE AND THEY ALL BECOME AWARE OF ITS IDENTITY. He then puts it into his pocket from where it is subsequently removed much to his discomfiture.

A STORY OF CRIME

TED ANNEMANN

One of my favorite "story tricks" for many years is the one I'm describing here together with the patter angle, which is really the most interesting part of it all.

First I'll give the effect, then the method, and finally the story. But, as I've said, the story is the dressy and all important part. A card is chosen, returned, and the deck shuffled by a spectator. Running through the cards face out ,the performer removes the four Aces. These are shown separately and singly. The spectator cuts the deck at the center, and the four Aces are replaced, face up, at this spot, and the cut is replaced. The deck is not even picked up from the table, but for effect it's given a bit of riffling with one hand. The deck is spread face down and in the center are the four face up Aces—BUT among them now is seen a face down card. The fan of five cards is removed. The spectator names the chosen card, the fan is turned over and the card in the center, mysteriously located, is the chosen one.

Method: So much for the effect without the story. You'll have to take your cards in hand to get the working in a practical manner. The card is selected and returned and is brought either to the top or the bottom by your favorite method. If to the bottom, glimpse it, cut the deck and give it to a spectator for shuffling. If brought to the top, do the same. In other words, all you need at this point is the name of the card. I vary this sometimes by forcing the card, then give the deck to the assisting spectator and ask him to replace the card himself and give the pack a good shuffle.

After the shuffle, take the deck, and pattering about finding four cards which will represent four prominent men I run through the cards and cut the first Ace to the bottom. Suggest that you will use the Aces to represent the people. Now go right through the deck again looking for the selected card as well as the other three Aces. Each time you reach one, snap it loudly to the bottom or face of the deck. Your audience hear you get only four cards to the face of the deck which they believe to be the four Aces (however, ONE of these 4 cards you've so openly found is the selected card). Now take these five bottom cards in a bunch from the deck, which is placed aside for the moment. Hold the packet of five face down and, as you remark that you will use the four Aces and introduce them as people, shift one or two from the top to the bottom of the packet so to bring the chosen card to the top or back of the bunch. Now hold the packet face out in your left hand, with the fingers at the bottom side, the thumb at the top and the forefinger at the outer end.

With the second finger of your right hand, slide off towards you the first Ace which is on the face of the packet and put it on the table or the floor, face up. Do the same with the second and the third Ace. Count them as one, two, three and four as you do so. The last card, however, is grasped at the ends with the right second finger and thumb and put on top of the others. You have thus counted and shown four Aces. Pick up the packet and hold it face down in your left hand, with all the fingers at one side and the thumb and its base at the other. Now remark that you will introduce the people in person.

Slide off the top card with your right thumb at the front end, turn it over, end for end, and square it face up on the packet. Mention who it is while the right second finger and thumb picks the card off by the ends and places it down on the table face up. Do the same with the next card, also naming it according to your patter. Turn the third Ace over in the same manner and explain who it represents. However, as you lift this card off you've got to steal the selected card along with it. Do it as follows: Take hold of the face up Ace with the right second finger and thumb, as before, at the ends but nearer to the right edge of the card. Hold firmly to the two top cards (the second one being the selected card and face down) while the left forefinger slides the bottom card—an Ace) out a bit on the left side. This frees the two top cards, and they are lifted as one card and laid on top of the pile on the table. Lastly the single card remaining in the left hand is turned over, face up, and named before adding it to the pile of Aces on the table.

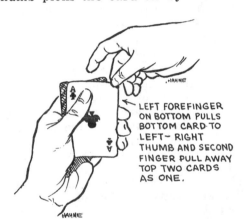

LEFT FOREFINGER ON BOTTOM PULLS BOTTOM CARD TO LEFT— RIGHT THUMB AND SECOND FINGER PULL AWAY TOP TWO CARDS AS ONE.

The spectator now cuts off half of the face down deck, and the pile of squared up Aces are placed, face up, on top of the lower half of the cut. The remaining cards are replaced, sandwiching the Aces in the center. The deck is now riffled without moving it from the table, and when it is spread out across the table an odd card is seen to be face down between the center Aces. The five are removed in a fan, and when the spectator names the identity of the murderer (the selected card) you turn the fan over and the right card flashes into view. Now go on with the patter, and you'll see, with the cards in your hand, how it all fits together and makes a smooth running story to cover the necessary action.

Patter Story: "This is a story of crime; a tale concerned with criminals and the law. The deck is to represent the underworld, and in it, there are 52 law makers and law breakers all trying to outwit each other. First, I want you to remove one card, and look at that card as a murderer of the worst type. A man who is the cause of a great manhunt. No one is to know the identity of this much wanted man but yourself. After you've seen his face, drop him back into the underworld. This shuffling is to show the shake-up in the police department after present officials have failed to capture the criminal. Perhaps someone else had better mix them too, though. You, sir, give them a shuffle, to prove that he's really lost in the dark alleys of iniquity, and is not being protected by politics.

At this time I want to introduce four great men in our story. These gentlemen are always trying to do their bit towards wiping out crime, and this will be a test of what they can do. I use the four Aces to represent these men, (when an Ace happens to be selected card, use the four Kings) and shall introduce them to you personally. Here are the Aces, one, two, three, and four. Introducing them singly, we have the Ace of .... (here, always use the same order of names, no matter what order of Aces), who is the Mayor of the metropolis in which we are living. Next we have the Ace of ...., who is the District Attorney. Then comes the Ace of ...., who is the Commissioner of Police, and lastly, the Ace of ...., who represents a reporter from the .... (localize the name of paper)............, for one must know what is going on.

If Mr. .... will now lift the lid from off the underworld for a moment, I'll place these four just men, with apologies to Edgar Wallace, in the middle. This action of riffling is supposed to represent great activity in police circles, while the manhunt is on and the criminal is being pursued. The drag-net is, of course, spread over the city, so we, in turn, spread the deck over the table, and here, deep in the underworld, we find the four men with a suspect between the District Attorney and Commissioner of Police. Who it may be, or how he got there, we don't know, but they picked him up somewhere. And now, Mr. ...., will you name, for the first time, the murderer? The .... Look, they've got him!

THE 32 CARD MYSTERY

AUDLEY WALSH

Effect: The performer borrows any deck and proceeds to deal four piles of eight cards each. The onlooker selects any one of these piles and, picking it up, the performer has him think of a card when they are fanned face outward. The four piles are grouped together and again dealt into four piles. Fanning each pile for the spectator to glance at, the performer asks him to state when he sees his thought of card. The others are discarded and this pile dealt into two rows of four cards, one under the other, and with all of the cards face down. The spectator indicates a row, then two cards in that row, and finally one card. He names his card thought of, turns over the one left on the table, and it proves to be the one!

Operation: This effect practically works itself with the exception of a simple bit of information which the performer gains at the outset. Follow the above primary maneuvre in the effect. Have one of the four piles selected. Pick it up and fan four of the cards face down in left hand and four in the right. Now ask the spectator to think of just one card that he sees. Lift the two fans together, hold them for a second and lower them again. You won't miss once in a hundred times knowing it which of the fans the card has been noted. When you drop the fans, put the one in which the noted card lies **under** the other. Reassemble the piles, putting one on top of the one in hand and drop this packet on top of both remaining piles. This routine is always followed. The cards may now be false shuffled and cut provided the order is not changed. Deal a row of four cards face down, on top of these another row and so on until the 32 cards are again in four piles of eight cards each. Pick up each of the piles and fan them facing the spectator. When he sees his cards he says so whereupon the other three piles are discarded. Now deal this pile of eight face down into two rows of four each from left to right, one row under the other. The selected card will **always** be in the lower left corner. Have the spectator indicate a row, then two cards in that row, and finally one of the two left. In each case, the well known dodge of either leaving or discarding the row or cards selected is resorted to and the last card left on the table is the one the spectator thought of. This effect, smartly worked, is clean cut and but one trial will convince you of its value as an impromptu table trick.

THE CARD ANGLER

STUART ROBSON

Effect: The performer has the usual card selected, marked, and returned to the pack which is shuffled and dropped into a hat for further mixing, as the magician says, in order that they may be shaken around without the possibility of being controlled by the hands.

From his pocket the performer now takes a roll of ribbon about two feet long, and unrolling it, may tie one end to his wand or a table knife to represent a fishing pole of sorts. The end of the line is lowered into the hat, and the performer asks the spectator to name the selected card.

Slowly the line is raised, and dangling on the very end is seen the chosen card with its face to the audience. Removing it, the performer gives it to the selector as a souvenir of a magical fishing trip, and suggests that the owner may now have his catch stuffed and mounted as a trophy.

Method: The effect is quite new and original, and the working is too clean for words. The selection and return of the card is done in the regular way, and the chosen and marked card then is passed to the top of the deck in the usual way.

A felt hat or derby is now taken and the deck dropped face down inside. Any amount of side or circular shaking will not mix the cards a bit, but the audience can hear them hitting against the sides and it is all very realistic. The performer can always see the top card staying right there. Put the hat on a chair or table so that one end of the chosen card is pointing towards the audience.

The ribbon used should be of half inch wide stock, and preferably red in color. At one end make a half inch fold, and in this pocket sew three bee-bee shot.

At any Dennison store or stationery house, get a fifteen cent roll of Scotch Cellulose Tape, manufactured by the Minnesota Mining and Mfg. Co.* Get the half-inch size in red. This is positively the greatest sticking medium on the market to-day, bar none. Take a one inch length of the tape and let it curl naturally. It will curl with the adhesive side outward.

Now stick the tape onto the ribbon end which is weighted, so that the curl of the half inch left free reaches one-eight inch below the end of the ribbon. Roll the ribbon loosely from the unweighted end, and have it in your pocket or at hand.

Proceed with the effect as described. Tie the ribbon to a wand or knife with the adhesive at the rear. When you lower the line into the hat, have the end of the ribbon meet the chosen card as near as possible to the front end. Don't jerk it or work fast but let it rest surely on the card. Now raise the card out slowly, remove and return it. Just a touch of the adhesive is necessary and it is surprising how it works.

*Unchanged from 1943 edition. Prices have risen and are likely to continue changing.

ACES OF EIGHT!!

OTIS MANNING

This is one of those rare effects wherein the performer does it all and never requires the taking of a card. It is simple, the sleights are nil, and the routine, while not astounding, is neat and gives the impression of great skill with the pasteboard. It is impromptu and uses only eight aces. Remove the aces from two decks, and while the backs of all should be alike, in a pinch backs of the same color will do. If a pinochle deck is handy, take the eight aces from it.

Routine: The eight aces are laid face up on the table. Calling attention to the fact that there are two aces of each suit, they are gathered up and the spectators are allowed to square cut as often as desired. Placing the cards behind his back, the performer, by sense of touch, brings them out in pairs of like suits. Again they are gathered and cut. This time the performer states that he will bring them out in like colors but different suits. For the third time the cards are placed together and cut. This time he states he will bring them out in pairs of red and black each. The fourth time the cards are picked up and the performer says that mixing means nothing as any of them can be found by the sense of touch. He cuts the cards a few times and then spells them off, moving a card at a time from top to bottom and spelling R-E-D, turning the last card face up on the table. It is red! He then spells B-L-A-C-K in the same manner and the last card turns up black. This is continued through the packet until the last card is left, which is black. For the last time the cards are assembled and cut several times by the spectators. Putting them behind his back, the performer instantly brings both hands to the front and in one hand are the red aces while in the other are the black ones.

Method: A routine like the above makes a very clever effect for close up parties and night club tables. The first three effects are worked by the same means.

First, all the Aces are face up on the table. Pick them up one at a time into a face up pile on your hand—Clubs, Hearts, Spades, Diamonds, Clubs, Hearts, Spades, Diamonds. Just have the last four in the same suit order as the first four and have the colors alternated. Have the packet cut any number of times. Put the cards behind your back face down in your left hand, count down four cards and hold a wide break with your left little finger. The right forefinger goes into the break and pulls off the top card of the lower packet and, at the same time, the second finger is on top of the first packet and the two cards can be drawn off together and tossed face up on the table. Repeat this three times and all suits come out in pairs.

The second time the pairs are picked up and placed face up on your left hand, but the colors are alternated—Red, Black, Red, Black. Again they are cut and the performer does the same as before behind his back. This time the colors are alike but the suits are different.

Throughout this routine always tell, as you put the cards behind your back, what you are going to do—then do it! The third time, pick up the two red piles and on these put the two black piles. Have the packet cut and repeat the action as before. This time each pair will be of mixed colors. Drop them on the table so they are scattered.

Pick them up and place them face up on your left hand in this order: a pair of reds, one black, a pair of reds, one black. Turn the packet face down and then pick up the remaining pair of blacks and drop them on top. This serves to apparently mix them a little more. Now cut or false shuffle them but don't disturb the arrangement. Spell out the colors as described above, starting with RED and laying the last card of each spelling face up on the table in a pile. The pile, at the finish, is thus evenly mixed as to color. Turn the pile face down and have it cut several times. Then place it behind your back. As they are alternately mixed it is only necessary for you to run them over, putting one on each side of your right index finger, and then bring out the two packets of separated colors. Learn it smoothly and do it as one continuous effect without stopping or hesitating. You'll like it!

WORTH KNOWING: An excellent substitute for a Card Shiner is "lacquer" nail polish. Paint an elongated circle upon the inner surface of the first joint of the left forefinger with this transparent polish. Apply smoothly, permit to dry, and apply a second coat if the "thumb prints" are too prominent. With a little experimenting it will be found that the indexes of cards may be easily read in this makeshift mirror. When the deck is held in the left hand and someone is allowed to open the cards at any point and note the index, a bit of handling will show how the reflection can be gotten to give you the card's identity. With the lacquer applied to the right forefinger, cards can be glimpsed as dealt from anyone's shuffled deck.—Dr. Ervin.

LES CARTES PAR HASARD

STUART P. CRAMER

Effect: The spectator gives his own deck a thorough mixing. The magician asks for the deck and riffling it before the spectator's eyes, requests him to glimpse and remember one. These is no force, the only important thing being to make him actually see a card and keep that card in mind.

Dealing the cards into four piles, the performer picks up each in turn, fans them towards the spectator so that he can get one more glimpse of the card to impress it more strongly on his mind. Each pile is cut, and all are stacked one inside of the other. In other words, pile No. 2 is sandwiched in before the cut is completed. This double pile is then cut for the insertion of another pile, and so on with the last. Now, for the first time, the performer looks at the faces of the cards. The mentally selected card can now be revealed by conversationally pumping, or else the spectator can name the card which is immediately shown, either in the performer's hand, reversed in the deck, on top, or on the bottom.

Method: The last sentence above gives it away. You end up with four cards, one of which is bound to be the chosen card. When you riffle the deck for the "sight" selection, you open the deck at about the middle. Riffle slowly as you ask him to think of some card that he sees, and ask at once if he has one. The card must be one of the 16 cards lying from the 9th to 24th inclusive from the top of the deck. Deal the cards in four piles. Fan them, face out, cutting each pile before placing it down. From the pile which contains the chosen card, cut TWO cards from the left side of the fan (bottom of pile), and place on top. Now, in picking up the piles and assembling them as described in the effect, the chosen pile is the last one. It is cut, and the rest of the deck is placed on the bottom half and the top half of cut replaced.

The chosen card will now be one of four cards, either the two on the top or the two on the bottom. Put the botton card in the deck reversed, so as to be face up; palm off the top one, and put the deck on the table. Having noted them in fanning through, you are now set for the finish, by asking for the name of the thought of card.

WORTH KNOWING: If you go in for chances, do your card tricks minus three cards—the 9 of Diamonds, the Ace of Spades and the 2 of Clubs. Whenever possible, ask the spectator to name a card rather than select one. The moment one of the above three is named, and it will happen, hand them the deck to be mixed. Cause the card selected to vanish from the deck they are holding and take it from your pocket. It stuns!

A PARADOX OF PAIRS

DR. JACOB DALEY

In this version of "You Do As I Do" only one deck is used and but a moment is needed for the preparation, if it can be called that.

Take any deck and note the two face cards as you hold them facing you. These should be preferably a red and a black card. Run through the deck and pass to the top or back of pack the two cards of same value and color. Thus, for example, the top and bottom cards might be the Fours of Clubs and Spades, and the second card from top and second card from the bottom might be the Tens of Hearts and Diamonds.

Start by dovetail shuffling the pack so as to retain the top and bottom pairs in their respective places. Then place the deck on the table and ask the spectator to cut it into two piles. At this point you pick up each half and shuffle it overhand style and there is a bit of skullduggery in this that is far from being difficult. Pick up the top half first and overhand shuffle, running the two top cards one at a time and shuffling the rest on top. This puts them on bottom in reversed order. Shuffle once more but the fingers (of the hand holding the cards) against the face or bottom card, hold it there while the rest of the under portion is drawn away and shuffled off on top to the last card which is left on top, and this half of pack is re-placed on the table. The other half is picked up and given only one shuffle. The fingers of the hand holding the cards rest against the face of the packet and retain the bottom card, while the under portion of the packet is drawn away and shuffled off on top to the last card. Replacing this half on the table, both halves are now apparently well mixed. However, the top card of each packet (if arranged as described before) is a red ten, and the bottom card of each is a black four. Up to this moment everything has been perfectly aboveboard as the deck was genuinely shuffled to start, then cut by a spectator, and each half shuffled again.

The spectator is asked to pick up a packet and you take the other. Each of you deal a card at a time into a face down pile together until the spectator wishes to stop. Immediately you prove that an unseen force is at work by turning each packet face up on the table and showing two red tens. Now you ask him to count the remainder of his cards onto the table singly in a pile and at the same time you do likewise. If he has the most, he is to place his top card (as deck stand now) face down on the table without looking at it. You turn over your top card (making a two card turnover), show it, turn it over again with back up and deal it on the table. Now he turns up his card and it is a black four. You looked surprised and say that to be correct your card should also be a black four. Turn your card over and it is seen to have changed to a four matching his card. If you had the larger packet in the counting, you merely do your turnover first and lay the card out, asking him to turn over his after and finish the same. If both packets have the same number of cards you call attention to the fact that he cut them himself and that the two packets have a strange attraction for each other. Any way you have him, the cards match and the number of cards in each pile only serves as the excuse for the counting to reverse the packets and make possible the last part of the trick.

THE PSYCHIC TOOTHPICK

TED ANNEMANN

Years ago I learned to do this magnetic effect with two toothpicks. Only lately did I apply it to the location of a card, and I found a new and perfect impromptu table trick You'd better carry a few toothpicks of your own, though, for the best places rarely have them, and for effect carry them in an impressive little box.

Effect and Routine: Put a toothpick on the table pointing directly at you.   Now put another on top of the first, at right angles, and balanced so that it doesn't touch the table at

either side. Stick your right index finger out straight, and rub it against your head for a second. Hold it an inch or so from the near side of the right end of balanced match. At the same time, open your lips just a thin trifle, and breath steadily and quietly. The balanced match will swing towards your finger as though it were a magnet. Practice this a few times until you get the swing of it. You'll find that very little breath is needed for the working. Now take two toothpicks from a little box of cotton and place them in the position just described. And make the toothpicks swing, as above, when you pass the selected and shuffled card over it. Watch the customers examine the toothpicks, which you then carefully put back in their box.

THE "ELM" CARD CHANGE

E. LESLIE MAY

For a quick close up and impromptu trick this one is hard to beat. It is far from being complicated and that alone helps make it great in the eyes of the audience. It can be done any time with any deck.

Effect: The spectator initials the face of a card he selects and replaces it in the pack. The performer now selects a card, initials it also and shows it to all. This he places in his own pocket and then gives the deck to the spectator to hold. This person now attempts to say where he thinks the two initialed cards are, but he is wrong, for when he ribbon spreads the deck on the table he finds the magician's card reversed in the center of the spread. Reaching into the performer's pocket the spectator finds his own initialed card!

Routine: Have someone shuffle the deck and remove a card. The performer takes back the deck as the spectator initials his selection. Holding the deck in his left hand, the performer takes the selected card in his right hand as he explains that to really put the card in to the deck at random he will do so with the cards behind his back. Both hands go behind his back for a moment and then the left hand brings the deck forward and one card is seen to be protruding about an inch near the center of the pack. This card is now pushed into the deck and lost. Actually, however, the chosen card is on the top of the deck, for when the deck was behind his back the performer drops the chosen card on TOP of the deck and, inserting his fingers in the center of the deck, pulled out another card part way.

Remarking that he will now take a card, the performer turns over the top card of the deck—really double lifting the two top cards. He initials the face up card, letting everyone see it. Now, while this card is still face up on the deck in his left hand, the right hand shows the right trouser pocket to be empty. The two face up cards, as one, are now turned face down on top of the deck. Then the left thumb pushes the top card off the deck about an inch, and the right hand as openly puts it in the right trouser pocket. Now under cover of cutting the deck, the top (performer's) card is reversed and the cut completed. The deck is at once handed to a spectator to hold.

Questioned as to the location of the cards the spectators will always be wrong. He is told to ribbon spread the deck across the table and there, staring up at him, is the reversed card initialed by the performer. As a finale he reaches into the performer's pocket and finds his own card.

THE CARD UNHARMED

TED ANNEMANN

I've been using this effect for several years as a press and publicity stunt. I can't claim it for myself as it is a variation of several ways, but it has got a strong climax and I've yet to run across anyone else using it.

Effect: When I do it, I ask for a business card as it is most effective when using the card of the witness. An ordinary letter envelope is used (6¾ size), and it is held open for the spectator to look into while he drops in his card. The envelope is sealed. Taking a pair of scissors you clip one end from the envelope, shake out the card, and then cut the other end off so that the portion left is about an inch shorter than the card itself. Now you put the card back in this makeshift tube so that about a half inch of each end of the card is sticking out.

Holding the envelope flatwise with the flap side up, your right hand takes the scissors and deliberately cuts the envelope in two— the left hand holding it so that the two pieces will not fall. I grip it firmly near one end with the left first and second fingers, and the other end between the thumb and third finger. Then I cut across between these two spots. The scissors are dropped and the envelope is held up with the flap side towards the spectator, the pieces still together. Slowly they are pulled apart and the card is seen perfectly whole and is returned to the spectator. The very strong part is that a borrowed card is used and its two ends are seen throughout.

Method: The envelope is faked by first cutting a slit with a razor blade across the address side from top to bottom (except for about one-eighth of an inch) in the center. Now the address side and flap are cut from another envelope and insert-

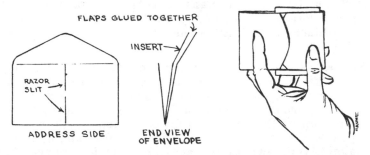

FLAPS GLUED TOGETHER

INSERT→

RAZOR SLIT →

ADDRESS SIDE

END VIEW OF ENVELOPE

ed into the whole one, the flaps being glued together. This envelope can be shown carelessly if the slit on the back is covered with the fingers, and the spectator sees nothing when he drops his card inside. After sealing, one end of the envelope is cut off short about an inch and a half to one side of the slit. The card is removed and the other end of the envelope is also cut off about an inch and a half on the other side of the slit. Now the card is re-inserted but in reality it goes through the back compartment on this occasion. Holding the envelope with the flap side up in the manner described above, the right hand takes the scissors. The lower and pointed side of the scissors is inserted under the envelope but above the card and the whole thing cut through. When the halves are then pulled apart, the card, whose ends have been constantly in view, is found unharmed.

I've used this so much, and found it to be such a perfect offhand stunt for committees and newsmen that I've gone to the trouble of faking up envelopes except for the slit, and mailed them to myself. Tear off one end, insert a piece of cardboard and make the slit. Carry several with you and, when ready to perform, take the envelope from your pocket, remove a dummy letter, and use the envelope for the trick. You'll find it well worth the small amount of trouble, and once used, you'll keep it on hand most of the time.

This effect can just as easily be done with a regular playing card, an automobile driver's card, a lodge card or any personal card belonging to the spectator. The apparent mutilation strikes right home!

RESTLESS COLORS

F. JACKSON

Effects that get away from the all too common "Take a card" theme are none too many. This is very much on the usual lines where a packet of red cards changes place with a packet of black cards, but the changes are numerous and more confusing.

Effect and Routine: Ten (say) red cards are shown, but attention is not called to their number. They are placed face down on your left hand, the third finger being inserted under the two top cards. Ten black cards are shown and apparently placed on top of the red cards for a moment while the right hand pushes the remainder of the deck to one side, as it is not used again. Unknown to the audience, the left fingers have tilted the two red top cards open bookwise and the black cards were dropped on the remaining (8) red cards, the left fingers immediately closing and depositing the two red cards on top of the blacks.

The positions of the cards from back to face are two reds, ten blacks, 8 reds. The performer fans the entire left hand packet, faces towards himself to separate the colors, but he cuts so that the top two cards of each packet are of the opposite color to the remaining ones. Both piles are placed side by side on the table and face upwards. Now in order to prove that each pile contains, only cards of one color, the performer goes through the following moves which are explained in Stanley Collins' Four Ace Trick.

Each pile is taken in turn, face down in the left hand. The cards are dealt from the bottom of the pile with the right hand until six have been dealt face up on the table. Then comes an important move. The 7th card is drawn back by the second finger of the left hand and the right hand takes the 8th, 9th and 10th cards as one and deals them on the face up pile. The remaining card is carelessly flicked and placed face up on the pile. The same routine is followed with the second packet. The two piles are now arranged thusly: Pile 1 (from back to face): 6 red cards, 2 blacks, 2 reds. Pile 2: 6 black cards, 2 red, 2 black. Any other moves which might bring about this position could be used.

The face card of each pile is now removed and placed, still face up, in front of its pile. The two piles themselves are now turned faced down, and it is explained that the two face up cards have a great influence over the piles and they are always in sympathy.

First the two face up cards are transposed. Then the two piles are picked up in turn, put face down in left hand, and by means of the glide, the second card from the bottom of each pile is dealt face up to apparently prove the packets have followed their indicator cards and also changed. The exposed cards are transposed again, but this time it is only necessary to deal the bottom cards to prove again that the packets have done the same. This is repeated once again, and still it works. For the last time the performer then transposes the exposed colors, and causes them to change, this time turning over the packets and letting the rest of the cards be seen in each.

It is suggested that no distinctive cards such as Ace, Kings, etc., be used, and at no time should attention be called to the number of cards in use. After the "glide" there is no further use of sleights as the remainder of the routine works automatically. For large audiences a small display stand can be used, and the placing of this offers a good excuse for combining the packets at the start.

THE TORN DECK TRICK

JULIAN PROSKAUER

When "Sawing a Woman in Half" was in vogue, Mr. Proskauer introduced a striking card trick which he called "Sawing a Deck in Half." Through the years he has added several points to this trick until today the effect is as follows:

Effect: An unopened pack of cards is handed to someone in the audience who breaks the seal, removes the pack and gives it a good shuffle. A card is now selected and across its face is written the name of the person making the selection so that there will be no question of the cards' identification later. The card is then returned and the pack given a good shuffle. The magician now cuts the deck in half and places the halves at opposite ends of the table. The assistant chooses one half which he picks up, while the other half is picked up by the performer. The magician then bids the assistant to do as he does, and proceeds to tear his packet of cards in half. The assistant does likewise after a struggle. Mixing all the pieces of both halves, the magician commences to discard the torn cards, piece by piece, and asks someone to stop him at any time. When they call "Stop," he lays that piece on the table, and then continues discarding more pieces until he is stopped a second time. Adding this second piece to the one on the table, he holds them both up and they not only match, but turn out to be the card originally selected—still bearing the name of the person who drew the card.

Routine: Any deck may be used, and if it is a new one in cellophane wrappers the effect is all the stronger. After the card is selected, you hand a pencil to the assistant with instructions to "Write your name on this card so that we may identify it later." The card is replaced, brought to the top and retained there while the deck is given a good shuffle. The deck is now cut into two portions and one placed at each end of the table, as a spectator is given his choice of either portion. Of course, this is a "magician's choice" and you force him to take the lower half of the cut while you pick up the half with the selected card on top. Now say to the assistant "Do as I do," and proceed to tear your portion in half. This brings a good laugh for usually the assistant "stalls." If he does tear his half it's still a good thing for you to pick up all the pieces and mix them with your piece, always keeping the halves of the selected card on the top of all. Now divide the handful of pieces into 2 portions, retaining one half of the selected card on top of each portion. The rest is simply showmanship and presentation! Pick up one portion of the torn cards and begin to discard the halved cards onto the floor, one at a time, requesting someone to call "Stop" at any time. Second deal as you discard so that when "Stop" is called you can lay aside the first half of the selected card which you have retained on the top of the packet. Let the rest of this handful of cards trickle to the floor. Now pick up the second portion of cards and repeat the same maneuver, laying aside the second half of the selected card when "Stop" is called again. Discard the remainder of the torn cards. Pick up the two halved cards laying on the table, match them and read off the autograph written on its face, proving it the very same card originally selected. Pass them out for identification if you wish.

A CARD IN FLIGHT!

BOB HUMMER

Effect: After having a card selected, the performer very openly drops the deck into a borrowed hat or receptacle. Asking the person how many spots were on the noted card, the perfomer reaches into the hat and pretends to take out that number of spots and flips them away. The spectator is now asked to remove the deck and see if his card is there, but it has vanished! Another spectator raises the window curtain and, astonishingly enough, the selected card is seen to be sticking to the outside of the window looking in!!

Method: If in a home where it is possible, steal two cards from the owner's deck—the Two of Spades and the Two of Clubs. Excusing yourself at some opportune moment, plant the Two of Spades for the climax between the upper and the lower frames of the window on the outside. Fake the club card by sticking to it two small triangles of black paper with saliva. These pieces, over the club pips, turn them into spade spots. Jet black paper cut from the newspaper ads is ideal, because when it is moistened it sticks well and will roll into minute pellets. Add this card to the deck upon your return and force it any way you please but don't let the spectator look at it himself. Take it from him and step back, holding the card so all but you can see the face of it. This little distance prevents a close inspection, but at three feet the card is certainly a spade. Drop the card on the deck and give it an overhand shuffle which leaves the fake Two of Spades on the bottom. Drop the deck into the hat face up and ask the number of spots on the chosen card. Reach in, and taking one piece of paper, roll it into a pin head ball between your fingers and flick it away over your shoulder. Do the same with the second spot and again with the third. Tip the deck out onto the table face down and have the card looked for by the spectator. It has gone and you are ready for the finale with the card being found looking in through the window.

THE SPECTATOR'S CHOICE

STEWART JUDAH

Here is a cute impromptu effect which can be done at any moment and should find favor with more than a few.

Effect and Routine: Deal out six heaps of five cards each, face down. The spectator now picks out any two cards from the rest of the deck and places one each on top of two of the six heaps. He then writes down the names of these two cards on a piece of paper which is placed on the table writing side down. As he is doing the writing, you gather up the six heaps so that two of the five card heaps go on each of the six card heaps. Place these two packets together, making one packet.

Remarking that you will select two cards from those picked up, you fan spread the packet in your hands and note the eleventh and the twenty-seventh card from the face of the packet as you fan them from left to right. You now write the names of these two cards (the 11th and 27th) on a second piece of paper and place it writing side down on the opposite corner of the table.

Now deal out the cards in two face down heaps, one card at a time, beginning at your left and alternating. The heap on your left now contains the spectator's cards, and the heap on the right contains your cards. Tell the spectator he is too choose either your pair of cards or his, and whichever he chooses you will contrive to leave on the table at the finish of the trick. If he chooses his cards, discard the right hand packet, and pick up the left pile and redeal the cards exactly as at first. Discard the right hand packet, and redeal again and continue this redealing and discarding of the right pile until only two cards are left in the left hand pile. These two will be his cards. Do not turn them up however, until you have the spectator read off the names of the two cards he wrote on the slip of paper.

Emphasize that he has had a free choice throughout. If he points to your slip, or says to use your cards, follow the same routine as outlined—but discard the left pile each time. If he points to the slip which contains the names of his cards and then points to the heap on the table which contains your cards, tell him that the two cards named on the slip will be the one left behind and that you will follow his choice and discard the right hand pile throughout. No matter how his choice goes, you have him beaten!

QUEER QUEST

STEWART JAMES

This trick has a stunning effect, is strictly impromptu and should be presented as a mind-reading test more than a card feat.

Effect: Any deck is handed to a spectator to shuffle; he then turns his back, removes any card and puts it in his pocket. The performer takes the deck, and hands it immediately to a second person who also gives the deck a shuffle. This person then cuts off a bunch of cards, looks at the face card of the cut off packet and holds these cards against his body for the time being. The performer takes the remainder of the deck and hands it to a third person for mixing. Taking them back, the performer fans them facing this third spectator who is asked to think of any card he sees in the fan. The deck is assembled and the three selected cards are located by the performer.

Routine: Everything is strictly fair up to the third person's selection. In fanning through this packet, the performer silently counts the number of cards in it. We'll assume there are 22 cards. He also notes the face card of the packet and remembers these two points. He now hands this packet to the second spectator and tells him to put it either on the top or on the bottom of the bunch he is holding, and then cut the deck twice.

At this time, the performer states that he is desirous of having the three cards together in the pack so that all three minds will come together at one point rather than three, thus making the location easier. The third person is given the deck and asked to run through the cards, remove his mentally chosen one and hand it to the second person. The first person is asked to take his chosen card from his pocket and also give it to the second person. Now the second person is asked to take the deck, locate his own card and put the other two selected cards next to his, one on each side. Closing up the deck, he cuts it several times more and hands it to the performer.

The performer takes the deck and fans through it, face towards him. He first locates the key card he has remembered and cuts it to the face or bottom of the deck. Then, counting from the face towards the back of the deck, and including the bottom card, he counts to the 22nd card (the number of cards he counted in the third man's group). The 22nd card, the 23rd card and the 24th card are thus the three selected cards, with the second man's card in the middle of the three. These three cards ar now cut to the top in that order.

Snap the top of the deck and tell the second man you have

his card. He names it and you show it by making a double lift and turning the two top cards over and placing them face up on top of the deck.

The left hand holding the deck now turns over so that the 2nd person's card, just shown, now faces the floor. The right fingers reach under the deck, withdraws the card just shown, reverses it and replaces it back on the deck in the same spot from where it was withdrawn. Now when the pack is righted again, by turning the left hand, the above maneuver has resulted in covering the second of the two cards originally reversed on top of the deck by the double lift. That card is now face up, second from the top and is cut to the middle and glimpsed with a left thumb riffle.

Knowing what the remaining two selected cards are (one of which is reversed) the performer asks a question regarding the suit or color of the first person's card to find out which of the two known cards is his. If the first person's card is not the reversed one, turn to the third person and ask him to think hard and name his card. As soon as he names it, fan the deck and reveal his card reversed in the center of the fan.

Now cut the deck IMMEDIATELY UNDER the reversed card and place the bottom stock on top. This brings the first person's card to the top of the pack. Hold the deck behind your back, have the man name his card and then produce it in a fitting manner.

YOUR FORTUNE, MISS!

AUDLEY WALSH

Once more there comes along an effect which has been tested thoroughly, and the directness of its presentation has much to do with its success. One who can tell fortune is always the lion of the gathering, and it is seldom that a magician is not asked if he is so gifted. Just giving a straight "spiel" reading is one thing, but I've found it 100% more effective if one can answer a direct question in giving the talk. And the following routine will be found attractive because it can be done practically impromptu.

Effect: A pack of cards is borrowed, and the performer stands behind a small table across which he works to one or two spectators at a time. The sitter shuffles the deck, and then gives it to the performer who hands him a piece of paper on which he is to write a question and fold it once each way. The written query is openly burned by the spectator himself, whereupon the performer fans the deck and has five cards drawn from different parts, and dropped face down on the table. The spectator looks at these, places them in a row still face down, and then starts turning them over one at a time in any order. The performer gives a short reading as each card is turned, and finally is able to look at them all and answer the important question that has been on the spectator's mind.

Routine: Taken all together, it is really the routine and presentation of this effect that makes it a worthwhile number. There are many booklets and pamphlets that give meanings for cards. However, in most cases, just a little imagination and a short, tactful fairy story, made up while you peer wisely at the cards, will suffice. After all, the knockout part, it also being the convincing point too, is when the question is answered.

Beforehand have two pieces of paper about 2 inches square. Fold one piece each way and put it in your left trouser pocket. Borrow a deck and have it shuffled. Put the second piece of paper before the spectator as you palm out the dummy paper from your pocket and hold it concealed in your left fingers. Take back the deck with your right hand and place it, face up, on your left hand thus hiding the dummy slip. Tell the spectator to write a question on his slip and fold it. Turn away towards your left and, as you turn, your left thumb pushes out two or three of the face up cards and your right hand turns them over, backs up on the face of the deck. Turn towards the spectator, take his slip with your right hand, put it on top of the deck (really on top of the reversed cards) clipping it with your left thumb. Gesture towards the ash tray with your right hand and ask the spectator to light a match. As your right hand comes back, transfer the deck to it from the left hand—turning it over in the process, and bringing the dummy slip into view.

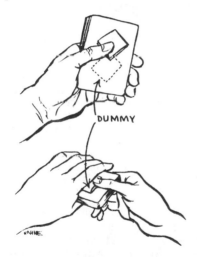

DUMMY

Just as soon as the deck is in the right hand, the left fingers pick off the dummy slip and deposits it in the ash tray where it is burned. As the dummy flares up, the deck is fanned out between your hands with the exception of the last few cards, and the spectator is asked to pull out five cards at random. Again you turn away, asking that he place them in a face down row after looking them over. While your back is turned you'll have time to read his question and also right the two bottom cards. Now pocket the spectator's slip. When you again face the spectator and begin to read her fortune, just lay the deck down on the table and push it to one side. Give as good a reading as you are capable of as the young lady turns up one card at a time; and at the finish give an answer to her question for the grand climax!

The actions for this presentation are so simple, and natural, that it makes a perfect reading method for single sitters. Those who are conversant with the Nikola Card System will find that the Key words for the various cards will give you a good lead for the reading of each card. I wouldn't be surprised if someone does take this idea and use it with as great success as did Mogul with the torn center method.

A TEST OF POWER

EDDIE CLEVER

Effect: This trick is an impromptu version of one in Annemann's remarkable book, "Sh-h-h, It's A Secret." The subject is asked to think of any card in the deck and write it's name on a slip of paper which the performer hands him. This is folded and dropped into a glass or placed in full view. The performer now writes something on a piece of paper which is placed elsewhere. The deck is spread face up on a table and the spectator is given ten chances to pick out the performer's card. He fails. The performer now spreads the cards faces down, picks one card, has the spectator name his thought of card, and it is right.

Method: Used are three pieces of paper, a deck of cards, and the simple finger switch of papers which is too well known to need much discussion. The performer has them in his left trouser pocket to start. One is folded and the other two open. The two opened pieces are removed and placed on the table. One is handed to the spectator for the writing of his card after which he folds it. Meanwhile, the performer has secured the dummy in his left hand from pocket and, taking the folded slip from the spectator, switches it and drops the dummy in the glass. Immediately picking up the remaining open slip from the table, the performer writes his own card's name, folds, switches for the spectator's slip and drop this in view, retaining the slip upon which he has just written. And the card whose name the performer writes is on top or at the back of the deck (and may be any card).

The performer spreads the cards from left to right with the faces up, so that the last card or two remain hidden at the end of the spread. At this time the spectator's slip is a dummy, the performer's slip belongs to the spectator, and fingerpalmed in his left hand the performer has his own slip. The spectator now indicates face up cards, one at a time, and the performer says "No" after each, until ten have been selected. The performer now picks up his own paper apparently (actually it's the spectator's paper), opens it and calls off the name of his own card. By this subterfuge he is able to note the name of the card the spectator wrote. He now refolds the paper, switches it and tosses his own paper to the audience to verify, retaining the spectator's slip just read.

Scooping up the deck, the performer hands it to the spectator to verify the presence of the card in the deck. However, knowing the spectator's card at this point, the performer scoops up the deck in bunches which enables him to leave the spectator's card on top. This action also transfers the performer's card to center! The performer now spreads the deck face down and picks up one card which he places face down on the spectator's outstretched hand. Picking up the spectator's slip (really the dummy) the performer switches and opens the actual slip which he reads and hands still open to the audience. The spectator turns over the card on his hand and it is the same.

On paper this routine may sound a bit complicated but it isn't. From the audience viewpoint the action is direct and nothing is done of an untoward nature. The theme is interesting and different from the usual card problem. And when the spectator is picking out cards in an effort to find the one thought of by performer the interest holds. It is all presented as an example of how difficult it is really to find a chosen card, and when a person can't pick it with ten chances and a face up deck while the performer does it with one chance and the cards face down, the point should be proven!

WORTH KNOWING: Sidney Lenz, the bridge wizard, used to have a pet trick for his transatlantic trips. He had a selected card disappear from the pack and appear in the selector's locked stateroom. Mr. Lenz would time it right and drop the palmed card on the steward's tray when tipping him in the cocktail room. The steward, in on the frame up, would snap it under the door face up, sending it half way across the cabin floor.

SUBCONSCIOUS MYSTERY

DR. WILLIAM BATES

Effect: Four cards are freely drawn from a previously shuffled deck while the cards are in spectator's hands. The performer does not touch the deck and the cards are drawn face down on the table so that no one knows what they are. While the performer has his back turned at a distance, one of the cards is drawn to the edge of the table, still face down, and an identifying mark placed upon its face. Then it is mixed with the other three, so that its identity and position are unknown even to the one who selects and does the marking. Returning to table, the performer deals the cards separately in a row, places several more cards on each one, shuffles the piles face down, and then, by some unknown power, causes the spectator to unerringly select the pile in which the marked card is lying.

Patter: I have long been engaged in the study of the obscure manifestations of the mind. My dealings with and studies of the human brain convinced me that the subconscious mind possesses a power not ordinarily recognized even by the medical fraternity. If I were to tell you that the subconscious keeps accurate track of every minute detail of your life, you would hardly believe it—yes, it even goes further—it penetrates into such depths as to border on the mysterious. This I will demonstrate to you in a manner easily followed by using a deck of playing cards. (Ask for the loan of a deck). Kindly shuffle them well, spread them face down on the table, and draw out any four cards face downward. Now place a mark on the under (face) side of one card in such a manner that you do not know what card you are marking, but can identify it later.

After you have marked the card, shuffle the four, still face down (while he does this square the deck on the table) so you do not know what your card is, and then place them on the deck. (Turn your back while this is done). You have carried out the instructions? We shall proceed. (Deal the top four in a face down row again). Do you know which of these is your marked card? It's important that consciously you do not. Some people think that I look at the cards some way, so I'll deal a few cards on each and have you mix each of the piles by themselves.

The marked card now lies near the center probably of one of these piles. Your ordinary, or conscious mind, has lost all track of it, but your subconscious mind has followed every movement, a sixth sense, if you will, and knows exactly where the marked card is! Just make your mind as blank as possible and simply indicate the first pile your subconscious mind dictates. (The pile is now revealed as containing the selected card).

Method: I have never presented this effect as a trick, and have never yet failed to mystify and entertain a group with it. They invariably attribute it to some psychological power and give the performer credit for a lot of "it." It seems as if the more educated and erudite the onlookers, the harder they fall.

Most readers will have recognized an old friend of all magicians, the Four Ace Trick in a really new dress. Simply have three extra cards palmed off to pocket before starting the effect. Upon your return palm them onto deck. Deal off the first four. Pause and patter. Don't be in a hurry. Then deal the next three on the last card dealt. Three more go on each of the others. Have the piles shuffled separately and keep your eye on the correct one. By having him "indicate" a pile instead of "select" you are free to use the old "take or leave" way of forcing. Or put the pile second from one end and use the "between one and four" method of selection.

NUFIND

AL BAKER

Put this problem in between other effects and watch it befuddle the wise ones.

Effect: Any deck is used. Following a genuine shuffle, the cards are given to someone and the performer turns his back and walks away. The assistant is asked to deal the pasteboards face down into two piles side by side, one card to each alternately, and to stop dealing whenever he pleases. At such a time, the spectator is told to look at the top card of the pack he holds undealt, remembering it well. He then replaces the noted card on the deck. Either one of the two dealt off piles is now placed on top of the deck and the remaining pile on the bottom, sandwiching the pack. Finally, the spectator gives the entire assembled deck a complete cut.

The performer returns to the fray, and taking the deck, runs through the cards but once. Asking the person to think of the color, the performer throws out a card saying, "That's the color." Asking the person to think of the suit, the performer throws out a card saying, "That's the suit." The spectator now is asked to think of the value. This time a card is thrown face down instead, whereupon the spectator names his chosen card. He is asked to turn over the face down card, and it proves to be correct!

Method: This effect is deceptive because there can be no apparent control exercised. The secret, however, takes up less

space than the description. The performer has noted the two
top cards as keys. The shuffle is a dovetail leaving them in position on top of the deck. One key thus becomes the bottom
card of each dealt off pile. Subsequently, one of the two key
cards must fall on top of the chosen card when the cards are
dealt as described above. The deck is cut once by the spectator. Running through the face up pack, from face towards
back, the performer locates the chosen card for it lies in front
of the first key card reached. The rest is merely build up.

Tricks With Two Decks

FOLLOW ME

JEAN HUGARD

Most of the tricks along this line use only one spectator and the performer. Now it is possible to use two spectators for a double effect. Two ordinary decks are needed. The working will suffice to make clear the effect itself.

Hand one deck to one spectator and have him shuffle. As he finishes this, hand the second deck to the other person to mix also. While he shuffles, take back the first deck and give it a further mixing while obviously waiting for second person to finish. You note the top and bottom cards of your pack. It is easy to merely note the bottom card, shuffle it overhand to the top, and note the new bottom card. Now take the deck from the second person and place your "keyed" deck in his hands. Ask the first person to cut off half of the pack and hold. At this time, the two spectators each have half a deck and you have a full deck. You know the top card of first person's packet and the bottom one of second person's.

Tell them to do exactly as you do. Look at the first person, take a card from the center of your pack and look at it. He does the same. Put it on top and cut the pack. He does likewise. Now look at the second person and repeat the procedure. Now have them put the two halves together and cut them once more. Take the pack from them, at the same time handing the first man your packet. Tell him to run through it and remove the card he looked at. Handing the rest of the pack to the second person, he looks them over and removes his selected card also. You fan your deck and remark that at the same time you'll take out the two cards you picked by chance. Lay your deck aside and hold the two cards with backs out. The first man turns his card so all can see. You turn one of your cards and it is the same! The second man turns his card. Your remaining card matches!

Remembering the two key cards your task has been but a pleasure. When you run through the deck they have looked at and handled, you have only to remove the card to the left (or above) the known top card, which is that looked at by the first person, and the card to the right (or below) the known bottom card, which belongs to the second person. This double bit of business will upset a few at least, and make for a much better effect on the whole.

SYNTHETIC SYMPATHY

TED ANNEMANN

Effect: Borrowing a red deck and a blue one, the performer apparently forces a spectator to take a card from one of the decks which matches the magician's selection made from the second deck. In short, the magician apparently knows exactly which card the spectator will choose.

This trick was one of Annemann's finest effects. It's convincing, direct and has a stunning climax. Follow the moves with the cards in hand, for they are really very easy to do although they are difficult to explain. Once mastered, you'll have an effect that's a humdinger.

Method: Hand out the blue deck to be shuffled. Take it back and then hand out the red deck for a mixing. Hold the blue deck in your right hand with the thumb at one end and fingers at the other. The deck should be back up and held just as though you intend doing the overhand shuffle. The red deck is now taken back with the left hand. Hold it face up by the sides between the left thumb and fingers so that the deck rests well into the left palm and the fingers extend beyond th side of the pack. Now, as you make a slight turn to the right, you tap the long edge of the right hand blue pack onto the face of the left hand red pack. Simultaneously, the fingers of the left hand reach up and grasp the bottom card of the blue pack and slip it onto the face of red pack held in your left hand. Immediately turn your left hand down, so the red deck faces the floor, and ask the spectator which pack you will use—the red deck in your left hand or the blue deck in your right hand.

Interpret his choice to mean the blue pack, and spread this one face down across the table from right to left. Now turn the red pack in your left hand towards yourself and run through it to find a card. First note the card on the face of the deck (this is the added card from the blue backed deck) and fan through the cards from left to right till you find its duplicate. When you have located it, slide the bottom (added) card onto it with the thumbs under cover of the fan. Now cut the deck with your right hand just in front of the two duplicate cards, and transpose the lower half of the deck to the back and close up the fan. From the audience viewpoint it appears as though you ran through the red deck until you found a card and then merely cut the pack to bring your selected card to the front of the deck.

Hold the deck face up in your left hand, without letting anyone see your selection. The card on the face of the deck is the blue backed card from the tabled deck, while the card behind is its red backed duplicate. With your right thumb, left up the bottom edge of these two cards, as one, and push them up about an inch so that they protrude beyond the edge of the pack. Turn the deck face down with the left hand and withdraw the protruding card(s) with your right hand, grasping them as one card between the thumb and second finger. Lay the red deck face up on the table with the left hand.

These two cards you have withdrawn are handled as one card, from now on, and are kept with the red back of the top card always towards the audience. They are now placed in the left hand so that the lower long side of the cards rest on the left fingers while the left thumb rests on the upper and opposite long side. The left forefinger extends to the outer short edge of the cards and helps keep them lined up.

A spectator is asked to push out any one of the fifty-two cards from the blue pack spread on the table, but not to look at it as yet. You pick it up with the right hand and, keeping it face down, place it back outwards against the back of the red card(s) in your left hand. Pull it towards you about an inch so that neither card is out of sight for an instant.

The left forefinger now moves inward about a quarter of an inch and presses against the face of the inner of the two duplicate cards (the blue backed one) which you have

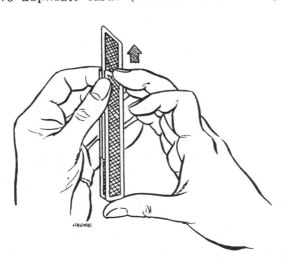

been so carefully handling as one card. Now the right hand is brought up to the backs of the cards, which are facing the audience, as though to steady them. The right second finger (which should be moistened) presses against the backs of the two visible red and blue cards, at the point where they overlap, and gets set to push them both forward simultaneously. The right thumb moves down to the inner end of the visible blue backed card (the spectator's selection) and gets ready to act as a stop for the following move. See the illustration!

As you ask the spectator to tell which is his card and which is yours, an easy push forward is made with the right hand. This action causes the duplicate blue card nearest the left palm, which is being retained in position by the left forefinger, to remain stationary and thus line up with the blue card selected by the spectator. In other words, it has moved from a position of alignment with it's red backed duplicate to a new position in perfect alignment with the spectator's freely selected blue backed card. (Shown in illustration). However, there has been no apparent change from the audience viewpoint, as the backs of the two cards they have been watching will remain in the same identical position.

Recalling that your card was selected first, you draw out the red backed card, show it and lay it on the face up deck. Now, still holding the remaining two blue cards as one, you turn them over with the right hand and show that the spectator's selection was identical with yours! Immediately lower the right hand so as to bring the card(s) face down and use it to scoop up the blue deck spread on the table. Insert the card under the right end of the spread and close up the ribbon of cards to the left, which will bring the spectator's card to the face of the deck as you turn it face up on the table. The face cards of both decks match, and everything may be examined as there is nothing to find!

AN EASY LESSON

MARTIN GARDNER

This is a trick of the do-as-I-do variety. The effect is presented as an easy lesson in the art of card magic, but actually the audience is left completely bewildered.

Two ordinary decks are used. The spectator shuffles one while you shuffle the other. Try to glimpse the bottom card of the deck he holds after he has completed his shuffle. If you fail to do so, remember the bottom card of YOUR deck, and trade decks with him.

At this point you ask the spectator to follow your moves closely and precisely, repeating them after you. The deck is fanned in the left hand with the face of the cards toward you and a card is selected. This card is withdrawn and placed on top of the fan which is closed immediately. Unknown to the audience, however, the card which you selected and placed on top was the duplicate of the card which you glimpsed on the bottom of his deck. We shall refer to this card as the key card.

The decks are given a single cut and exchanged. Actually you execute a false cut, but since he is concerned with cutting his own deck the move will not be detected. Personally

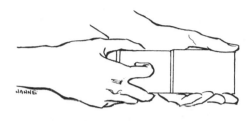

I prefer to use an old gambling cut that is made as follows: the deck is held horizontally in the left hand, backs to audience as shown in the illustration. The thumb is on top and the fingers below. The right hand draws the lower half of the deck to the right, and with a slight upward flourish it slaps this half on the table. The hand then returns, takes the remaining upper half and places it on the cards on the table. The left hand never moves. Correctly executed the false cut actually looks more genuine than a true cut made with the same motions!

After the decks are exchanged they are again fanned in the left hand, and again the selected cards are withdrawn and placed on top. What you really do is this. You first locate the key card. The card immediately beneath it will be the spectator's card. Square these two cards together and remove them as a single card, placing them on top of the fan.

When the fans are closed and the decks are placed on the table, they will be prepared as follows: On top of your deck is your selected card and beneath it is his selected card. On top of his deck is his chosen card and beneath it is your card!

Each of you now slide your card from the deck to the table. Pause a moment and tell your audience that you are going to teach them the way in which magicians find a chosen card. Explain that it is only necessary to glance at the top card of your deck and it will be a duplicate of the card selected by the spectator. Turn over your top card and then the spectator's card to show that they are identical. Now ask him to try the trick on you. He turns over his top card and you smile and say, "By George—you've got it!" Then turn over your card to prove it.

This double coincidence will be quite a surprise to those who have seen the simpler forms of the trick. Naturally you caution him not to tell others how the trick was accomplished!

Impromptu Tricks Using A "Short" Card

The use of a short card for a "key" when working with a borrowed deck offers the magician many advantages, and the "key" can be prepared very easily at a moment's notice. It's presence is never suspected and, when handled correctly, it eliminates considerable sleight-of-hand so that the magician may devote most of his time to the presentation of the effect being exhibited.

There are various types of short cards that are easily made, and one or more of them should be in every magician's bag of tricks. Some are more suitable for certain effects than others. They are:

A.   The regular short card, with which most of you are familiar. This is made by trimming the narrow end of any card by about 1-32 of an inch. By carrying a small pair of nail scissors you are always prepared to trim a card obtained surreptitiously from your host's deck. When out of the other's presence, just go to work on it. This card can be pocketed and added to the host's deck later in the evening when you are called upon to do a few tricks. When using this type of "short", you will have to tap the ends of the deck on the table top a few times to be certain of getting the short card into the correct position for working. However, proper misdirection will cover this simple maneuver.

There is another method of trimming a short that avoids this tapping procedure. Instead of cutting it across, just cut out a small concave section from the center of each end of the card. With this type, the cards can be squared in the hands, and the short is always ready to be riffled to.

B.   The "Broken Corner" short card is probably the most satisfactory for impromptu work. Simply bend one corner of the card and break it a bit. This makes an excellent short card "key." To be perfectly sure of it, both diagonally opposite corners should be broken so that no matter which way the cards are facing you can always find the short card by riffling the proper corner of the deck. Break the upper right corner and the lower left corner, or the two opposite ones, depending on how you do your riffling. This card does not have to be tapped down in the deck for, like the Concave End Trim, a natural squaring up will set it for working.

C.   The "Corner Short" principle makes another excellent key card. This is a combination of both the former types described in that the short is cut with a scissors on the two diagonally opposite corners. This can be done while you are out of the room. It has all the advantages of the Concave Trim and the Broken Corner card, and is absolutely certain in operation. By preparing two cards as follows, you are set with two "keys." Slightly trim off the upper left and the lower right corners of one card, and the upper right and the lower left corners of the other. Now, by riffling at the left upper corner of the deck you will always get the one, and by doing the same at the right upper corner you can get the other.

So much for the "short" card. The tricks that follow employ one or more of them and are among the finest of impromptu effects.

THE MIRACLE SPELLER

VINCENT DALBAN

Seldom a trick comes along with a truly genius-like idea behind it, and I honestly think that everyone who reads this now will do it immediately and continue to use it in preference to many others. The only requisite is a deck in which there is a short card.

Effect: While the performer's back is turned a spectator spells out his name—which the performer need not know—dealing (into a face down pile on the table) a card from the pack for each letter of the name. The card that falls with the last letter is looked at and memorized. The balance of the pack is dropped on top of the pile on the table and the whole pack squared up and cut. The performer turns around, and taking the pack spells out **his own** name, dealing a card for each letter. The card that falls with the last letter is turned up AND IS THE CHOSEN CARD!

Method: Shuffling the pack at the start, the short card is cut to the bottom of the pack. Now explain to the stranger what he is required to do, at the same time illustrating the instructions by spelling off a name—any name for example, but it must have one letter less than your own name. Just figure out a name with a letter less than the number of letters in your name and always use it. When this name is spelled off the balance of the pack is dropped on to the pile on the table. This whole pack is squared and handed to a spectator. The short card is now so many cards up from the bottom of the pack according to the name spelled off.

After the spectator has spelled off his own name as described in the effect, noted the card and dropped the rest of the deck on top and cut, the performer takes the pack again and cuts the short card to bottom once more. Then remarking that his own name is magical he spells it off, turns over the last card and there is the originally selected card.

Because the number of letters used by the spectator is immaterial, you may even ask him to spell his mother's maiden name, the month of his birth, or some such bit of data of which you could not possibly know.

"NUTS TO YOU"

GERALD KOSKY

Effect: Giving a plate full of walnuts to a spectator, the performer asks him to pass them out to the others in the audience, retaining one for himself. This having been done, the magician hands the assistant a pack of cards for mixing.

Taking back the cards, the performer says, "I want you to select a card from this pack in the following manner:—you may deal the cards onto my hand, one at a time, until you have a desire to stop; or I can deal the cards onto your hand until you say "Stop;" or, if you wish, you may insert this knife into the pack, and the card at that spot will be the one used."

The card is thus chosen as spectator wishes, an_ shown to the audience. The patter continues, "You passed out to various spectators of this audience a score or more of walnuts, keeping one for yourself. You also shuffled the pack and chose one in the manner best liked by yourself. Now I want you to take the walnut you have, place it in your right hand, gaze at it, and try to visualize how the card you chose would look inside that walnut. Have you done so? I'm sure that if you have made a clear mental picture, the walnut you have selected will not disappoint you. Just crack it open (giving him a nut cracker). And inside the cracked walnut it found a miniature of the card picked out! Finish, I want to congratulate you on your extraordinary power of visualization. You should do something with it."

Routine: Here again we have an effect that people remember and talk about because of the objects used. The working is a matter of ease because the walnuts are freely selected by both the audience and the spectator; none of the audience walnuts have anything in them, and the deck is a regular one with no duplicates.

The nut chosen by the assisting spectator is exchanged. When the spectator brings back the empty plate, the performer takes it in his left hand, and at the same time asks for the walnut, taking it in his right. No one knows what is to happen anyway. Pattering as he places the plate aside, "Your assistance is greatly appreciated, I can assure you, and in return I'd like to autograph this for you. Baseball players autograph balls, movie stars autograph pictures, and it is rather in keeping that a magician autograph a nut." As the performer puts this gag over, he puts down the plate with his left hand, right hand goes to his pocket with the selected nut which is left there as you bring out a duplicate nut and a pencil stub. The nut is written upon and returned to the spectator as your patter is concluded, same having been delivered slowly and pointedly.

The walnut substituted for that selected from the plate by the assistant has been prepared by splitting it cleanly with a knife and hammer. A miniature photo of a card (all magic dealers have these reproductions) is inserted in the kernel and the halves of the shell are then glued together.

The cards are unprepared except for the one you must force. This is a short card and found upon return of the shuffled deck by saying, "Did you cut the pack?" Regardless of the reply you cut the cards to bring the short to the top, and your cutting appears subconsciously done and is never noticed. If the spectator wants to do the dealing, you side steal the card from the bottom of the pile in your hand under cover of, "Were you influenced to stop at this particular card?" As you say, particular card, you place the stolen card on top of your heap. If the spectator wants you to deal onto his hand, deal seconds if you can. If not, shuffle the top card to the bottom of the deck. Now deal fairly onto his flat palm. When stopped, look directly at him and say the same thing as in the other variation, side steal the card from the bottom of your pile, reach out and add to his pile and openly draw it away as if you were only taking off his top card. This is very cute when done deliberately and cleanly. If he wants to insert a knife, keep the card on top, and in opening the deck book fashion slip the top card to the top of the lower half.

Having been forced, the card is now shown to all and the effect concluded. Try this out a time or two and you'll use it.

COMPOSITE ROUTINE

TED ANNEMANN

The impromptu masterpiece of subtlety, "The Thought Card To Pocket" needs no introduction I'm sure. However, my own presentation wherein I repeat the trick three times, using three different methods, may be of interest to you.

In bare effect, a spectator shuffles an ordinary deck, thinks of a number, and notes the card at that number from the top of the deck. The performer takes the deck, places it behind his back and removes a card which he places in his trouser pocket. The spectator's card is now looked for but has vanished, and the performer pulls it out of his pocket.

Method: In the three methods I use for the repetition each has one or more strong points that stand out in the working. If all three methods could be combined one would have the perfect trick, but by repeating the trick twice, the audience is more and more puzzled as they try to check, and when it is over they only remember the strong points of each method. and combine them into an unsolvable problem.

The first method is best known and came out around 1902 in England, being sold for about five dollars. The spectator shuffles, thinks of a number from one to fifteen and notes the card at that number. Placing the deck behind his back, the performer removes one card from the bottom, brings it to the front with the back showing and slides it into his right trouser pocket; immediately palming it out onto the top of the deck. Now the spectator is asked what number he originally thought of. One at a time the performer deals cards off the deck face down, and at the number named tosses the card to the spectator, asking if that is the card he noted. He says "No," and the performer say. "Naturally not because I put your card in my pocket." And as the spectator looked at the card given him, the performer palmed off the next card, top card of the deck (the selected one), plunged his hand into his pocket, where he had supposedly placed the card and came out with it at his fingertips.

Now hand the deck to a second person, have him shuffle and note a card from 1 to 10 from the top. Take the deck and place it behind your back, but this time rapidly count off the top ten cards, square them, and bring them around AS ONE CARD and put them in pocket as before. Ask the person what number he thought of. He tells you, but then you say, "Here you do the counting." As he takes the deck and begins to count off the cards, you drop your hand to your pocket and count through the ten cards along with him until you reach the correct card. Hold on to this card and when he says the card isn't there, you draw out the selected card from your pocket.

Take the deck back, and while you ask for someone else to help you palm back the extra cards onto the deck from your pocket. In the deck is one short card, or one with a broken right corner at each end, which can easily be done with a card from the borrowed deck. Get this on the top of the pack. Tell this third person to think of a number and, when you turn your back, to count off the cards one at a time face down until he has dealt one less than the number thought of. He does so and you tell him to look at the top card of the deck, and then replace the pile of cards from the table onto the top of the deck. You turn, take the deck, put it behind your back, riffle along the end until you stop at the short card. Take out the card below the short, show back of it like the others but put it only half way into your pocket, so it can be seen. Spectator looks for card but it is gone. He himself takes it from your pocket.

THE MIGRATING PASTEBOARD

TED ANNEMANN

Once again I introduce an effect that has been tested under fire and which has proven a good item for small club and close-up programs. It uses one of my favorite subterfuges—that of introducing an odd card into a borrowed deck—than which there is no other principle more intriguing.

Asking two members of the audience to assist, you have one on each side and announce a most baffling problem with the borrowed deck. With the cards face up you deal them onto the spectator's hands, the man to your right getting the black cards, and the man on your left getting the reds. You ask if everything has been fair to date and receive an affirmative reply from both. The packet of red cards is now given a shuffle with faces towards the audience and is then encircled with a rubber band, after which they are held by the left hand spectator. The man on the right is now asked to say 'STOP' as you riffle the black packet, and note (as well as remember) the card stopped at. This packet is also secured with another band and given him to hold. Mystic words are said, passes are made and everyone holds their breath. The right hand man is told to look through his packet and remove his card. It is gone! The left hand man is now told to look at his card and see whether or not there is a black among the reds. There is! The first man names his card. The second man shows the black stranger. Climax! Nice? I think so because it has always been received very well.

Borrowing the deck for this trick makes it a practical drawing room and club number. In the latter places have the secretary, president or the person from whom you obtain the deck, act as one of the assistants to emphasize this point. Besides yourself an extra card is necessary, and it should be a low spot card and preferably a black one such as the Three of Spades. It may be of any back design. I always carry four cards about with me. Two are of bridge size with red and blue backs and the other two are of the regular size also with red and blue backs. Thus it is possible to match a deck in size and general color. This extra card is a 'short' but made with trimmed corner or a concave trim at the center of ends. Palm it onto the top or back of the deck you have borrowed. Keep the deck face up and, fanning through the cards, locate and pass to the face of the deck the genuine duplicate of this extra card.

Have the spectators standing on each side of you with their hands outstretched. You deal the cards from the face out pack, the reds to the left and the blacks to the right. After the

first, and until the last, they can be dealt in bunches, but the man on the right gets the black packet with the genuine card at the back and the fake duplicate at the face. They both admit that everything has been fair. You take the two packets from them, one in each hand. The black packet is held backs up in your right hand, ends between thumb and second finger. The left red packet is face down on your left hand. Ask the left hand person which color packet you shall use. At the same time you tap the right hand packet's side onto the back of the left packet, and the left fingers come up around the back of the packet and top slips the card off onto the back of the left packet. The spectator names a color. It doesn't matter. If he says 'RED' you hand black packet back for a moment and with the faces of the red cards to the front, overhand shuffle about half and drop the rest on top (or face) all of which brings the genuine black card to about the center. Take a rubber band from your right trouser pocket, snap it around the packet and give to him to hold.

If the spectator says 'Black', say that you will have a card chosen from this selected packet but first you will have the red ones secured and then proceed in exactly the same manner as outlined above. Now take the black packet again. At the face of this packet is the fake duplicate. Cut the deck bringing this locator card near the center and turn the packet face up.

Riffle the front end from bottom to top and have the right hand spectator say 'STOP' at any time. It is simple to riffle this packet through quickly several times as you say this and whenever he says 'STOP' you riffle to the short card and stop. Thus the fake duplicate is looking up and staring him in the face. He remembers it (we hope). The deck closes and it is turned face down. Right thumb riffles up the end nearest the performer until the short card drops and the deck is cut, the right hand masking the back of the fake duplicate now on top. At this time, however, you are talking about the card that has just been noted in the black packet and you ask the man with the red packet if anyone has been near him. He says, 'No.' At this time you palm the top card of your packet to pocket as you reach for the second rubber band. Secure the black packet and give it to the right hand man. The effect is done as far as the mechanics are concerned. Reread the description for the finish and the deck is returned to the host or hostess with thanks.

DECEPTO

BYRON CHURCHILL

Here is a nice divination stunt for sandwiching between other tricks.

Effect: The deck is spread face down on the table from left to right. The spectator pulls out any card and turns it face up on the top card of the deck. Now another card is selected in the same manner, but not looked at, it being dropped face down on top of the face up card. The spectator then squares the deck and one complete cut is made to bury the face to face pair. The performer holds the deck behind his back for a moment so that, he says, the face up card may talk to the one face down and meet him. Holding the deck to his ear for a second, the face up card then apparently whispers the name of the other card to the performer, for he immediately names it correctly and lets the spectator find it so.

Method: Almost every card worker uses a key card of some sort to allow of out of the ordinary effects impossible otherwise, so I have no qualms about using a short card for this. A short card, whose identity you know, is brought to the top of the deck after mixing and the deck spread on the table. Any card is withdrawn, noted, and placed face up on the top (short) card. Any other card is drawn and, without being looked at, is placed face down on the top face up card. The deck is squared and cut. Behind your back you merely riffle the end of the deck to the short card, break and exchange the top card of the lower portion with the bottom card of the upper portion. Now you hold the deck to your ear and name the short card. It is above and facing the original face up card when the spectator examines the deck later.

Note by Annemann: I think a repeat on this would be effective as there is nothing to catch. Instead of the usual short card, use two "opposite corner" short cards as explained in "C" at the heading of this chapter. Get them both to the top of the deck, remembering their order. Follow the same working. as for the first effect. Then spread the deck after naming and have a spectator remove the face down card above the face up one. Cut the deck at this spot bringing the second face up card again on top, and repeat exactly as before, this time getting the second short card and naming it.

LIES! LIES! LIES!

HENRY CHRIST

A card is selected, noted, and returned to the pack which is given a shuffle. The spectator takes the deck and gives it several cuts while the performer turns his back. He instructs the person to deal the cards from the face down pack into a face up pile, calling their names as they appear. But—when the selected pasteboard shows up, the spectator is to lie. In other words, for once he is to disregard the truth, and instead of calling a spade a spade or suitwise, he is to call that particular card by another name. The performer, secure in his great knowledge of lying, announces that he will be able to detect a false note in the voice and stop the proceedings at such a point just as surely as though the spectator was being tested by a mechanical Lie Detector.

So it goes. And an audience believes it provided the performer presents it with sincerity. The patter possibilities are unlimited! Everything depends upon a key or locator card. Personally I break the very corner of a card if using a borrowed deck and use it as a short. Have it on the bottom when starting. A card is chosen from the fan. Undercut half the deck, have the card replaced on the top half and drop the bottom half on top of this. Now cut the deck just under the replaced card, overhand shuffle a little over half of the deck and drop the rest behind the cards shuffled. Give the deck to the assisting spectator and ask him to cut it a couple of time. As the key card is above the selected card, the performer hears it when it is called and knows the "lie" is on the following call.

A second method is with the use of the League Back Bicycle cards. The wing reverse in the center of the back can be seen at a distance of twenty feet with no effort at all. The deck is reversed for the return of the card and the spectator may overhand shuffle to his heart's content. He is told to hold the deck face down and pick up the cards one at a time, look at them, and call out their names. Then the card is placed on the table, or on the back of the deck. In this case, the performer faces spectator and knows the selected card the instant it is held up.

THE MODERN EYE POPPER

TED ANNEMANN

Performers who have used the effect of a card being placed second from where it jumps to the top will like this really new version which takes away the necessity of much skill.

It is necessary only to have a regular short card in the deck, (see "A" under short cards). Have it on the bottom and then have the usual card selected. The noted card is returned to the top of the deck which is undercut, effectively burying it. Another cut and a riffle shuffle at the ends can be given, for with thumbs at the ends, the short card will not be separated from the selected one. Now riffle and cut deck so that the short card is at the top, and the selected card is second from the top.

Say that you have located the card because by its strange power it always comes to the top of the deck. With the right thumb at one end and the second finger at the front, lift the top card and show it. Really though, the second card is picked up and the short card on top comes with it! Don't try to pick up two cards, just pick up the top one and the two will come up together. Still holding the selected and found card with the right finger and thumb, use its left long edge to flip over the top card of the deck which your left thumb pushes out a little. Call attention to this one, which apparently is the second card of the deck. Flip it back face down and drop the card held in your right hand on top. Now slide the top card back a little, and slide out the second card and place on top. Pick it up by the ends as before (only the one card will come up this time) and it is the chosen card back on the top! Put this down for a second and look to see if the second card on the deck is the same as before. Lift by the ends and two cards come up as one and the second card is seen to be the same.

Replace this and pick up the chosen card from the table and place it back on the top. Again slide the second card out and place it on the top. Again lift by the ends (short card is now back on top) and once more the chosen card is back.

Again flip over the next card on the deck and again it is the same card. Replace all as before. Now very slowly take off the top card alone and slide it half way into the center of the deck. Now if you can make a decent genuine double lift you can show the second card apparently on top which proves the selected card is at the center of the deck. Put the second card face down, shove the card completely into the deck, tap the deck and turn over the top card showing, that the chosen card is back for the last time.

This is a very beautiful and worthwhile improvement for those not too skillful with the strictly sleight-of-hand method.

THE CARD THAT ISN'T

RUSSELL WISE

Effect: A card, say the Ace of Hearts, is drawn, replaced and the deck shufflled and cut by the performer who announces that the top card is the one chosen. It is not, however, but proves to be, say the Ace of Spades, which is laid face down on the table. The deck is now handed to the spectator with instructions to spell out his card, dealing one card for each letter. He spells out the Ace of Hearts, letter by letter, and turning up the last card finds the Ace of Spades. Realizing that there cannot be two Aces of Spades he turns up the card on the table and this proves to be the Ace of Hearts!

Preparation: An ordinary deck of cards may be used or one containing a short card. For the sake of illustration, I shall use a short card as well as the Aces of Spades and Hearts in describing the routine.

Prepare by placing the short card on top of the deck and above it the number of cards required to spell ACE OF HEARTS. Eleven cards! The short card should now be 12th. Place the Ace of Spades on top of these and lastly, on top of all the Ace of Hearts. Now you are ready.

Routine: Force the Ace of Hearts either by a slip pass to center or in any favorite way. Have it returned so that it can be passed back to the top position which will leave the deck exactly as at the start. Now make a double lift of the two top cards, show the face of the second card (Ace of Spades) and say that this is the chosen card. When they see the Ace of Spades they'll deny it. Turn the two cards (supposedly one) face down and deal the top card, which they think is the Ace of Spades, ónto the table. The card dealt will really be the Ace of Hearts, unknown to your audience. At this point you riffle quietly to the break caused by the short card and slip pass the top card to this break just above the short card. (When slipping the top card to the break, it can be done simply by riffling up with the right finger to the breaking point; then the left fingers, which come around the right side of the deck, slip the top card to the right spot merely by the right fingers lifting up the top portion minus the top card and then dropping it again).

Now hand the deck to the spectator with the request that he spell out his card, letter by letter. He says it was the Ace of Hearts. He spells as directed and turns over the card following the last letter. He gets the Ace of Spades! This makes the second Ace of Spades to show up so he naturally grabs for the card on the table—and finds his own card, the Ace of Hearts!

Card Transpositions

IMPROMPTU PASSING

L. VOSBURGH LYONS

Effect and Routine: A member of the audience comes forward, and may be seated before a small table. He brings a pack of his own cards and two envelopes. He mixes the cards and gives them to the performer, who counts off ten cards and puts them on the table. The spectator is asked to spread them face down and, while the performer's back is turned, to look at one card. The performer turns his back, and at this time counts off nine cards from the top of the deck which he is holding in his left hand and palms them in his right. The spectator is now asked to gather up the ten cards on the table and give them a good shuffle.

As the shuffle is completed the performer turns around and holds out the deck with his left hand for the replacement of the ten cards on top. Immediately, the right hand takes the deck, adds the palmed cards to the top, and places it face down on the table.

The envelopes are now picked up and the spectator is asked to number them 1 and 2. Then he is asked if he knows which one of the ten cards on top of the deck is his card. He says, "No." Picking up the deck, the performer counts off the ten top cards face down as before, singly and deliberately. However, after the first three or four are counted, the same snap is made for one count, but no card is passed. Thus only nine cards are counted as ten. These are handed to the spectator to seal in envelope Number 1, which he pockets. Now the performer remarks that the spectator has ten cards sealed in his pocket, one of which he has previously selected, and that no one knows where it may be located among the group.

Again the performer counts ten cards, one by one, from the deck and drops them on the table face down. The spectator is asked to pick up envelope Number 2. As he does so, the performer palms one card off the deck with his right hand and adds it to the ten cards on the table as he picks them up and gives them to the spectator to seal in envelope Number 2. Simultaneously, the performer sets the remainder of the deck on the table with his left hand. After envelope Number 2 is sealed, the performer takes it and puts it in his own pocket.

The performer points out that the spectator has ten cards in his pocket, among which is one selected card; and that the performer also holds a sealed packet of ten cards. Now the object of the trick is to cause one card to pass from the spectator's envelope to the envelope being held by the performer. And, in order to prove that a card really does pass, the performer will cause the selected card to make the invisible flight!

The performer orders the card to pass, the spectator tears open his envelope and counts his cards. There are only nine! Then he names his thought of card, looks for it and it's gone! The performer now opens his envelope, pours out the cards, counts them slowly—one by one—and there are eleven! Repeating the name of the chosen card, as he fans the eleven cards, he picks it out for all to see.

ACME THOUGHT CARD PASS

DR. DALEY and TED ANNEMANN

For many moons a popular card effect among club and drawing room performers has been to pass three thought of cards from a stack of 15 to another stack of 15, both packets of cards being sealed in envelopes. Here is an impromptu method, using any deck, that is a favorite with Dr. Daley. Only two cards pass, but the method is very clean, practical and most effective.

Get a stack of about six business size envelopes. Use any deck, but prior to the presentation put any two cards into the top envelope (with the flaps facing you as you hold the stack in left hand) and then turn the flap down in back of the envelope. Put any eight cards in the second envelope. The flaps of all but the top envelope are left open outward. The stack of envelopes now appears ordinary.

Start by handing the deck to a spectator who has stepped forward. Have him shuffle and deal two separate piles of ten cards on the table face down instead of fifteen cards as usually used. Ask him to pick up either heap and step into the audience.

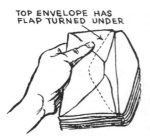

TOP ENVELOPE HAS
FLAP TURNED UNDER

He is to fan the cards facing two different spectators and have each merely think of any card which pleases them. When the spectator returns to the front, the performer is holding the envelopes, and taking the ten cards from the spectator they are inserted in the top and flapless (turnback and under) envelope. This action is normal and the flaps of the open envelope will hide this move although there is little chance of anything wrong being seen. The right fingers immediately grasp the open flap of the second envelope and this is pulled clear of the stack and handed to the spectator to seal and pocket.

He really gets the envelope containing eight indifferent cards while the group of ten goes into the top envelope where two extra cards are added. You now pick up the other pile of ten from the table and put these in the next envelope under the top one. The flap of this envelope is open while the flap of the top one is still turned under making the move very easy. This time the top envelope is removed and the stack pocketed. You seal the envelope and go over what has happened. Two piles of ten were dealt, one selected, and therein two cards mentally chosen by two different spectators. The spectator has the packet sealed and in his pocket while you have the second group of ten. You are now to cause the thought of cards to leave his envelope and come over to yours. The spectator removes his envelope, opens it and counts the cards. Only eight are there! The spectators name their thought of cards. Your assistant looks through his fan of eight and announces them gone! You now hand your envelope to someone else who opens and counts to find twelve! And on looking them over the two thought of cards are found!

Just in case it ever happens that the two people in the audience think of the same card, there is one out. When this occurs, hand your envelope at once to someone else to hold. Take your assistant's envelope, open and make a false count of nine. Only one apparently has gone. Hand the cards to the assistant so he can check and verify the disappearance of the card named. Then take the envelope from other spectator, open and false count eleven. Then hand them to the spectator to verify the arrival of the card. They will never count them again, but just look for the card, however it will rarely happen. The trick, as it stands, makes an excellent club number.

CARD PASSE-PASSE

OSCAR H. PAULSON

Effect: Counting fifteen cards onto the hand of a spectator, the conjuror asks him to recount them, to verify the number. To prevent mistakes the conjuror again counts on spectator's hand, requesting that two cards be handed him from the pile. They are vanished and reappear among the spectator's cards which are counted once more. This effect is repeated, and finally the fifteen are vanished and found in the helper's pocket.

Method: It is all in the count, so to speak. To commence, at a suitable time slip fifteen cards into somebody's outside coat pocket. This is comparatively easy at a get-together. Then pick upon this person to assist, and tell him you intend to give him fifteen cards, and ask him to hold out his hand palm up.

Count the cards one at a time onto his hand, counting as follows, "Fifteen, fourteen, thirteen, twelve, eleven, ten, nine, eight, and 2 are ten, and 2 are twelve, and 3 are fifteen." On these last three counts, you drop 2 cards, 2 cards, and 3 cards respectively. There will be smiles at this novel bit of counting, but you ask him to verify by recounting one at a time in the orthodox manner, onto your left hand. This he does, and there really are fifteen.

At this point, your right hand is in your trouser pocket where, beforehand, you have put four cards. Palm two of them now, while the spectator is counting the cards onto your hand, and when he has finished, add them to the pile on your left hand. Say to him, "I see you are suspicious, sir, so I will count them again. Fifteen, fourteen, thirteen, twelve, eleven, ten, nine, eight, seven, and 3 are ten, and 2 are twelve, and 3 are fifteen."

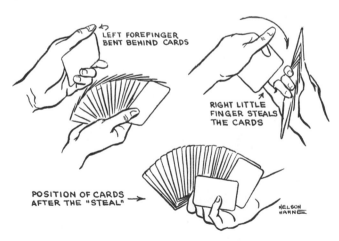

LEFT FOREFINGER
BENT BEHIND CARDS

RIGHT LITTLE
FINGER STEALS
THE CARDS

POSITION OF CARDS
AFTER THE "STEAL" →

NELSON
HAHNE

The spectator now actually holds 17 cards, and you ask him to give you two of them. These are vanished in any suitable manner. I usually pick up the remainder of the pack from the table, fan them out in my right hand, while the left hand holds the two cards to be vanished. Now with a downward sweep of the fan steal the two cards, as the left

hand turns back outwards. After a bit of fanning the left hand
is shown empty and the deck is laid aside.

Say, "Now the two cards have returned to your packet of
cards." He counts them one at a time onto your left hand and
there are fifteen. While he is counting this time, again palm
out two cards from your right trouser pocket, and add to
the counted pile. Again you count to him, "Fifteen, fourteen, thirteen, twelve, eleven, ten, nine, eight, seven, and
three are ten, and two are twelve, and three are fifteen."
Ask him for two cards and vanish them as you did the first
time, or in a different manner. He confirms the fact that the
cards have returned to his packet by counting them and finding fifteen cards again. Finally you take the fifteen cards off
his hand and vanish them, saying, "The cards are very fond
of you, even though you have continually doubted them. No
doubt that fondness has resulted in their returning to you."
He looks through his pockets and finds the 15 cards you
have previously loaded there!

Poker Demonstrations

DRAW POKER PLUS

MARTIN GARDNER

As a demonstration to a lay audience of the magician's ability to control the cards in a game of poker, I think this effect is extremely convincing.

Begin the demonstration with four Aces on top of the pack, unknown of course to the audience. Shuffle the cards in any manner you wish, holding the top stock, and then place the deck on the table. Let someone perform the first operation of a cut. As you pick up the halves, hold a slight break between them with the tip of the little finger (Erdnase, page 94 has an excellent method of doing this). If you prefer, you can keep the break by crimping the upper half of the deck slightly.

Deal four hands of poker rapidly and place the deck on the table. Just before you lay the deck down, however, the left thumb slightly fans the few cards that remain above the break. Glance at these cards and count them quickly. Then square the deck and place it aside. This assumes that the spectator cut the cards either in the center or slightly above the center of the pack. Most of the time they will do so. Watch him as he cuts and if he cuts below the middle simply replace the cards and request that he cut them more evenly.

Let us assume that the cards have been cut near or above the center. After dealing the twenty cards that form the four poker hands, there should remain between six and twelve cards above the break.

Turn over the four hands and arrange each hand properly if it shows anything of value. While you are doing this quickly analyze the first, second, and third hands (the fourth hand is your hand) and decide on approximately how many cards each player (if there were a player behind each hand) would discard for the draw. Then juggle these numbers about in such a way that the total number of discarded cards will equal either the number of cards that lie above the Aces, or that number minus one. We shall see in a moment why it is possible to leave this leeway of one card.

Let us suppose that you have counted eight cards above

the Aces (i. e. above the break after the hands have been dealt). Perhaps the first hand holds two pair. It is obvious that a player holding this hand would draw only a single card. Perhaps the second hand holds a pair. A glance at the third hand reveals that it contains nothing. Since the first hand MUST take a single card, you know that six or seven cards remain to be discarded from the second and third hands. So you assume that the second player holds only his pair and draws three cards, and the third player holds his highest card and draws four. Or you could permit the second hand to hold a high card (in addition to the pair) and draw two, and then give the third player a new hand of five. In other words you must invent plausible excuses for the number of cards discarded by each hand, so that when these hands are dealt their cards it will bring the Aces to the top of the deck (or to the top with a single card above them) so that you will catch them on the draw.

If the Aces are on the top, then hold the high card of your hand and deal yourself the four Aces. If there is a card above the Aces, then discard your ENTIRE hand and deal yourself five cards. In either case the four Aces come to you. Deal them slowly and dramatically.

If you are a convincing talker you will get away with all this. It combines well with Annemann's poker deal, explained in his book "The Book Without A Name." Employ his deal until four of a kind show up in one hand. Gather the hands with this one on top, false shuffle, and present the draw poker deal here.

DEAD MAN'S HAND

HENRY CHRIST

When "Wild Bill" Hickock was shot from behind by Jack McCall, in the Deadwood days of outlawry, it stopped the life of a picturesque character, but started the legend of the "Dead Man's Hand" and made possible this most original card story and routine.

In the Mann & Lewis Saloon of Deadwood, South Dakota, "Wild Bill" Hickock was playing poker with some friends. His back towards the one and only door made it possible for the murder just as Bill was preparing to make his "draw" to a hand consisting of the ACE OF CLUBS, the ACE OF DIAMONDS, the EIGHT OF HEARTS, the EIGHT OF SPADES, and the QUEEN OF HEARTS. This hand has since been known as "Aces and Eights—the Dead Man's Hand," and it is with this hand of five cards that a strange

story and occurrence takes place at any time or place, and
with any deck of cards.

Effect: As you unfold the story of "Wild Bill" Hickock
and his untimely end, you tell of the five cards he was holding when shot. Using any deck, you run through the cards,
face up, and while talking find and throw out face up the
Ace of Clubs, Ace of Diamonds, Eight of Hearts, Eight of
Spades, and the Queen of Hearts. These cards have since
been known as the "dead man's hand" you explain, and
somewhere, in another world, "Wild Bill" is undoubtedly interested in the group of five upon which he had his mind
centered when shot. It can be the only explanation for the
experiments to which you shall put them.

A nearby spectator is asked to pick up the cards and
mix them face down. He then selects any one at random,
looks at it, and drops it on the deck which you cut to lose the
card. The remaining four are not shown, but dropped on top,
and the pack again mixed.

Now you recall the nickname of the cards, and deal four
cards from the top of the deck in a face down row from left
to right, spelling a letter with each card—D E A D. On top
of these four you deal four more, spelling—M A N S. Four
more are dealt, spelling—H A N D. Now you apparently call
Bill into your presence by spelling four more—W I L D, and
still another four—B I L L. You have thusly dealt out five
rows of four cards each, the rows being dealt on top of each
other successively.

At this time you state that Bill's interest in the cards invariably results in the location of the one removed by the spectator, for after all, when Bill was shot, he was contemplat-
ing on what card he would discard for the draw. The spectator names the card he selected from the five. You turn over the next card on the deck. IT IS CORRECT.

Continuing, you gather together the deck and give it a bit
of mixing. You state that the second strange coincidence is
truly that. The "dead man's hand" only appears by chance once
in a million times. And when it does, strangely enough, it falls
to a person whose back, at the time, is towards a door! Very
deliberately you now deal out five hands of poker to as many
persons sitting around the card table. One of them, of course,
having his back towards a door, or as close to such a position
as possible.

Everyone present invariably remarks about this, and the
tension can always be noticed. You look at this person seriously, say that he has his back towards a door and that
there's one chance in millions that history will repeat. Ask
him to pick up and look at his cards, imagining himself to be
"Wild Bill" Hickock for the moment. He picks up the hand,

looks at it, and at that moment A SHARP CRACK OF A
PISTOL BREAKS THE SILENCE!

And if you, dear reader, don't think that the onlookers
will jump, and the man holding the cards bounce more than
all the others, it's just because you haven't tried the stunt,
or seen somebody else do it!

Method: The secret working is an ingenius non-sleight
method that practically works itself. Take a deck in hand
and follow through. It will work the first time for you.

Turn the deck face up and start running it through to
find the five cards. Count the first sixteen cards from the face
of the deck, and hold a break at that spot while you continue through the deck, throwing out any of the five cards as
you come to them. If any are missing, go back and find them
among the first sixteen, adding enough more cards to make
up for any removed. Turn the deck face down keeping the
break with left little finger.

The spectator takes the five cards, mixes them face
down and selects one. At this point you undercut off the
sixteen cards below the break, have him drop the card on
top of the deck, and you drop the group on top. On top of
these have him put the remaining four face down cards.
You can now give the deck a dovetail shuffle leaving the top
21 cards undisturbed, and finish with a false cut if you wish.

Deal out a face down row of four cards and spell
DEAD. Then a second row on top spelling MANS. With the
third row spell HAND. With the fourth spell WILD. And
lastly spell BILL. That deals off 20 cards. Patter along as
heretofore given, and when the selected card is named,
throw down the next card from the deck face up. Now pick
up the four heaps, one on top of the other in any order and
drop them on top of the deck. Put the face up selected card
on top, AND THE DECK IS STACKED AUTOMATICALLY
FOR THE POKER DEAL!!!

Left as it is, the "dead man's hand" will be dealt to the
first man of the five who are dealt cards. You have had ample
time to note which five you will deal to, among those who
are near, and which one of the five has his back towards a
door. Thus you can put on top of the assembled deck enough
cards from one to four to bring the hand to the second, third,
fourth or fifth person as you will. Outside of that it is entirely a build-up of tension through seriousness.

The gun shot? Just one of many possible gimmicks. All
magical novelty shops carry cap shooting appliances for
jokers. They have been built in cigarette packages, decks of
playing cards, etc., any of which you can put down near you

before starting the routine, and merely pick up at the right moment.

Suggested though is one of two appliances that will serve continually and anywhere. One is a small tin box about 1x½ inches and quite flat. It is loaded with a cap and placed under any object. When the object is lifted, the explosion occurs. In this routine, carry the box set to go, with a rubber band around it. Just before you start, slip it under your foot or the leg of a card table if you work on one. The other gimmick is a very small pistol worn as a watch charm and which sells for about 50 cents. It uses small blanks, is less than ¾ of an inch long, and will make a noise louder than the one that got Bill down.

This tiny gadget can be carried loaded with the hammer down, and just before starting you can cock it. At the finish of the deal, while you are still talking, and all eyes are on the fated spectator who has the hand, you have only to toy with it and pull the trigger on time.

As has been said before, this is one of the most original tricks to make an appearance in many a moon. It hasn't failed yet to go over with terrific effect as long as the performer takes the whole thing seriously and presents it as a strange thing. And people being superstitious as they are helps one on to success.

Spelling Tricks

GIVE A NUMBER

HARRISON

This smart effect, wherein a chosen card appears at any number in the pack selected by a spectator, is based on a clever gambler's sleight.

Method: Have a card chosen freely, returned, and bring it to the top of the deck. Now ask the spectator how far down in the pack he would like to have his card appear. Let's say he decides on 18.

Hold the pack in your left hand and draw off the cards one at a time with your right hand counting out loud as you do so. When you reach 17, transfer these cards to the bottom of the deck. This will leave the 18th card on top and the se-

lected card on the bottom. Moisten the right forefinger and draw off the 18th card between the first and second fingers of the right hand, immediately placing the deck between the thumb and forefinger of the same hand and then toss it on-to the table. When you release the deck, let go of the card you have clipped between the fingers. The weight of the deck causes the bottom (selected) card to adhere to the index finger of your right hand where it is immediately clipped by the thumb. Ask the spectator to name his card, and turn over the card you are holding and show it. It's the selected card.

"AD LIB" SPELLING

DR. JACOB DALEY

Effective and Routine: Use any deck, and have the spectator give it a thorough mixing. Fan the deck for a free selection. The card is put back and, in any way suitable to the individual performer, it is brought to the top or bottom. At this point, the card is glimpsed as the deck is handed to the spectator so that he can give it another shuffling. Taking back the deck, and secretly knowing the selected card, you fan the cards face up as you remark, "As I go through the deck I want you to note that your card is still there somewhere. Don't stop me or let anyone know what it is or where it is. Just be satisfied that I didn't take it out before you shuffled."

As you are talking along you watch for the selected card as the cards go by. When it comes along, you keep right on but start counting with the selected card and spell its full name, you note the card on which you have finished spelling, and then continue to do the same thing over with that card. When you reach the end of the deck, just start over again and finish the spell. The spectator will quickly tell you he has seen it after the first run and before you've gone far on the second. Just cut the deck at the spot where you finish the second spell.

Now explain that he is to do the rest himself, and that any card can be found merely by spelling it. The performer continues, "Take any card, for instance the Six of Spades (naming the second card you spelled). You just deal the cards one at a time and spell out the name. On the last card, you turn it over and there it is." As you have spelled out the name of the card mentioned, it shows up! Drop it back on top of the pack, drop the pack on the dealt off cards and give them to the spectator. He names his chosen card, spells it out and automatically arrives at his card. He'll afterwards swear he shuffled and kept the cards always.

PREPOSTEROUS

MARTIN GARDNER

Of all spelling ideas this has claim to being the most novel to date. The hardest part is to bring the selected card to 3rd from the top. You may use your own method, but I have a fair appearing way that you may like. Make a key card by pencil doting the upper left and lower right corners of any one. Have it on the bottom.

Spread the deck and while your back is turned have one drawn and placed on top of the spread. The deck is squared and cut by a spectator. Turn around and spread the deck a second time. "Is that what you did while my back was turned?" Go through the same operations. But although you appear to draw out a card carelessly and put it on top, you pull out the card second above the key which you spot in the spread. Turn it over before it is free from the spread so that it levers the upper portion of the spread slightly forward as shown. Place the card on top. When you square the deck, the upper portion will be jogged a bit forward, and when you push the two halves together, the thumb in back holds a small break between the halves. The deck is cut at this break bringing the chosen card third from the top.

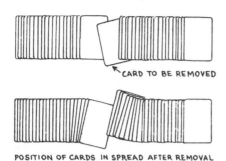

CARD TO BE REMOVED

POSITION OF CARDS IN SPREAD AFTER REMOVAL

You will find this a handy way to control a selected card for other effects. It enables you to bring the card to the top or any desired position with perfectly natural moves. In this particular trick you produce the selected card in the following manner.

Hand the deck to someone with the request that he deal the cards from the top of the deck to the table, dealing any number he may wish between five and ten inclusive. After he has done so, pick up the packet of cards from the table and by shifting single cards from top to bottom of the packet, spell out the words of a short sentence. At the termination of each word turn over the NEXT or top card of the packet and discard it. At the conclusion of the sentence ONE card will remain in your hand. When turned over it is disclosed as the selected card!

You will have to memorize six sentences and their corresponding numbers. They are:

If the number of cards in the packet is 5 the sentence is, "Your card it left."

If 6, "This is the selected card."

If 7, "This last card will be yours."

If 8, "The last card is the selected card."

If 9, "The last card will be your chosen card."

If 10, "The last card will be the card you chose."

Remember to shift a card from the top of the packet to the bottom for each letter, and when the word is completed, the NEXT card is shown and discarded. The remaining card—believe it or not—will always be the one selected.

Note: A further amplication of this idea will be found in "Jordan Plus Gardner"

NEWSPELL

MARTIN GARDNER

For a quick, clean, and cute spelling maneuver this will fill the bill and appear different from the usual type.

Have a card selected and replaced. Shuffle the deck and ask a spectator the color of his selected card. Red or Black, you spell off the color dealing a card at a time face down on the table or on his hand. Then ask him the suit. This is spelled off also. Lastly ask if the card was odd or even. Again you spell off whatever he says. He names his card and you have it.

The card is selected freely but, as you run the cards from hand to hand, silently count thirteen and hold a break with your little finger. Now when the selected card is returned you can cut off these top thirteen and have the selected card replaced fourteenth from the top. Dovetail shuffle, not disturbing these top fourteen.

You will see by the following table how the spelling is accomplished. There are only eight possible combinations and as given they either end on the thirteenth card or the fourteenth.

REDHEARTSODD

REDHEARTSEVEN

REDDIAMONDODD

REDDIAMONDEVEN

BLACKCLUBSODD

BLACKCLUBSEVEN

BLACKSPADEODD

BLACKSPADEEVEN

The one exception is the Odd Red Heart. It ends on twelve, and necessitates a double lift to show, or a second deal as you ask for the full name of the card and then deal it face up.

The only other thing to watch is when the card selected is a Spade or a Diamond. Always ask "Is it a Spade" or "Is it a Diamond?", using the singular. Then you can spell it that way. One trial will show this to be a nice deception.

JORDAN PLUS GARDNER

TED ANNEMANN

Effect: A shuffled deck is cut into two portions and one card selected from each half. The cards are returned, the halves shuffled and cut several times, and yet the performer is able to "spell out" both selected cards in quick order. A single tryout before well versed card men will prove this to be an excellent impromptu group stunt, and far different in effect and method from the usual run of the mill trick.

Routine: You fan through a borrowed deck and remove the Joker or extra cards. In this action you simply count from the face of the deck and note the 27th card from the bottom. Close the deck and have someone step forward to the table. Spread the deck across the table face up from left to right and ask the spectator to pick whichever half of the deck he wants to use. Whichever he points to, scoop them up, making a break below the noted 27th card, and thus the deck is subtly separated into two packs of 26 cards each.

Ask the spectator to look through his portion (don't call it half) and take out one card that appeals to him. In the mean-you pass among the audience and have someone else select a a card from the other half of the deck in the regular manner. They note and remember it, replace it, and you return to the front, shuffling this half. It is only necessary that you bring the selected card to the top upon its return and then shuffle two cards onto it, leaving it third from the top of the packet. Hold your cards in your left hand. Ask the standing spectator if he

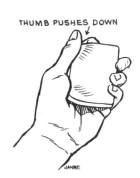

THUMB PUSHES DOWN

has chosen a card, at the same time crimping upward the rear left corner of your 26 card packet. The base of the left thumb does this, while the tip of the same thumb is on outer left corner of packet pushing it downward. The result is a slight crimp at rear of the packet but not at the front. Hold out your left hand and ask the spectator to put his selected card on top. Then tell him to put the rest of his packet on top of all. Thus two cards have been selected and returned without much loss of time or motion.

Saying that it is customary to mix the cards a bit,· cut off about nine cards and drop them face down on the table. Cut off about nine more and drop them to the right of the first pile. The third time cut at the break which shows at the back end of the pack, and as the right thumb lifts the packet at this spot, you glimpse and remember the face card of the bunch. Drop this packet to the right of the second packet on the table. Continue cutting the remainder of the pack into three more heaps, which are placed in a row under the first three. We shall call them and place them thusly:

1 - 2 - 3

4 - 5 - 6

Assemble the piles by putting 1 on 3, 5 on 6, 2 on 3, 4 on 6, and then 3 on 6. This really puts things back about where they were but the mixing allows you to learn the identity of the standing spectator's card, via the glimpse, which is 26th from the top. And the third card under it is the one selected by the second person.

Ask the standing spectator to think intently of his card and hold out his hand. One at a time you deal the pasteboards onto it face down, spelling a sentence and then the card. When finished he acknowledges that you are correct, and, turning over the top card of the deck, there it is! (You'll be surprised how many people ask you how you could possibly know the card, let alone find it)

Knowing the name of the card, and the fact that it is the 26th from the top, makes this very simple. The names of cards have a spelling range of but 6, from 10 to 15 inclusive. Depending upon this detail, you merely use one of six sentences before the name of the card, invariably ending with the 25th card dealt. Turning the next brings up the card itself!

YOU PICKED OUT THE .... any 10 letter card.

YOU SELECTED THE .... any 11 letter card.

YOU TOOK OUT THE .... any 12 letter card.

YOU PICKED THE .... any 13 letter card.

YOU CHOSE THE .... any 14 letter card.

YOU DREW THE .... any 15 letter card.

As you reveal this card, take back those you have dealt off and put the 26 on the bottom of those in your left hand, leaving the second chosen card third from the top. One of the nice things about this combination is that it almost takes care of itself and wise people are fooled because you never are seen to be keeping control of any cards.

Ask the second person to step forward, and as he does,

give the deck a dovetail shuffle or two, keeping the top three cards at least in place. Hand the deck directly to this person and ask that he or she deal the cards face down onto your hand. It is necessary for you to have from 5 to 10 cards inclusive dealt onto your hand. I have found no trouble in merely saying that I want a few cards, and for the person to deal. As they deal the fourth card I say, "Just stop when you please." So far, I've not had anyone go beyond the six following cards. A cute point is to have them deal slowly and say the name of their card to themselves with each card dealt. This will keep a person from going very far.

When they have finished you work with the packet in hand, mentioning that it contains only as many cards as the spectator wished you to have. Now, deliberately and openly you shift single cards from the top to the bottom of this packet, spelling out the words of a short sentence. At the termination of each WORD, turn over the NEXT or top card of the packet and discard it. At the conclusion of the sentence one card will remain in your hand. The spectator names his chosen card, you turn the one card up, and it is the same!

You have six more sentences for this second revelation, depending upon the number of cards dealt onto your hand. The chosen card is third from the top of the deck at the start of the deal off. Remember to shift a card from the top to the bottom for each letter, and when the word is completed, the NEXT card is shown and discarded. The last card remaining will be the selected one.

The sentences aren't difficult to learn, and in this case, the bit of memorising will pay good dividends.

Simple Prearrangements

CARD MINDED

MARTIN GARDNER

The effect of this trick is as follows. The magician shuffles a deck of cards thoroughly and asks someone to cut it into two piles, chosing one of them for himself. From this pile a card is selected and removed. It is then inserted into the other pile which may be shuffled by the spectator. The magician takes this pile and fans it, faces down, in his hand, and asks another spectator to assist in an experiment in telepathy. The person who chose the card is asked to concentrate upon it while the fan is raised so that the second spectator may have a full view of the faces of the cards, or the second spectator may take the fan of cards in his own hands and move over to the far end of the room. He is asked to make his mind as receptive as possible, then to run his eye over the cards. If his mind focuses suddenly on a single card he is to remove that card from the fan and place it face down on the table. When this card is turned over it proves to be the chosen one! No, there are no stooges, and the trick seldom fails to be successful.

Method: The deck must be arranged beforehand with the reds together and the blacks together, it matters not which is on top. While pattering give the cards a good false shuffle. An easy false shuffle for a half and half set up like this one is a simple over hand shuffle and run of a few cards. Just start a fair over hand shuffle. As you near the center of the deck, start running the cards singly. Only eight or nine of these are necessary and then fairly over hand shuffle off the rest. This reverses the position of the red and black packets each time it is done, but that doesn't matter. Just pass the center of the deck with a run of single cards, and fairly shuffle at start and finish.

After the shuffle have the deck cut into two piles. Force the larger pile on someone, and fan it for the selection of a card. A few cards of the opposite color will be either on top or bottom, so keep these few cards closed and fan the packet at the other end. The card is replaced in the smaller pile. Naturally it will be the only card in the pile of odd color. Have the pile shuffled and call upon someone to assist you who appears likely to have a sense of humor.

Build up the climax with a talk on telepathy and then fan the cards so that only the spectator can see the faces. He will spot the off color card immediately. Wink at him if you get the chance, but he should catch on anyway if you phrase your directions carefully.

Have the card placed face down on the table or stand it against a glass and have it named before you turn it over. Unless you plan to repeat the trick (and it will easily bear a repetition) shuffle the cards immediately to destroy the set up.

TATTLE TALE CARD

EDWARD REESE

Effective is the work-up of this conception, and it is done with a borrowed deck. The bit of setting up can be done during another trick or in a spare moment.

Effect: The magician is blindfolded, whilst shuffling the pack. He hands it to a spectator and asks him to deal about half of the cards, say 26, on to the center of the table. Then the spectator is asked to take any number of cards, from one to ten, from the middle of the cards remaining in his hand and hide them in his pocket. After this he is told to drop those cards he is still holding beside those on the table; then to choose whichever packet he wishes and hand the other to the blindfolded magician. Each places his packet behind his back, and brings forward one card at a time from the top of his packet to coincide with the card the other brings forth. The first person to run out of cards declares that fact. The other brings forth his next card. The magician states that he is so familiar with cards that they tell him all that goes on in the pack. He asks the spectator how many cards he hid in his pocket. The card last brought forward is turned over and proves to be the tattle tale card telling by its number of spots, the exact number of cards hidden in the spectator's pocket.

There is almost nothing to this as only ten cards are arranged on top of the deck at the start. On top is an Ace, then a Two, then a Three, etc., up on the ten spot. Pay no attention to suits.   From here on the trick works itself. False riffle shuffle while being blindfolded, but keep the top ten cards in place. The spectator counts half (26) of the deck on to the table which puts the setup on bottom of the table packet with the Ace at the face. After one runs out of cards the next card the other brings forth tells the number hidden in the spectator's pocket from the other packet. Just be sure the deck consists of 52 cards with no Joker.

THE TOUCH THAT TELLS

TED ANNEMANN

Effect: The performer deals sixteen cards face down in a four card square. The rest of the deck is handed to an onlooker, who secretly places any number of cards, from one to ten, in his pocket, and holds the remainder of the deck behind his back. The performer now touches the cards laid out, in a mixed up order, and each time one is touched, the spectator brings forward one card from those he holds and drops it in a face down pile. This is continued until he announces that the card he has just put down is the last. The finger of the performer is, at this time, touching a card, so he turns it over. The number of spots on this card is the same as the number of cards secretly pocketed by the spectator!

Although the performer cannot possibly know, when he touches a card, whether the spectator's card to follow will or will not be the last one to fall, this being very evident to the audience, the trick works with but very little mental exertion on the part of the performer.

Method: The secret is simple in that only ten of the sixteen cards laid out are essential, they being of any suits, but in values from Ace to Ten. Lay them in any order that you may wish to invent, just so you easily can point to them in rotation beginning with the Ten spot and running down to the Ace.

Have these on top of the pack so that you can false shuffle (the dovetail is good) and leave them in position. Then deal off the four rows of four cards each, having the ten cards necessary in their respective positions. This leaves 36 cards in the deck which are handed to an onlooker. He secretly puts into his pocket any number from one to ten inclusive. NOW—— when you start touching cards (always before the spectator lays one down from behind his back), the first 25 may be any of the 16 cards in any order. BUT—the 26th card you touch is the Ten spot, the 27th is the Nine spot, the 28th is the Eight spot, and so on down to the Ace. Somewhere among these ten, the spectator will stop you as he deals his last card, and while your finger is still on a card. If you have done as described, you will have your finger on the card that tells the number of pasteboards the spectator secretly pocketed.

Always, for the effect, pick up this card without showing and ask how many he pocketed, remarking at the time that the card you hold is of the same number. He reveals this and you turn over the card. That's the climax.

CARD BOX SYMPATHY

ORVILLE MEYER

This effect while a complete number in itself makes possible two things heretofore considered impossible. Using a P. & L. metal box you can actually change ONE or TWO cards and leave the rest UNCHANGED. Secondly you can change cards that have been initialed.

Two decks are used in the effect. One has a red back and the other is blue. Taking the blue deck the performer removes a card which he openly shows and has a spectator initial. Picking up a metal card box, the performer places the card face up within where it is fairly seen by all.

Now from the mixed and face down red deck a person in the audience selects a card. Without its face being seen, the performer initials it and it is dropped face down on the card selected by the performer. The lid of the box is closed and the performer hands it directly to a spectator to hold while he explains that his card was selected first from one deck and initialed by the spectator to prevent substitution. In turn the spectator freely selected a card from the other deck and this one was initialed by the performer.

The spectator opens the box himself and **finds the two initialed cards and they are both alike! And both decks are found ordinary and unprepared.**

Preparation: It would be best to follow this explanation with a card box and cards at hand.

In the regular compartment in the card box lies a card face down from the red backed deck. This card bears the performer's initials and shall assume it is the Five of Diamonds.

In the false compartment and lying face up is an extra Five of Diamonds the color of its back does not matter.

Now, if the false lid of the P & L card box is not closed but merely let down carefully, the box can be held on the left hand and either the false or regular compartment opened at will—it looking all the same to the audience regardless of which is done.

Method: In starting, the performer runs through the blue deck and removes the Five of Diamonds. He states that this is his selection and, showing it openly has a spectator write his initials on the face for later identification. While this is done the performer picks up the box and, opening it at regular compartment but not allowing the inside to be seen, takes back the card and slips it face up UNDER the red backed Five of Diamonds already there.

The lid is allowed to close but performer immediately reopens it as an afterthought, but this time he opens the false compartment, and shows the audience the Five of Diamonds face up in the box.

Now the red deck is shuffled and spread down while the spectator pushes out one card of his own free will. Picking it up the performer says that as the spectator initialed the first card, he will initial this one. This the performer pretends to do and then, without letting it be seen, opens the false lid again and drops the red backed card face down on top. This time the false lid is pressed firmly shut and the box handed a spectator to hold.

Now when the spectator opens the box the two cards found are both Fives of Diamonds and both bear initials. The decks may be examined but are now complete and unprepared. The puzzling part of all this is that the performer shows his card openly, the audience sees it face up and alone in the box, and the spectator initials it and then later checks these markings.

It will fool magicians and people who know the card box for the purpose of merely changing a card.

WIRED THOUGHT

TED ANNEMANN

Do you happen to have a set of the old card from the pocket indexes among your souvenirs? And have you, by chance, one of the popular card in the pocketbook effects? If you have but the first, you have the makings for a stunning press and drawing room stunt. And if you also have the latter, a neat variation is possible.

Fill the indexes, not with the usual cards, but with folded slips of paper on which are written the names of the cards, like this: "The chosen stranger will think of the ——" 53 of these papers are indexed and the containers pocketed. Now find yourself at someone's home or in a news office. Write a prophecy, fold it and drop it in a hat or bowl, but finger palm it out. Now ask the observer or host to think of some friend and to call them on the phone. This unknown (to performer) person is asked to think for a few moments and then name any card that comes to his or her mind. You immediately request the host, or caller, to ask the stranger if they had any particular reason for picking that card or if it was just a blind selection. This allows a full twenty to thirty seconds stall, and you have secured and palmed the correct paper from the index in your pocket. You pick up the hat or bowl with that hand and, dropping the paper to the bottom, give the container to the spectator to read aloud to the person at the other end of the wire. Imagine that person's feelings!

Or fill in the indexes with playing cards as usual. Don't

exnlain what you will do, but just have someone called who na. es a card. You take your pocketbook out and inside is found the correct card! Telephoning a stranger (to you) is wh it makes this perfect.

THE NEW NIGHTMARE EFFECT

TED ANNEMANN

Some six years ago (1929) I put out an effect I called "The Nightmare." It was quite popular for a time and then died out as tricks do. I worked out a different twist to it and it has proved a novel stunt for tables and close work.

Effect: Writing something on the face of a card from the deck, the performer hands it to someone to hold for a few minutes without looking at it. Riffling through the face up pack, another person says, 'Stop" at any time and looks at the card staring them in the face. They are asked to remember it well. The deck is closed and without a move, placed on the table. Turning, the performer asks the first person to read the writing on the card: "The card chosen will be the Three of Clubs." The prophecy is correct! Now the performer says he has gone further. The deck dealt through a card at a time face up and the Three of Clubs is gone! "And where is it?" queries the mystic. "I made it change places with the card I originally wrote upon!" And the first spectator shows the card he has been holding from the start and from which he read the writing AND IT IS THE THREE OF CLUBS! And all this happens with a borrowed deck of any design which makes it a veritable nightmare for anyone!

Method: Used is a fake card carried by the performer ready to be introduced into any deck. I carry two, one for bridge decks and one for regulation size. Two cards are glued together at one end the face of one against the back of the other. The back of the two is cut across the free end to make it a short card. We shall call the back card the Three of Clubs.

Borrow a deck and have your card ready to add to the face of the pack. After this explain that you will make a written prophecy. Fan through the deck and find the regular Three of Clubs belonging to the deck. Without letting the card be seen, write across the face "The card to be selected will be the Three of Clubs."

Hand this to somone to hold or pocket without them seeing the face. Now cut the deck which brings the fake card near center. Turn the deck face up and riffle at the front end from bottom (or back) to top. Tell the person (preferably the owner of the cards) to tell you to stop at any time, and as you riffle through you take it easy until stopped when you let them all go to the break caused by the short card.

Just keep the deck open at the front end and ask someone to note card stopped at and looking up. It will be the back card of the glued pair. When it has been noted, let the deck close and lay it on the table. Have the first person take the prediction card out and say, "Just read the writing on the card." They do and the second person acknowledges it as correct. Now, and most everyone will think the trick is over, comes the climax. Explaining that the card has vanished or has been purloined in an expert manner, the performer takes the deck face up (and turned so the glued end of the double card is towards the spectator) and deals through into a face up pile a card at a time—and the chosen card cannot be found! Then they are told it has changed places with the written card AND IT HAS! While this is being grabbed for and looked at, the fake card is stolen from the deck.

Editor's Note: This effect may be obtained also by using a short double face card. Reverse it after the selection has been made and you are all set. This is but one example of how double face cards can be utilized with a borrowed pack, and making it a short card offers unlimited possibilities in the field of impromptu tricks.

Addenda

THE FORCE THAT COULDN'T BE DONE

BY CLAYTON RAWSON

Here is a really good force, one that is so bold, simple, surefire and obviously not a force at all that it has fooled some of the best eyes in magic. The principle, on which this force is based, appeared in Anneman's book "202 Methods of Forcing." In one of the 202 methods the force card was on the bottom of the deck facing up. With the deck held by the performer under a handkerchief, a spectator cut some cards off the top and the performer turned the bottom half of the deck over. Extending his hand the performer had the spectator lift off the top card, thus forcing the correct card. Right here we reach the weak point of this force—the lower half has to be righted again, and even Annemann admitted that a wild arm swing or other haywire gestures wouldn't hide the fact.

In my method, which I call "The Force That Couldn't Be Done" you don't need a wild arm swing, just a smooth easy one, plus two pinches of misdirection. No handkerchief is employed.

To prepare: The three bottom cards of the deck are reversed and face the deck, with the bottom card being the force card. Hold the deck in your left hand is in Fig. 1. Have the spectator cut off any number of cards and lift them an inch or two above the rest of the deck. Now say that just to be sure that the spectator cut when he wanted to and not where you wanted him to, that he still can have the privilege of taking off a few more cards or dropping a few back on. They always do this and that's the clincher that makes them swear later they had a free selection of the card.

And here's how you do it. Your right hand is held palm up about a foot away and your left hand swings over and points at the outstretched palm. Simultaneously you say. "Put your cards there, please." The command, the pointing finger, the swing of your left hand, the sudden shift of the spectator's attention, and the fact that he's given something to do all make him and the other onlookers completely miss the fact that you've turned the bottom half of the deck over. Well, almost over. See Fig 2. The left thumb has gone under the deck and tilted it to the right onto the finger ends. The deck has made a little more than half of its half turn. As the spectator places cards on the performer's right hand, the left swings back to its original position and the deck completes its half turn, dropping down and lying now on the fingers instead of the palm. (If your hand is small use the narrower bridge decks.)

The thumb immediately slides the top card straight forward, see Fig 3, while the forefinger presses inward on the end of the deck and prevents more than one card from sliding out. You must use a back design with a white margin, of course. Now, while the spectator is looking at his card and showing it to the others you turn your back so as not to see, and take this opportunity to turn the left hand portion of the deck right side up, replace the top half and reverse the two bottom cards of the deck so that they are all facing one way.

The above force is used in Clayton Rawson's unique card trick entitled "The Card From Hell" from the Jinx No. 46. Had the trick met the impromptu requirement of this collection, it would most certainly have been included herein.

THE "SO SIMPLE" FORCE

LYNN SEARLES

In this force, the moves are so natural and to the point that even you, yourself will, at times, wonder at its working. Take any pack and, noting the bottom card, overhand shuffle it to the top. Or, if you wish, use any peek so as to know the top card. Again, if you are using your own deck and intend forcing some particular card, have that card a short one so you can put it on top when ready.

Hold the deck face down in the left hand between the thumb on one side and the fingers on the other. Approach a spectator with the request that he cut off any number of cards, and then have him replace them face up to mark the cut. You now have a pack with each half facing outward.

Now turn the left hand back up and spread the cards in a ribbon on the table. Thus you have turned the deck over, giving it a new top, and by pushing out the face down card

at the division of the face up and face down packets you force
the card desired, as it is actually the card which was on top of
the deck.

Not alone can this be used as a force, but as a minor
trick. Knowing the top card you may write a prophecy, have
deck cut, make the spread, push out the card, have prophecy
read and the card turned over. It also makes a neat and fast
discovery. Bring the selected card to the top and then have
the spectator cut and apparently find his own card in this
manner.

INDETECTABLE SHIFT - PALM

TOM BOWYER

This sleight is an improvement on the Erdnase Diagonal
Shift-palm. The steal can be accomplished with everyone
watching your hands, yet it is positively indetectable!

When a card has been chosen, riffle the deck for the person
to return it, but squeeze at the inner end so he cannot force
his card in all the way. It should protrude about half an inch,
or as much more as you like, from the outer end of the deck.

Hold the deck in the left hand with the forefinger bent
under it, the thumb on one side, the remaining three fingers
on the other. Cover the cards with the right hand and immediately drop both hands FROM THE WRISTS, so the outer end
of the deck is towards the floor. At the same time, push the
protruding card to your left with the right little finger, until
it presses against the left thumb, then shove it diagonally in-
wards through the deck with the right forefinger, until this
card is also pressing against the left little finger.

The left hand then releases the deck entirely, the left
forefinger pressing the cards into the right hand as it straight-
ens out. The only parts of deck now visible will be the corner X

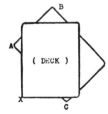

shown in illustration, and the corner diagonally opposite.

The right hand holds the deck between
the thumb around the corner X and its third
finger is near the outer left hand corner.
As for the chosen card, the right forefinger
rests on corner A, and the little finger
presses against corner B so that corner C
is against the base of thumb. The left hand
now takes the deck by gripping at corner
X between the thumb and forefinger. The right hand remains
stationary while this is done, but its first three fingers straight-
en out slightly to allow the deck to be removed. It will be
found that the chosen card will be left palmed in the right
hand, securely held at corners B and C.

ANNEMANN'S MIRACLES
OF CARD MAGIC

Just A Word . . . .

It is with genuine pleasure that we present this second volume of feature card effects from Ted Annemann's files. With its companion volume, "Annemann's Full Deck of 52 Impromptu Card Tricks," it makes available for ready reference a wealth of headline material to be cherished by every magician. Each and every trick was selected personally by Ted Annemann for its striking effect, its stunning climax, or for some other unique feature that spelled ENTERTAIN-MENT. For this reason, and this alone, you will find in the one hundred and ten tricks in these two books a collection of card magic that is unsurpassed in entertainment value. Truly, this is magic as your audience like it!

The present volume is not restricted to impromptu tricks alone, although one-third are in that category, but it brings to you many of the more brilliant feats whose successful presentation depend upon the magician's unsuspected allies . . . shorts, double faced, stranger, duplicates and otherwise easily made and ingeniously faked cards. These, interwoven with Annemann subtleties and misdirection, provide the means for creating miracles otherwise unobtainable. Regardless of whether you are seeking card tricks for close-up or stage presentation, you'll find a full array here. And included for good measure are two complete routines, conceived and used by Ted Annemann, which alone are worth many times the price of this entire volume.

MAX HOLDEN
JOHN J. CRIMMINS, JR.

Contents

IMPROMPTU TRICKS FOR EVERY OCCASION

THE WHISTLE

TED ANNEMANN

Two cards are chosen from any deck by two spectators. After noting them, the cards are returned to the deck and the latter given a good shuffle during which the two cards are brought to the top of the deck. I use the Hindu Shuffle for this which does away with the need for a pass or a shift. It is necessary, however, for you to know which spectator selected the top card for this will be the first one revealed.

The deck is now given a dovetail shuffle and one card is allowed to drop in between the two top cards, separating them. At this point you say that if you were an expert manipulator you would have a chosen card on the top of the pack. As you say this you are holding the deck face down in the left hand, so you proceed to double lift the two top cards and show the face of the second, or indifferent card. This is the usual method in which the two cards are turned over as one and left face up on top of the deck. After both spectators agree the card showing on top is not theirs, you turn over your left hand and show them the bottom card of the deck with the same negative results.

The face-up pack at this point is protruding out of the thumb side of your left fist, so to speak, and the right fingers go below the deck and visibly slip out the card which is now on the bottom, actually the top reversed card. This is now turned over so that it is face up, and then returned to the bottom (top) of the deck. This card, of course, is the one that was first shown, via the double lift, and which had been left face up on top of the deck. However, the action just described apparently rights the deck for, when the latter is now turned over so as to be face down, everything seems to be in order. You have shown both the top and bottom cards of the deck apparently, but you end up with one of the chosen cards reversed second from the top. The other chosen card is third from the top, as matters now stand, but we will forget this one for the time being.

You now explain that you will attempt to find one of the chosen cards, not by sleight-of-hand, but by a "Whistle." You mention that you have a different way of whistling for each of the 52 cards in the deck. As you say this, cut the deck several times by bringing up small bunches of cards from the bottom to the top, which action moves the reversed card to about the center of the deck. Then ask the person who selected this card to name it. When he does so, you think for a moment and then give any peculiar whistle you can. Now spread the deck on the table, or floor, and his card is found face up in the middle of the spread.

Continue right along by saying that many people do not believe in the whistle theory and that they are right to a certain extent, for most of the invisible force actually comes from the spectator who originally touched the card. As you patter along on this angle, pick up the deck by scooping the spread from left to right until you reach the face up card. This packet, including the face up card, is picked up with the left hand, transferred to the right hand which drops it on the right hand end of the spread. The left hand continues scooping up the spread, from the point where the reversed card was, and closes up and squares the deck. The action as described leaves the reversed card on top of the squared up deck, which otherwise is all face down. As you go through with this maneuver, you say, "When a person touches a card he makes it feel different from the others. The card in question takes on a personality of its own, and tries to become an outstanding individualist in its own world of 52 cards. And the one way it can be different from the others is to turn over and become face up while the rest are face down."

As you finish with this explanation, you are holding the pack in your left hand. The right hand now apparently picks up the top, face up card, and inserts it in the deck facing the same way as all the other cards. Actually, however, what you do is not quite so innocent. A double lift is made and the two top cards, (the second one of which is the other selected card,) are picked up with the right hand as one card. The right

TWO CARDS HELD AS ONE — CARDS ARE BACK TO BACK

hand holds them as such, and in the same position temporarily, while the left hand turns over bringing the pack itself face upwards. The right hand now inserts its face up card (really two) into the now face up pack, see illustration, and thus apparently everything is in order once again. However, the second person's card, which was under the card pushed into the deck, is now reversed in the pack. In short, you have very openly replaced the first card and at the same time have maneuvered the second card into position for its revelation.

Ask for the name of the second card chosen, turn the deck face down, and ribbon spread it across the table top. The second chosen card now appears face up in the center of the spread, and your trick is finished!

The subtlety of the effect lies in the fact that you are always one jump ahead of the spectators, and each of the reverses is finished before the audience expect it. Then, too, the fact that you repeat the trick with the second person's card makes the trick the stunner that it is, for everyone has seen all the cards face down on the first spread and, so far as anyone can ascertain, no tricky moves come into play, Lastly, you do not have to keep track of the second person's card. The first reversed one does that for you!

THE MYSTIC TWELVE

AUDLEY WALSH

The late Nate Leipsig claimed that this effect was one of the most puzzling of all impromptu feats with cards. It is extremely simple once you know it, but magicians will wrack their brains in an effort to figure it out by complicated stacks and mathematics.

A spectator shuffles the deck and removes any twelve cards. These twelve he shuffles again and, while your back is turned, puts any number of them into his pocket. He again shuffles the remaining cards of the packet, notes the face card, then squares up the bunch and places it on top of the deck. He now picks up the deck and deals from the top two rows of six cards, face down on the table. Ask him to touch any one of the cards on the table. The rest are picked up. The spectator now turns over the card he touched and, as soon as you see it, you not only announce how many cards the spectator has in his pocket, but also name the card he looked at.

The beauty of the trick lies in the fact that the turned card really tells nothing. After the spectator has taken out 12 cards, you pick up the remainder of the deck and, while he shuffles the packet he holds, you nail nick the top card at about the center of each end. Lay the deck on the table as you explain what you want the spectator to do, and then turn your back as he places any number of the twelve cards he holds in his pocket.

Next, following your instructions, he shuffles the remainder of his packet, looks at the bottom card, replaces them on top of the deck, and then deals out two face down rows of six cards each. As he starts to do this, you turn around and watch for the nicked card to be dealt. Mentally counting this card as one and then adding the number of cards that are laid out following it until 12 have been dealt on the table, gives you the number of cards the spectator has pocketed. For instance, if the nicked card is dealt third, there will be nine more following it . . . thus the number of cards he has in his pocket is 10. Furthermore, because of the manner in which the cards are laid out, from left to right, on the table, the selected card will always precede (be to the left of) the nicked card. Thus, when the spectator is asked to touch any card, you have accomplished a miracle if he should happen to place his finger on the back of the card preceding the nicked one. Just ask him to hold his finger on it while you gather up the remaining cards. Now announce the number of cards he has in his pocket, ask him to name his selected card, and then tell him that's the card he has his finger on. He turns is over, and it's correct!

If, on the other hand, he touches some other card, then gather up the remaining ones in such a manner that the selected card is the bottom one of the packet. Glimpse this card, without letting anyone else see it. Now ask him to turn the card he touched face up and pretend to divine from it the number he has in his pocket as well as the name of his selected card.

CARD OF THE GODS

DAI VERNON

Any deck is well shuffled by a spectator who then cuts off about a third of the cards. He is asked to look them over and finally settle his mind upon any one card in the packet he is holding.

You now take the packet, fan it, and appear to be trying to locate the thought-of card. Actually you look for two spot cards of like value, preferably from 6 to 10. These are kept together and are moved about in the fan, which is held face towards you, so that the second of the two cards will occupy its own number from the top of the packet. Thus, if you use two "nines," one should be placed eighth and the other ninth from the top; if two "eights," one should be seventh and the other eighth.

Professing failure in your search, you say that you'll deal the cards into a face up pile, and ask the spectator to watch for his chosen card and note its position in the pile. The spectator thus watches for his card to remember the number it will fall at, while you take the opportunity of noting the total number of cards in the pile.

You now replace the packet of cards just counted face down on top of the deck, and proceed to shuffle the entire deck in the following manner. It is extremely simple and there is little to forget. Undercut about half of the pack, slip one card, injogging it, and shuffle off the rest. Cut under the jogged card, shuffle run the number of cards you stacked, injogging the last, and throw the rest on top. Square the deck somewhat and cut below the jogged card, placing the two piles thus cut onto the table. Remember which packet represents the top half of the cut, and which packet represents the bottom of the cut.

Now tell the spectator that strange as it seems, and impossible as it sounds, you are sure he has the intuition necessary to locate his own chosen card. Tell him to pick up one of the two piles, warning him that unless he picks the correct one the test must fail. However, you insist that you are certain he'll choose the correct heap.

You are perfectly safe regardless of which heap he selects. If he indicates the pile representing the top half of the cut, you merely turn it face up revealing one of your stacked pair as the bottom card. If he picks the other heap, you turn over **its top card only** which is the other one the set pair. Saying that the card thus revealed will find his thought-of-card, you ask him what number his card occupied in the original pile. It may have been seventh, tenth, fifteenth, etc.

Using this number and the value of the card showing, you subtract the smaller number from the larger, count to the resulting figure in one of the piles, and the card at the number proves to be the one of which he is thinking.

The designation of the pile in which the counting is done is arrived at in the following way. If the number given by the spectator is less than the value of the card turned up—the counting is done in the pile representing the lower half of the cut. If the number given by the spectator is higher than the value of the card turned up—then the counting is done in the pile representing the top half of the cut.

Telling the spectator that he will always be correct in his pile selection is important, and has much to do with the impressiveness of the feat. The turned up card either finds the thought-of-card in the opposite pile, or in its own, and this is logical in each case. If in the top pile (which has been turned over completely and face up) the packet is turned face down for the counting. If in the bottom pile(the top card of which is the only one turned face up) the top card is turned face down again before the counting is done.

THE DIVINING PASTEBOARD

S. LEO HOROWITZ

The deck is shuffled and fanned for the spectator to select any four cards from any position in the fan. The spectator thinks of one of these four cards, whereupon they are all well mixed with their faces down so that no one can possibly know the location of the mentally chosen card. The four cards are now returned to the fanned deck and the latter is squared up.

The performer now puts the deck behind his back, saying that he'll attempt to find the thought-of-card through the use of another card which he calls a "diviner". His right hand brings forward a card which the audience remembers as a "three" spot. Replacing the "three" behind his back, the performer turns it over and inserts it in the pack in a reversed position so that it is face up while the remainder of the deck is face down. The deck is now brought forward and spread face down across the table top. A three spot is seen to be reversed near the center of the spread. Saying that the spectator's thought-of-card has been found, the performer has it named aloud and proceeds to prove his assertion!

This location is very subtly arranged to leave little or nothing for the spectators to catch. The preparation consists of turning any five cards face up on top of the deck. These are now covered with a face down three spot, and the six cards are crimped at the inner end so that they may be lifted together when necessary.

Begin by giving the deck a dovetail shuffle, keeping the top stock of six cards in place without revealing that some of them are reversed. Now fan the deck below these top six cards, and have a spectator make a free selection of any four cards. Still holding the fanned deck face down in your left hand, you take back the four selected cards with your right hand, fan them and show them, and ask your assistant to make a mental selection of any one of them. While he does so, you make a mental note of the order of the four cards from the back to the face of the fan. It is only necessary to remember their values, such as 9-5-7-2. You close up the fan of four cards, and place them, as a group, face up on top of the deck.

The right hand now squares up the deck and apparently turns the four top cards face down on the deck. Actually, however, ALL the crimped cards are turned over with them at one and the same time. Thus the five reversed cards originally occupying the second to sixth position from the top of the deck are now face down on top of the deck, and are separated from the four selected cards by the "three" spot card which formerly was the top card of the deck.

Without further ado, you say that perhaps the four selected cards should be mixed up a bit, so you nonchalantly deal the four top cards off the deck onto the table. Ask the spectator to place his hands on the cards and mix them around, face down, until even he has no idea which is his mentally chosen card. You now fan the deck once more, with the exception of the six top cards, and have the spectator pick up the tabled cards one at a time and push them, still face down, into different parts of the fan. Thus, to all appearances, you have had four freely selected cards returned to different parts of the deck, and one of these four is being thought-of by the spectator.

You now place the deck behind your back, and shift the top card to the bottom of the pack. The card now on top is the face up three spot. Pick this off, turn it face down, and bring it in front of you with your right hand. Show it saying you will use it as your "diviner" card, and that you intend to push it face up somewhere into the deck behind your back. Pretend to do so, but actually just place it face up on top of the deck, give the deck one complete cut and square up the cards. Now bring the deck forward and ribbon spread it, from left to right, across the top of the table. The face up three spot will show up at about the center of the deck, and at this point you ask the spectator to name his mentally selected card.

As soon as he names his card you, having memorized the order of the four selected cards, know immediately the position it occupies to the left of the face up three spot. (The four selected cards having retained their original position below the reversed three spot during the cut.) We will call them A, B, C and D.

If A is named, you simply show that the three spot has found it, as it is the first card to the left of the "diviner" card.

If B is named, you say that the three spot has located it. So saying you count to it, starting your count on the face up three spot and calling this "one," the next card "two," and the next (chosen) card as "three." Turn it up and show it.

If C is named, say that the face up three spot has located it. Push the three forward out of the spread, and begin your count with the next card and count down to the third card—the chosen one.

If D is named, do the same thing, counting off three cards below the reversed one, and turn up the next one — the chosen card.

Thus, you have a perfectly natural "out" in each case.

TWO CARDS IN FEAR

DR. JACOB DALEY

This is a double location with the cards found in different spots. It has always seemed to me a bit incongruous for a knife to be thrust into a pack only to find the two selected cards on either side of it. With two cards chosen and shuffled back into the deck it is quite a little miracle just to have them come together.

In this version of the stabbing trick, two knives are used and two spectators assist. The only requisites outside of an ordinary deck of cards are the two knives. These should be of the artistic type with different colored or shaped handles. Paper knives offer a wide choice. A sheet of newspaper about the size of a quarter sheet of a tabloid is at hand.

Two spectators step forward to assist in the feat. One stands on your right and other on your left. We shall call the left one — No. 1, and the right one — No. 2. The latter returns his card first and it is brought to the top, then another card is added on top of it during a riffle shuffle. The deck is then undercut for the return of No. 1's card (onto the top of the deck), the lower half is dropped on top, and a pass made which brings the two chosen cards, with an odd one between them, to the top. A Hindu shuffle may also be used instead of the pass. As matters stand now, the No. 2 card is third from the top, the No. 1 card is on top, and an odd card is between them.

The deck is now sprung lustily from hand to hand which serves to give it a downward crimp. Then, in straightening, only the upper two-thirds is sprung upwards. Finish this action by cutting the deck which buries the chosen cards about twenty from the top, and below the bridge which has thus been made. The deck must be so crimped that pressure at the ends will cause the cards to bridge at this one-third position from the top. See illustration. You may hide this bridge by pressure of  the right index finger on the center of the top of the deck while it is held betweeen the fingers and thumb at the ends.

Take the piece of newspaper and wrap up the deck. Give spectator No. 1 a knife. Hold the deck by the ends with your right hand and request him to plunge the knife through the **side** of the deck. As he is ready to do so, you put pressure on the ends, the deck inside the paper gapes at the bridge, and the spectator can't miss.

Transfer the deck and knife to the left hand, holding the deck this time by the sides from above. The No. 2 spectator now pushes his knife through from **end to end**, and as the first blade is but a third from the top there will be no difficulty in having the second knife penetrate below the first one.

The two knives form a cross, each being through the deck at right

angles to the other. See illustration. The stabbed deck can be held freely to show the situation. Then the paper is torn completely away. The deck and the knives are held face down in the left hand, handles to the left and rear. The blade crossing from left to right through the sides lies between the second and third fingers.

The No. 1 assistant names his card. The right hand grasps the blade of the side knife and, with the thumb holding the cards above it against the blade, the packet is turned over towards your body as you say that the chosen card never is above the knife, but always below it. With the little finger of the right hand flip over the top card of the lower half of the deck to show it as the first chosen one. If this is not natural for you, simply ask the spectator to remove it and show it.

The knife and packet in the right hand are laid aside. The remainder of the packet is left in the left hand with the No. 2 knife running through it from end to end. The other chosen card is second from the top in this packet.

As the No. 2 spectator is asked for the name of his card, the right hand covers the deck with the fingers at the outer end and the thumb at the inner end. The blade of the knife is between the second and third fingers. The left little finger is inserted **under** the top card (the odd card) and firmly against the back of the second card. As the card is named, the knife and top half of the deck is removed by hinge motion to the right to show once again that the card is not above the knife. This action covers a slip pass of the second from top card onto the top of the lower half. As you finish talking with "always below," the card is flipped over as previously described, or the hand is extended for the spectator to remove his card and show it.

I want to emphasize the "second card from the top slip pass." Slipping the top card to the center, or to the top of the lower cut, has long been a standard sleight, generally used as a force, or stop location. One had to watch his angles, though, for people on the performer's right always get a flash of the top card leaving if they aren't misdirected. By slipping the **second** card, nothing can be seen to move from any angle — the hinge movement of the right hand plus a slight turn over to the right, while the left forefinger is extended and points at the bottom card of the right hand packet, gives you more than ample cover for slipping the card. A few trials with your right side to a mirror will show how utterly deceptive this is. Those who still would like to keep to the old method merely have to bring the cards to the top of the deck without having an odd card between them. But once tried, I know this new topslip angle will be a favorite.

THE TWENTY CARD TRICK
WALTER GIBSON

This effect is one of high professional calibre; a sort of super-memory demonstration that has a tremendous effect upon any audience. Mr. Gibson based this routine on a trick featured years ago by a Professor Agostin. The presentation which follows is probably as smooth a one as it is possible to do.

Twenty cards are selected. They are gathered together on the pack one at a time, as you give each person a number upon receiving back his card. The numbers are given in rotation, from 1 to 20, and you ask each person to remember both his number and his card. After all the cards are collected, the deck is given a dovetail shuffle or two, and you place it in your pocket. Borrowing a handkerchief, or using your own you securely blindfold yourself. Now you call out numbers at random, and as each person hears his number he responds with the name of his card. The cards named are immediately produced in order from your pocket. No numbers are repeated, and none are missed.

Speed adds to the effectiveness of this trick, so have the cards selected as fast as possible as you pass up one aisle and down the next. Also make it obvious that each receives a free selection, which should not be hard to do as no forces are employed.

In gathering the cards on top of the deck one at a time, secretly bend up the corner of the eleventh card. Then when all are collected, lift off the ten cards above the crimped one and shift them to the bottom of the deck. Thus the eleventh card is on top when the deck is put in your pocket. A dovetail shuffle or so which does not disturb the top and bottom ten, or a false mixing of any kind, helps the effect at this point.

Now the blindfold is put on and the effect gotten under way, keeping the tempo speeded up as much as possible. As you become acquainted with the routine you will be surprised how fast you can really work it.

The method is not difficult, and is practically automatic. You need only follow a certain set routine in drawing out the cards combined with a memorized order, which you call out, of the numbers from 1 to 20.

Draw out the cards in this order:
Top card, second from the bottom, third from the top.
Bottom card, second from top, third from the bottom.
Top card, second from the bottom, third from the top.
Bottom card, second from the top, third from the bottom.
Top card, second from the bottom.
Top card, second from the bottom.
Top card, second from the bottom.
Top card, bottom card.
As you reach for the cards, call out these numbers:
    10-12-7; 11-8-15; 9-14-4; 13-5-18; 6-17; 3-19; 2-20; 1-16.

As you call the numbers, the spectators name their cards, and you withdraw them from your pocket, show each, and drop them onto the floor one after the other.

When you reach the last two cards, stop and say that but only a few can be left. Ask the holders of these cards to stand and call out the names of their cards. They do, and you immediately bring forth the last two cards together. As the cards occupy the top and bottom positions, this is a simple matter. Just press on one card with your thumb while your fingers press on the other, and pull the two cards free of the deck. Now bring them forth, get them below your range of vision (you can see down both sides of your nose, of course, in spite of the blindfold) and make a note of the face card of the pair. Transfer this card to your opposite hand, and then repeat its name saying, "That was number 1." Then show the other saying, "And the —— of —— was number 16." Remove the blindfold and, as the applause sets in, remove the remainder of the deck from your pocket and let it dribble to the floor. If you are going to pick up the 20 you already have dropped, you might as well pick up 52, and this finish is nice showmanship.

One last suggestion. Once you have become proficient and sure of yourself, you'll have many occasions when, during the selection, you'll get glimpses of the cards being taken. Remember two or three of them together with their numbers. Then, during the production process, say, of a sudden, "Who took the —— of ——? Call your number, please." And you have it. It's a cute variation.

Please avoid any and all "hooey" as a buildup. Simply make it a card problem of 20 cards being chosen and found. Make it more or less of a card trick to end all card tricks. In short, make it **the** card trick. It's an excellent effect if you are doing but one card trick in your act. Don't try to half it and use but 10 cards. It's the magnitude of the thing that counts, plus speed.

Editor's note:—One magician who has been featuring this trick for some time, has found that the production of the last two from among a shower of cards makes a striking finale. This, of course, is the old trick wherein you toss the deck in the air, reach into the resulting shower of cards, and end up with the selected cards adhering to your forefinger and thumb.

MATHEMATICAL BLACK JACKS
HENRY CHRIST

The method employed in this purely automatic trick is beautifully camouflaged and will confound those who try to duplicate it. For this reason it is an excellent impromptu table effect.

You borrow a deck of cards and tell a tale of the two black Jacks: "Back in the dim past these two cards were designed with a mathematical quality. The Jack of Spades holds an hour glass in his left hand, while the Jack of Clubs holds an object then used as a measuring stick. Thus, because these two Jacks signified the measurement of time and tides, they have mathematical properties possessed by no other cards even though the designs may have changed to some extent during the centuries." (Most cards, especially Bicycle and Fox Lake, can be shown to have these same characteristics even today). Incidentally, this theme material was contained in Zovello's "Mystery of Playing Cards," a valuable booklet for any person interested in playing cards.

Two black Jacks have been removed from the pack and shown during your discourse. Now they are put back and apparently lost during a shuffle. Actually, however, you bring them both to the top of the pack.

The Hindu Shuffle is excellent for this, providing you have the two cards inserted by one of the spectators.

You now cut the pack into face down piles, slip-cutting" one of the two Jacks onto the top of the lower half. (See Annemann's "A Card In Hand" in this book, which describes this sleight.) Thus the cards appear as in Figure 1, a Jack on top of each heap, although the spectators are unaware of this.

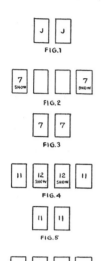

FIG.1

FIG.2

FIG.3

FIG.4

FIG.5

FIG.6

"The probability of finding one Jack," you say, "is 25 to 1." So you ask a spectator to mention any number between 1 and 10. We shall assume that 7 is chosen. With both hands, deal a card face down from each pile into a separate pile to the outside of the original packets. See Figure 2. The cards are dealt simultaneously. When the 7th card in each packet is reached, they are both turned over to show that neither is a black Jack. These two cards are replaced upon the outside heaps, and then the outside heaps are picked up and returned to the tops of their original piles. See Figure 3.

A second person is now asked to name a number between 10 and 20. Once more the cards are dealt singly and simultaneously to the sides. Let us say 12 was the figure called. When the 12th cards are reached, they are turned and again everyone sees that no black Jack has been discovered. See Figure 4. However, this time, after showing the cards, they are replaced **on the inner piles** from where they were picked up, and the outside heaps and now picked up and placed back on top of their respective piles. This simple change in procedure is never noticed when the effect is first presented before anyone, yet it is the key to the effect working for you, while not working for others although they may know or surmise the principle in general.

So far two people have tried to locate the Jacks but have failed. You now say that the black Jacks, having been mathematically endowed, take every opportunity to display their prowess. You suggest that the difference between the two selected numbers be computed. In this case 7 and 12, the difference being 5.

For the last time the cards are dealt off into their side heaps. On the 5th count, the two cards arrived at are tossed face up in front of all the piles. They are the black Jacks who have found themselves! (Figures 5 and 6 show these final moves.)

THREE PREDICTIONS

G. W. HUNTER

Holding a pack in your hands, you note the bottom card, and then request a spectator to deal three cards from the top of the pack onto the table about three inches apart. You do this yourself by way of illustration. Now gather up the three cards and shuffle the pack, bringing the bottom card, which you previously noted — we'll call it the Six of Clubs — to a position second from the top. Hand the deck to the spectator volunteering to assist, and request him to deal the three top cards in the manner you have shown.

When he has done so you remark, "I will now turn my back, and I want you to augment these three cards with as many more as you please. In other words, I want you to make three heaps of equal number, not less than four in each heap, but as many more as you like. When you have done so, I will, with my back towards you and without asking a single question, reduce the total number of cards to any small number you may suggest. And, furthermore, I will ask you to put any small number of cards in your pocket, and I shall tell you how many you put there. I will now turn my back, and please deal the cards softly, so that it will be impossible for me to know the number of cards you have on the table. When you have done so, kindly tell me." (Turn your back.)

When your instructions have thus far been carried out, remark, "You have a number of cards on the table, and it is, you will admit, utterly impossible for me to know how many there are. Tell me to what small number you would like me to reduce them."

We will suppose you are requested to reduce them to two. Proceed with your instructions, as follows: "Take three cards from each of the outside heaps and place them on the middle heap. Thank you. Now count the number of cards in one of the outside heaps, and take that number of cards from the middle heap and put them back on top of the pack."

When this has been done request him to replace the two outside heaps on the pack also. Then remark, "You have now but one heap of cards on the table. I don't know how many cards there are. (But, of course, you do know, for when the above instructions are carried out it always leaves nine cards in the remaining heap, no matter what number of cards above 4 there may have been at the commencement. This is the secret of the trick.) I want you to put the top half of those remaining cards in your pocket. If there happens to be an odd number, please put the larger half from the top into your pocket."

Carrying out your instructions, he place five cards in his pocket. You continue, "You requested me to reduce the number of cards on the table to two, so please take two more cards from the heap on the table and place them into the pack. Thank you. I have now fulfilled my predictions. You have two cards on the table and five cards in your pocket. I think you will admit that I'm correct. I will make one more prediction. Take the top card of the two on the table and put it back into the pack. Thank you. There is but one card on the table now, and I can visualize only the Six of Clubs. Please look at it."

Note: It matters not what number you are asked to work with. It is in your own hands when you have gotten the one heap of nine. For instance, if you were asked to reduce the number of cards to four, the thing is done when you have requested your assistant to take the larger half from the top and put them in his pocket.

For three he is instructed to take one card from the heap on the table and return it to the pack. For two he does as already shown. For one, take three from the heap and return to the pack. For a higher number — six, for instance, request your assistant to retake two from the pack and add them to those on the table.

The trick can be repeated. When you do so it is better to vary the operation the second time by requesting your assistant to take the smaller half from the top to be put in his pocket. The last feature — the naming of the card on the table — can be retained at the option of the performer.

MEPHISTO'S PREDICTION

CHARLES T. JORDAN

You will like this impromptu, non-sleight of hand card effect wherein you predict beforehand the position a chosen card will occupy in a freely shuffled deck. It's an excellent card table trick.

Any deck may be used as long as it contains a Joker. (In lieu of the Joker, the advertising or bridge score card may be used.) The pack is shuffled freely and a spectator inserts the Joker anywhere and then takes the deck, fans it and notes the card above and adjacent to the Joker. While he is doing this, you lay a folded piece of paper on the table upon the inside of which you have secretly written the number "11." After noting the card, the spectator closes up the fan of cards, cuts the deck and completes the cut, and then deals it into four face down heaps, a card at a time. You pick up the heaps reassembling the deck, give it a complete cut, and then fan the cards towards the person so that he can remove the Joker. He does so, whereupon you hand him the deck face down. He reads what you have previously written on the paper, counts down to that number from the top of the face down deck — and discovers his card at that number.

This prediction trick is practically automatic, if the above instructions are followed. The only thing you have to do is to be sure and reassemble the four heaps of cards by placing the fourth heap on the third, both of these on the second, and all of them on the first. After cutting the deck, fan it faces toward the spectator and ask him to remove the Joker. When he does so, run two more cards from the lower, or left part of the fan, onto the bottom of the upper, or right part of the fan, and then cut the deck at this point. This bit of maneuvering automatically brings the noted card to the position eleven from the top.

If you wish to repeat the trick, write the number "38" on another piece of paper, fold it and lay it on the table. This time, pick up the heaps in reverse order, the first heap going on the second, these on the third, and all on the fourth heap. Then follow the above routine exactly.

LIKE SEEKS LIKE

WALTER GIBSON

Here's a quickie that a lot of readers will add to their repertoire of impromptu tricks upon first reading; the rest of you will wait for someone else to attract attention with it before turning back and learning how to do it. It's particularly good for table work because it is done deliberately and convincingly.

You take six cards and hold them in a face down packet in your left hand. The fingers are at the left side of the packet; the thumb at the right. Now tilt the hand upward to show the bottom card, which is red. Promptly turning the packet face down, reach beneath the front end of the packet with your right fingers and pull out the bottom card. Show it again and place it face down on top of the packet saying, "Red." Proceed to show the next card on the bottom. It is black. Draw it off as before, give a brief glimpse of it, and put it on top of the packet saying, "Black." This routine you repeat with each of the remaining cards, alternating red and black, until you have transferred the entire six from bottom to top. Now turn the packet face up, fan it, and show that the cards alternate red and black precisely as represented.

Now comes the mystery. You repeat the above procedure in seemingly identical fashion; if anything, a bit more casually. The cards go from bottom to top, one by one; red, black, red, black, red, black. But when they are fanned face up, they appear in separate groups — the three reds together, and the three blacks together.

There is trickery, of course, during the second showing of the cards. The Glide is used, wherein the third finger of the left hand, beneath the packet, draws back the bottom card, so that the card above it may be removed by the right hand.

Nevertheless — of the six cards transferred, three are actually shifted. Of the remaining three, two are actually shown on the bottom of the pack. With only one card is the move made blind, about half way through the process. This is what makes the trick so effective and puzzling. The second transfer of cards from bottom to top seems identical with the first. That is why it's important to do the bona fide process at the beginning; then repeat with the special transfer.

With the proper cards in hand try it slowly in ordinary fashion, and then:

FIRST CARD (Red): Actually remove it from the bottom; show it with the right hand, and place it face down on top of the packet saying, "Red."

SECOND CARD (Black): Actually remove it from the bottom; show it with the right hand, and place it face down on top, saying, "Black."

THIRD CARD (——): Show a red card on the bottom. Tilt the packet downward. Draw back the card just shown by means of the Glide. Remove the next card, place it on top without showing its face, saying, "Red."

FOURTH CARD (——): Do not show the bottom card this time. Remove the bottom card (the one that was "drawn" back) and place it on top without showing its face. Say, "Black."

FIFTH CARD (——): Actually show a red card on the bottom. Remove it, show with your right hand, and place it on top, saying, "Red."

SIXTH CARD (——): Actually show a black card on the bottom. Tilt the packet downward, draw back the card, remove the next one and place it on top without showing it, but saying, "Black."

Now square the packet, mutter a hocus pocus or two and fan the cards face up. The three reds will be together, as will be the three blacks!

Note that moves 1, 2 and 5 are identical, and bona fide. Moves 3 and 6 allow showing of the bottom card before the Glide. Only move

4 is entirely a blind one, done carelessly as though a showing of the card were unnecessary.

WITH GIANT CARDS. The trick is performed with the same routine as above for stage presentation, the only difference is a variation in the use of the Glide. In this variation of the sleight, the right fingers push back the bottom card, on the two occasions when necessary, accomplishing it under cover of the packet. Some magicians use this simpler glide with regular cards. While ordinarily inferior it is suitable here because of the deliberateness of the presentation.

A CARD IN HAND

TED ANNEMANN

Many professionals claim that this trick is the best close up effect for presentation at night club tables that you could want. Just do it a few times and listen to the comment. It's extremely effective when worked for a lady.

The usual card is chosen and returned. In order to vary the selection and get away from the too familiar "take a card" request, I use a very cute wrinkle taught to me many years ago by Burling Hull. Hold the deck face down in the left hand and riffle the outer end. When the spectator stops you, lift up the upper portion and have the spectator note the top card of the lower half. The spectator replaces the card on top of the lower half, and the right hand comes over and replaces the top half of the pack. It is brought down at right angles to the lower half, and the left fingers come up against its back. The hands swing toward the right, the left fingers draw off the top or back card of the upper packet and add it to the top of the lower packet. This is done just as the hands are turned over, and the slip is completely covered. Immediately the slip is accomplished, the hands separate by about eight inches, the left turns so that the back of the hand is nearly upwards and, at the same moment, the left first finger is extended and points to the bottom face card of the right hand packet. You excuse yourself as you make this move, saying, "I didn't mean to look at this card, or let anyone see it. I don't want you to think I'm keeping track of your card by knowing the one next to it. We'll bury your card."

The left thumb now pushes the top card of the lower packet, supposedly the selected card, into the center of the upper packet as the two hands are brought in alignment. The left packet is now placed on top of the right hand packet, which brings the selected card on top of the deck. Or, alternately, the two packets are dovetailed together retaining the top few cards of the left hand packet until the end of the shuffle, which accomplishes the same results. The selected card is now on top, and you say, "I'm going to ask that you remember just about where your card is in the deck. You saw it go in, you know about where it is, so try to be certain of its location within two or three cards."

"Now take this card, the —— of ——, and push it into the deck about twenty cards above where you know your's is. I'll make your card move right up through the deck to that very spot." As you say this, you do a double lift, apparently showing the top card, and then turning it face down on top of the deck after naming it. Thumb it off, hand it face down to the spectator, and hold the deck before him. (In the fairest way possible you have given him his own card!) He stabs it into the deck and you tell him to hang onto it. Then you lift the packet of cards above the one he is holding, and show him the face card. It is not his card! Then you show him the top card of the lower packet, and this is not his card either! You act disconcerted and start to run through the pack, asking him what card he did have. He'll name it. You shake your head, blow towards the card he is holding and say, "Well, a magician has to have some way of getting out of a fix, so I'll make the card you are holding your card." He turns it over, and it is his! The effect on the spectator is just short of a knockout. To him, and to those watching, there is no conceivable way of your changing the card in his hand, and the misdirection throughout keeps the minds of all on the card buried in the pack.

Editor's Note:—As will be recognized by many, the above method of slipping the card from one packet to another has also been employed as a force, or to bring the top card indetectably to a certain desired spot in the center of the deck. It is quite well known today but, as many may not recall, the method used in the above trick is the original Hull routine which has been woven into a topnotch table trick in typical Annemann fashion.

DOUBLE REVERSE

WALTER GIBSON

Let's start off by being fundamental. Every magician is familiar with the original "reversed" or "turned over" card trick wherein the pack is held face up, but with a single card face down on top of it. When the spectator replaces a chosen card, it will naturally be found face up later

on. The magician's one problem is to hide or get rid of the face down
card which he used on the top of the pack.

This trick not only gets rid of said card; it utilizes it to double
the effect. The whole working is simplified to the limit, and has some
nice misdirection.

The effect, briefly: A spectator shuffles the pack, and divides it
into two heaps. He gives one half to you and keeps the other. Taking your
half, you fan the cards and say, "I'll pick a card and lay it down on the
table. You do the same with your half. Lay your card face down, as I do."
Both you and the spectator turn away during the process so that all is
very, very secret. You again face each other as the two chosen cards
are placed face down on the table. Now you pick up the spectator's
card and, without looking at its face, insert it into the half pack you
hold. The spectator picks up your card and pushes it into the center of
his half pack.

Extending your right hand you ask the spectator for his half pack.
Upon receiving it, you add your half on top of it, shuffle the full pack,
or give it a quick series of cuts, saying, "My card was the Nine of
Hearts — what was yours?" To which the spectator replies, "The Five
of Clubs", whereupon you ribbon spread the pack along the table top,
and there they are, face up, the Nine of Hearts and the Five of Clubs, well
apart in the pack.

Here's how: When you receive your half of the pack, you turn your
back (as does the spectator), and fan the deck noting and remembering
the bottom card. This card, say it's the Nine of Hearts, you turn face
to face with your packet of cards. You then withdraw any other card
without noting it and, holding it face down, turn around and lay it
on the table.

As you turn around to do this, you are holding the half pack in your
left hand, the thumb and fingers upward. That is, the half pack is simply
lying comfortably across your palm, but you are holding it so that the
single card you noted — the Nine of Hearts — is face down on top. The
packet looks normal, but it is really composed of one card face downward,
with the remainder face up beneath it.

You now pick up the spectator's card and push it, face down, into
the center of your packet where it automatically becomes "reversed"
because it goes in among face up cards. But when the spectator takes
up the card you laid on the table and buries it face down in his half

pack, he loses it. For the spectator actually pushes that card into a normal face down group of cards.

Now here comes the misdirection. Reaching with your right hand for the spectator's half of the pack, you swing your left hand towards the right, turning over your hand so that the knuckles are up. The move is simplicity itself, totally unnoticed because attention is on the right hand. Upon receiving the spectator's half which is face down, you coolly add your own face down half on top of it. Now everything is just as you want it. Somewhere in the upper half is the spectator's card — we'll say it is the Five of Clubs — face up. Half way down in the pack, and also face up, of course, is the Nine of Hearts. You now cut the pack a couple of times, even give it a shuffle, and obligingly name the Nine of Hearts as your card. The spectator names his card as the Five of Clubs, and when the deck is ribbon spread across the table top, both of these cards are revealed face up in the face down spread.

Thus you have used the card which you originally laid on the table purely as a "dummy" card to get a double effect of two reversals. As for the spectator, he can be very wise and still have a headache. No matter what he thinks about his own card, he can't get over the fact that he, personally, buried your card in his pile; yet it reversed itself anyway. The attention is thereby divided, leaving two problems instead of one; and in this very simple routine, the use of half packs allows misdirection; impossible with any of the older methods. Attention being divided between two people, the trick offers no problem whatsoever, except to the audience!

STOP WHEN READY

HENRY CHRIST

Here's a "stop" trick that will find favor with many, because of its simplicity and apparent fairness.

A selected card is returned and shuffled into the pack. Cards are dealt until the spectator calls "Stop," whereupon the very next card is found to be the selected one.

The selected card is brought to the top of the pack by your favorite method. Then you shuffle once or twice, preferably by riffling, and as you finish you add one extra card to the top so that the chosen card is the second one down. The deck is held face down in the left hand.

At this time you explain that you will not find the card yourself, but will have the selector discover it by intuition. Ask him to concentrate for a moment and then name any number up to 20. As he does so, you turn over the top card endwise, from front to back, so that it is face up on top of the deck, saying, "This isn't your card is it? Sometimes the card does get to the very top by chance and it makes things difficult." The spectator naturally says, "No," and you finish by saying, "Then we'll call that card No. 1."

During these few seconds you have prepared for a double lift of the top two cards and, as you make the last statement, you draw these two back about one and one-half inches on the deck, the sides being kept squared. The position of the cards now is this: the deck is in your left hand squared; on top is a face up card drawn back, and, unknown to the audience, underneath this drawn back card is the selected card face down.

Having called the face up card No. 1, you pull off the next face down

card from the front end of the pack, calling it No. 2. This is then turned face up and laid in that manner upon the first drawn back face up card. Likewise the next card is drawn off from the front end of the deck, and turned face up on top of the second card drawn. See illustration.

This same action is continued with each subsequent card withdrawn until the number decided upon is reached. This one is not turned up nor pulled forward over the front end of the deck. As you stop at this point, push forward all the face cards until they are square with the entire deck, saying, "You haven't seen your card among those dealt so far, have you?" As he answers, you fan the top part of the deck to show the face up cards. The answer must be negative, and the face up cards are drawn off into the right hand while the left hand extends the face down deck to the spectator assisting you. You say, "The next card is at the number you named, so turn it over yourself. By the way, what was your card?" The card is named and then turned. It has to be correct. The face down card, originally second from the top, and kept secretly under the first face up card turned over, has now become the top card of the face down deck, and resides at the correct number position as called by the spectator who chose it.

The important detail is to keep the deck in a position, or angle, almost flat towards the spectators so that the two cards held together appear to be but one card.

TWENTIETH CENTURY CARDS

TED ANNEMANN

Here is a nice card effect for club programs, and one that will be found different from the usual run of card tricks. All you need is a deck of cards, a ticket punch, and a two yard length of half inch ribbon threaded through a large darning needle.

A spectator freely selects a card and you hand him the ticket punch with the request that he punch a hole near one of the four corners of his card. The card is now returned to the center of the deck which is given a good shuffle. You now pick off one of the top cards of the deck and show it saying, "I know this is not the card selected by this gentleman because it has no punch mark in it." You likewise show the next card of the deck, emphasizing that this one has no punch mark in it either. You explain, however, that with the assistance of these two cards you will locate the chosen card in a novel manner. So saying you take the ticket punch and punch a hole in the corner of each card. You now introduce the ribbon and needle and proceed to thread the two cards onto the ribbon about a foot apart. A spectator assists in this by holding one end of the ribbon for you. The other end of the ribbon is now handed to another spectator nearby so that the ribbon, with the two cards swinging on it, is suspended between them in full view of everyone.

You now cover the two cards with a large handkerchief. While the card threading was going on you had set the deck on the table, so now you pick it up saying, "The selected card is still somewhere in this pack, but it will make itself evident as soon as it finds out what a good time these other two cards are having on this ribbon." Place the deck up under the handkerchief, give it a couple of sharp riffles, and then remove the deck whipping off the handkerchief at the same time. To everyone's amazement the selected card is seen dangling on the ribbon between the two cards previously threaded thereon. Everything may now be examined as there is nothing to find!

I believe this effect will find a spot in a good many programs because of its extreme simplicity. Everything is unprepared except one card. This has its back touched up with spots of diachylon in the corners, the middle of the sides, and in the upper center and lower center. Prepared thus, it is on top of your deck at the start.

One card is freely selected from the pack, and the spectator may write his name across its face. Hand him the ticket punch and ask him to punch a hole in one corner of the card about a half inch in from the

edge. Now undercut the lower half of the deck, and have the selected
card returned on top of the upper half (right on top of the diachylon
treated card), then bury the card by dropping the undercut lower half
on top. Square up the deck, give it a squeeze, and then shuffle it to
bring the double card close to the top. The deck, of course, being held
face down throughout. Now spread a few of the top cards of the deck
and your left thumb will "catch" the double card almost at once. Take
out this card with the right hand and show it as the first of your two
cards. Held face towards the audience no punch mark will be seen in
it, which is a convincing detail. The card stuck to the back of this card
is the "punched" selected card, but the back is not shown, and the card
is tossed face up onto the table. Another card is now shown in the same
manner, and this is tossed face up on the table also. Laying the deck
aside for a moment, you take the ticket punch and proceed to punch
a hole in both of the cards you selected, being careful to punch the hole
in the double card to coincide with the hole already in the rear card.

Both of these cards are now threaded on the ribbon, the double card
going on first so that the back of this card will face the front of the

second card. Thus the rear
(selected) card of the double
pair is now in position between
the two cards. Have the ends
of the ribbon held by two
spectators with the two cards
dangling freely in a very innocent and convincing manner.
In all the years that I have
done this trick, no one has
ever thought the cards to be

anything but what they seemed to be! Now cover the two cards with a
large handkerchief, place the deck underneath the handkerchief and
riffle it sharply a few times with one hand while the other seperates the
double card by pinching it and sliding the pair apart. The rear (selected)
card is now pushed along the ribbon until it is half way between the
two cards. The handkerchief is whipped off for the climax, and the
spectator's autographed card is discovered on the ribbon.

Aside from the dramatic effect wrought by the riffling of the
deck under the handkerchief, it is almost a necessity for it covers the
slight noise occasioned by the separation of the double card. Separating
this card with one hand will take a bit of practice, but the effect is well
worth it.

MODERN MONTE

CHRIS CHARLTON

The "Three Card Monte" effect has stood the brunt of many variations, and this method is one of the more convincing ways of performing it. Simply borrow three cards from any deck in use, preferably two spot cards and one picture card, and you are all set to entertain impromptu with the following baffling routine.

If you are adept at this game you may "throw" the cards several times in the regular way and then resort to Charlton's method for your climax, saying that perhaps it will be a lot easier to follow if the cards are kept face up.

Hold the three cards face up and squared. The left hand does this by holding the packet from above with the four fingers along the left side and the thumb on the right side of the cards. The forefinger rests at the pip of the exposed card, and the lower left corner of the packet rests in the crotch of the third and little fingers. The thumb rests about an inch and a half from the outer right end of the cards. Thus the left third finger, underneath, is in a perfect position to execute pressure on the under card. It will be seen that this is about the same position as used for the familiar "glide" sleight, except that in this case it is more practical for the under finger to exert a little backward pressure as the **thumb and first finger tighten on the sides and push the loose cards (top two) a bit forward.**

To experiment with this sleight, perform the move and take the two top cards as one by grasping them at the front end with your right thumb or forefinger. Slide them under the card (apparently two cards) left behind your left hand. Keep repeating this over and over until you do it with no concern or hestitation. It will be seen that the three cards show up, one after the other, in what appears to be a normal rotation.

Take the cards given to you (we will assume they are the Jack, Nine and Three) and say, "I'll show you the cards very slowly, and ask you to remember their positions. When I turn them over face down, pay close attention and note further that I do nothing to deceive you." Keeping the set in whatever order they happen to be, hold them as described and call the value of the top face up card as you move it fairly to the bottom. Name the next card that shows up and move this one fairly to the bottom. Now name the third face up card and likewise move this one fairly to the bottom. As you do this, the first card named naturally comes back into sight. Now turn the left hand over, bringing the packet face down, while the right fingers deliberately spread the cards into a fan. "Where is the . . . .?" you ask, naming the last card shown and moved to the bottom just before the packet was turned backs upward.

There will be no hesitation on the spectator's part as he selects the top or right hand card of the face down fan. And he will be right!

Remark, "I asked for a spot card that time as they always stay pretty well where they belong. Picture cards, exercise their noble perogative and are hard to depend upon. This time watch the Jack."

As you say this, cut the packet so that the Jack is at the bottom of the face up heap, and rests on tip of the left third finger which is curled around and under the packet. You are holding the packet face up, as described, and you now name the top card as before. This time you perform the sleight and draw off two cards as one with the right hand, and move them to the bottom of the packet. The Jack comes into view and is named. Again you perform the sleight, transferring two cards as one from top to bottom, and the second spot card comes into view. Perform the sleight once more, and the original card makes its appearance as the top card of the packet. Everything now appears to be exactly as in the beginning, so you turn the packet face down and fan the cards. The Jack, so far as the spectators are concerned, should be in the center, but it isn't. When this card is pointed out as the Jack, withdraw it and show it to be one of the spot cards. Do not show where the Jack is, just replace the card being held by the right hand on top of the face down packet.

Offer to repeat the moves once more. Turn the packet face up and go through with the three "double" moves. The Jack now shows up third, and after being named is moved (two cards as one) to the bottom of the packet. Turn the packet face down, and fan it once more. This time the Jack should be at the right end, but it isn't—it's in the middle! The three cards are now handed back to one of the spectators to be shuffled back into the deck in preparation for any ensuing tricks you may want to do.

MENTAL STUD

HENRY CHRIST

In this effect, which we are doing at every opportunity, Mr. Christ has brought into being a subtle problem with ramifications that cover all trickiness. In as much as the effect and method are being combined in this description, we recommend that you follow the moves with a deck of cards in hand.

Any deck is shuffled, and you offer to demonstrate a little "psychic Poker" showing how one accomplished in the reading of minds could very easily know exactly what cards were going to be played, or what cards in a player's hand were most important.

Four face down hands of five cards each are dealt onto the table, and these are picked up by the four spectators agreeing to play. Each is asked to peek at one of the cards in his hand, and then shufflle his cards. It is best to have them each peek at one card rather than fan out the hands, for some people have good card memories and might remember several of the cards in their hands, if not all of them.

While talking, bring out four coins, saying, "I hear people say so often they wouldn't play cards with me that I'm going to furnish the money so none of you will have anything to lose." Turning to the player at your left, give him one of the coins and take back his hand of cards. The coins may be of any denomination but should all be alike. However, the one difference is the dates on the coins which you have memorized, and in passing them out begin with the earliest date and end with the latest date. The first person therefore gets the earliest dated coin. But be sure you do not make it apparent that you are giving out the coins in any particular order. This is an important detail for you later.

The first hand of five cards you take back with your left hand, and give it a single, careless cut. The right hand now picks up the second coin and gives it to the second spectator, receiving in return the second packet of cards. Take these back with your right hand, spread them a bit in a slight fan face down, and then place them on top of the left hand packet. As you do so, the left little finger holds a break above the bottom card of the right hand packet. Square up the cards a bit, cut them at the break, and complete the cut. The right hand now picks up the third coin, hands it to the third person, takes back his packet, spreads them a bit face down, lays them on top of the left hand packet, and the left little finger again holds a break above the bottom card of this third packet. Again the entire packet is cut at the break, and the cut completed. The fourth coin is now handed to the fourth spectator, who is immediately on your right, and you take back his hand of cards. The same maneuvers are now gone through with the packet, ending up with your cutting the entire packet at the break and completing the cut.

To the players you have taken back the hands one at a time in return for the coins you passed out, and after each hand has been returned the packets have been added to each other and the final packet has simply been cut. Actually, however, the arrangement of the cards from the top down (back to face) is as follows, and we'll list them by numerals denoting the four players from left to right: 4-3-2-1-1-1-1-1-2-2-2-2-3-3-3-3-4-4-4-4.

Now deal out the four top cards in front of you on the table, from left to right and all face down, saying, "Stud will be the best form of poker demonstration for my purpose." Now continue to deal cards face up in front of these "hole cards" (laying them on the table towards the spectators and overlapping about half of the card's lengths on each deal) just as you would for a real game, until the packet of twenty cards have been laid out for the four hands.

The situation now is this: The four "hole cards" from left to right (that is, from your point of view) belong to players 4, 3, 2, 1. The first face up row across in front of the "hole cards" belongs to player Number 1 — the man on your left. The next row across belongs to player Number 2; the next row belongs to player Number 3; and the last to player Number 4.

Now ask the four players to put their coins in front of the row in which they see their peeked at cards. If a player doesn't see his peeked at card, then it must be one of the "hole cards" which are face down and, in this case, he is to return his coin to you. You step away and turn your back while they place their coins, or set them to one side awaiting your return.

Everything now is set for the climax. Picking up a coin in front of any row, you pass it up and down several times along that row, and then suddenly drop it onto the correct card! This is repeated with all other coins in view, and each time the player acknowledges that you have located, or designated, his card. Finally you look at the one or more coins in your hand which represent the "hole cards." Ask the player, or players, to think of his card and then drop a coin onto one of the face down cards. When he turns it up, he finds that you have located his card correctly. Do the same with the second coin, if you still have one.

From the foregoing explanations of the set up after the final deal, you should have no trouble in seeing through the deception of the climax. As you pick up the coins placed on the table in front of the various rows, all you do is note the date on the coin which designates the different spectators. Then merely drop this on the face up card in that row — 1, 2, 3, 4, —

which corresponds with that spectator's number. The same rule applies to the "hole cards" — 4, 3, 2, 1.

The dates of the coins is the little detail which allows you to step away from the table and turn your back while the coins are being set in front of the various rows. Upon your return to the table you may find two coins in front of one row. This, of course, presents no difficulty. Pick them up one at a time, note the date as you wave it to and fro over the row which tells you whether it belongs to player Number 1, 2, 3, or 4, and then drop it on the corresponding face up card. Then point directly at that player and say, "Your card." This really startling action was not possible with the old school boy trick of 25 cards dealt into five hands twice which is the basis for this modern version, nor was it possible to use but four hands of five cards each. The hole card angle makes this possible, and it throws completely out of calculation anyone who knows the old mathematical layout. At times a hole card will not be among those chosen, but the percentage is high in its favor. The showmanship of the first discoveries more than make up for the lack of face down discoveries.

THE RIBBON THAT MADE GOOD

ORVILLE MEYER

In this effect a spectator freely selects a card from a deck. After the card is replaced the deck is genuinely shuffled and cut several times. This may be done by the spectator himself. Saying that he will locate it, the performer removes a card at random. Upon seeing it, however, the spectator says it is not the one he picked out. A two foot ribbon is now fastened with a sticker to the back of this card and it is cut to the center of the deck. The spectator now names his selected card and gently pulls on the ribbon. He pulls out the card to which the ribbon is attached, and it is the chosen card!

No sleights are employed; there is nothing to cover up; no quick moves are necessary; and the chosen card may be initialed. A nice angle is to allow the spectator to keep the initialed card on the ribbon as a souvenir.

But slight preparation is necessary. Apply a bit of warm Diachylon to the back of the Joker, spreading it thinly in spots along the edges and in the center rather than over the entire back. With such a card on top of your deck you are ready to present this effect.

Have any card freely selected and its face initialed. Undercut about a half of the pack, have the card replaced on the top half of the deck, and drop the under half on top of all. The selected card is now near the center with the prepared Joker underneath it. Now pinch the deck tightly and the two cards will adhere. You can even give the deck an overhand shuffle without fear of separating them. After thus shuffling and cutting the deck remark that as usual you will try to find the selected card.

Fan the deck, and locate the double card which is easy because of it extra thickness. Remove it and declare it to be the one chosen. It shows up, of course, as the Joker. The spectator tells you that you are wrong. Now introduce the ribbon and sticker, and hand them to the spectator together with the double Joker. You need not be afraid of the double card coming apart, but if you are timid about this then place the double card on top of the deck and have him fasten the ribbon to the back of it with the sticker. Show the card to the spectator again after the ribbon is attached, and ask him if he is positive it is not his card. Lay the card back on top of the deck, and say you will bury it in the deck. Exert a little pressure on the back of the card with your left thumb as though pushing the card off the deck in dealing. This will separate the two cards. Pick off the top card (the selected one) with your right fingers and, holding it face down, push it into the center of the deck. (The Diachlyon treated Joker remains on top of the deck.)

Now hold the pack in a vertical position with its face card towards the audience, and with the ribbon coming out of the top of the deck. Have the spectator name his card. Riffle the top of the deck a couple of times, and then ask the spectator to pull up the ribbon. The correct initialed card makes its appearance rising out of the deck attached to the end of the ribbon.

TRICKS WITH DUPLICATES & SHORT CARDS

TRICKERY

TED ANNEMANN

Here's a pet of mine I'm sure you'll like. It's just the thing for one of those spots where you want to make a real impression with an unusual trick. You request one of the spectators to come forward and stand to your right. Have him look through the deck and note that it is well mixed. He then places five of the cards in his side coat pocket and hands the deck to you. You lay the deck on the table, and step away a bit as you explain to him that you want him to reach into his pocket and, while your back is turned, pick out any one of the five cards and show it to the others present. He is then to replace it in his pocket, insert it anywhere among the five cards, and bring forth the packet. You turn around now and face the audience. Take the packet of five cards, place them in your side coat pocket and remark that through some strange sense you are able to repeat the spectator's very actions. Reach again into your coat pocket, withdraw one card back outwards, and ask the spectator to name his card. When he does, you turn around the card you are holding and it is the very same card chosen by the spectator! The packet of cards is now added to the deck on the table, and you proceed with any further tricks you like for the deck is complete and may even be examined.

Four duplicates of any card, say the Ace of Spades, are used, but they are introduced and withdrawn in a manner so natural and subtle that their use is never suspected. I know, because I have fooled dozens of clever card men with this feat. These four duplicate Aces are in your right outside coat pocket at the start, and are in a standing position in one corner of the pocket.

The presentation of the feat is as follows:—Introduce the deck and fan it face up for the benefit of your assistant, who is standing to your right. Locate the regular Ace of Spades and, after closing the fan, cut the Ace to the top. Give the deck a dovetail shuffle and leave four more cards on top of the deck so that the Ace is now the fifth card down. Run off four cards from the top of the deck into your right hand without the spectator seeing just how many you take. Tell him that he is to put five cards into his pocket without showing them. Suiting your actions to your words, place the group of four cards into your right coat pocket, laying it on its side so as not to become mixed with the cards already there. Now withdraw one of these four odd cards from your pocket and show it, explaining that everyone is to have an opportunity to see it except yourself. Replace this card in your pocket, and immediate withdraw the four Ace packet, holding it face down, and put it on top of the deck. This leaves the five duplicate Aces on top of the pack.

Now give the deck another dovetail shuffle without disturbing the top cards, and then deal these five Aces from the top of the deck face down on the assistant's outstretched palm. He places them in his pocket immediately, as you turn your back. He then pulls out any one of the five cards which, of course, has to be an Ace of Spades, and shows it to all present. He then replaces it in his pocket, inserts it anywhere among the other four cards and advises you that his part of the experiment is completed.

You turn around and ask him for the packet of five cards which you take face down in your right hand. You place these, in a standing position, in your right coat pocket as you explain what you intend to do. After a bit of suitable hesitation, you finally bring forth one of the Ace of Spades, but hold it face down until the spectator names it as the one he selected. Then turn it around dramatically for your climax! Transfer it to your left hand as your right reenters the coat pocket and brings forth the four odd cards which have been laying there on their sides. These, plus the Ace of Spades, are thrown face up on the table, as you accept the applause for your uncanny ability and an almost impossible feat.

FOUR ACE STAGE PRESENTATION

TED ANNEMANN

This is my version of the "Four Ace Trick" for stage and platform use. Its novel manner of presentation will hold constant interest, and the method employed is more than fair and belies all suspicion of chicanery.

In effect, you request the assistance of four volunteers who are invited to the stage and asked to stand in a row facing the audience. A deck of cards is handed to the first assistant with the request that he run through the cards and remove the first Ace he comes to. Now, without showing this to anyone, he is asked to hold it face down on one outstretched hand. You then take the deck and pass it on to the second assistant who repeats the first man's actions; then the third and fourth assistants do likewise, the last man handing the deck back to you. Now each assistant is holding an Ace on his outstretched hand, the name of the individual Aces being known only to those holding them.

You now shuffle the deck, deal three cards face down on each of the Aces, and announce that one of the Aces is to be selected at random. Giving the deck a good shuffle, you turn up the top card the suit of which indicates the Ace to be used. Asking the assistant holding this ace to cover his packet of cards with his other hand and to stand to one side, you proceed to gather up the remaining packets from the other three assistants and add their cards to the top of the deck. A rubber band is snapped around the deck of cards and it is thrown out into the audience with the request that the spectator catching it will please stand up. The assistants are dismissed, except the one holding the chosen packet. The person standing in the audience with the deck of cards is now asked to remove the elastic band from the pack, and to run through it and toss each Ace into the air as he comes to it. Everybody watches, but nothing

happens. The Aces have disappeared! The deck is returned to the stage
and the assistant holding the chosen packet now shows his cards — and he
is seen to be holding the four Aces!

Of course, three extra Aces are needed, and they are employed without any special preparation. However, the deck itself is a "short" deck,
ie: one trimmed one-thirty second of an inch short. Any magic dealer
can supply you with such a deck. Remove from this deck the three short
Aces which are duplicates of the extra ones you will use, substituting the
regular length extra Aces in the deck in their stead. The three short Aces

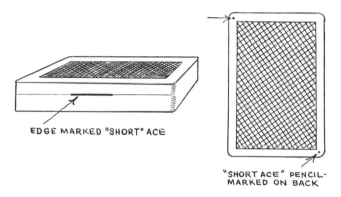

EDGE MARKED "SHORT" ACE

"SHORT ACE" PENCIL-
MARKED ON BACK

are placed in your right trousers' pocket, with faces of the cards towards
your body. Also have an elastic band in the same pocket. The fourth
short Ace, of which you have no duplicate, is marked with a pencil for
distance of about one inch along the center of both side edges of the card,
as illustrated, or pencil mark its back on the upper left and lower right
corners. The object being to enable you to spot this card when it is removed
from the deck, thus indicating which assistant has it. If the card is marked
on the edge it is a simple matter to note when it leaves the deck simply by
glancing at the side of the pack, as you pass the latter from one assistant
to the other. If it is marked on the back, you simply watch the backs of
the Aces as they are held by the assistants. And finally, to complete your
preparations, place any card of the same suit as the marked short Ace
on the bottom of the deck.

The performance of the trick is as outlined. Each of the assistants
removes an Ace and holds it face down on his outstretched palm. However, as the fourth assistant is searching for the last Ace, you casually
place your right hand in your trousers' pocket and palm out the three
short Aces. When the last Ace has been located and removed, take the
deck back with your left hand and add the three short Aces to the top

of it. At this point no one expects anything to happen, and you have very subtly convinced the audience, and your assistants as well, that but four Aces were in the deck. That's what makes the effect so strong.

You now give the deck a good false shuffle, retaining the short Aces on the top, and the bottom card in place on the bottom. Deal the three top cards (short Aces) face down onto the palm of the assistant holding the "marked" Ace, the cards going right on top of the Ace itself. Then deal three cards onto each of the other Aces, being casually haphazard about it and not necessarily dealing in order unless the "marked" Ace is held by the first assistant. Now announce that one of the Aces will be selected at random. Give the deck another good shuffle, bringing the bottom card to the top, and simply turn this top card over and announce the suit, introducing the selection by saying, "We'll make it a matter of chance by turning up a card at random, and the suit of this card will select the man. Will the person holding the Ace of this suit please step over there and hold his cards tightly between his hands." Again you have been fair because no one knows who has the different Aces except the assistants themselves.

Now have the remaining three piles returned to the deck, undercut just below this set of twelve cards and shuffle off on top. You will now find it an easy matter to cull out the Aces as you repeat the shuffle, the thumb and fingers easily stripping out the three long Aces and dropping them on top of the deck. While you are doing this (and don't look at your hands, as the stripping action is automatic) dismiss the three assistants thanking them for their help. Simultaneously, palm off the three extra Aces from the top of the deck with the right hand, reach into your trousers' pocket, get rid of the palmed cards, and bring forth the rubber band. Snap it around the pack and toss the deck out into the audience. So far as you are concerned, the trick is over, and you have no more to worry about. However, you continue to build up the effect to the grand climax.

The person in the audience catching the deck is asked to run through it and toss each Ace into the air as he comes to it. Of course, he does not find any, and returns the deck to you. Ask the assistant on the stage, who is holding the selected packet of cards, to step forward and show his cards. He shows the four Aces!

A strong point of the trick is that at the finish you are holding a complete deck of 52 cards, which may be examined, or which can be used immediately for any further tricks you wish to do. I've found it an unusually good program effect, one that can be sandwiched into your repertoire at any time. One trial is all that is necessary to convince you that it is good. The action of having four spectators in line and handling the deck is strong, and enjoys considerable audience participation which so many effects lack. The tossing of the deck into the audience is both novel and interesting, and the whole theme of the effect directs attention to the assistants affording you perfect cover for the few subtleties you must employ.

For those who want to present the trick without a "short deck," the action is the same up to the point where you collect the three odd packets of cards from the assistants you dismiss. In this case, when using regular cards, have the first packet dropped on top of the deck and then give the deck a little shuffle, running the three odd cards from the top to the bottom. This leaves the first Ace on top. Repeat this three times, ending up with the three Aces on top of the deck. It is now a simple matter to push these three top cards forward a bit off the deck, and to palm them just prior to reaching into your pocket for the elastic band. Then complete the trick as already explained.

Editor's note:—The forcing of the proper suit as explained above is excellent. However, for those who may not wish to retain the "marked" suit card at the bottom of the deck throughout the trick for the obvious reason that one or two of your assistants might note that it is the bottom card that turns up eventually, the following alternate is suggested. Simply use an "unmarked" suit card that has been crimped at one corner. Thus you can forget it temporarily, and then cut to it later after shuffling the deck legitimately. The audience will accept the apparently haphazard cut just as readily, if not more so, than turning up the top of the deck.

FLIGHTY ACES

LU BRENT

For a non-sleight and practical club or stage method, we have never run across an idea to compare with the following. While not differing radically from the orthodox Ace routine, this method of Lu Brent's will truly baffle the most observing audience.

The four Aces are withdrawn openly from the pack and are placed in a face up row on a display easel. Twelve odd cards are dealt from the pack in groups of three, each group being dealt face down on a different Ace in an overlapping position so that the top part of each Ace is visible. (The best type of easel for this effect is one that has a ledge about an inch from the bottom. Thus the Aces are placed on the ledge, and the odd cards are dealt against the Aces with the base of the cards resting on the table.)

A spectator is now invited to assist by naming any one of the four Aces. This is a free choice, and the Ace named together with its three accompanying cards are picked up, placed in an envelope and given to the spectator to hold. The remaining three Aces, together with their accompanying odd cards, are gathered up, placed in a second envelope and are retained by the performer. Upon a mystical formula being pronounced, an invisible flight takes place! The spectator's envelope is found to contain the four Aces, while in the performer's envelope twelve odd cards are found. Everything may now be examined, and the deck contains but its regular 52 cards and may be used immediately for further card tricks.

The requirements for this astoundingly clean effect are 12 extra Aces,, consisting of three sets of four each, three business envelopes, a pencil and, of course, a deck of cards. Now remove any 12 odd cards from the pack, reverse every fourth card, and seal this packet in one of the envelopes. Mark the face of this envelope with a large numeral "2", and put it in your inside coat pocket.

The twelve Aces are now arranged on the top of the deck, face down, ready for dealing and in a pre-arranged order depending upon the order you intend to use in displaying the four regular Aces during the effect. For instance, if you display the regular Aces from left to right as Hearts, Clubs, Diamonds and Spades, then your stack of extra Aces on top of the deck should be, reading from the top down: Club, Diamond, Spade; Heart, Diamond, Spade; Heart, Club, Spade; and Heart, Club, Diamond. The four regular Aces belonging to the deck are scattered through the lower part of the pack.

To perform, exhibit the two remaining envelopes and the deck of cards. Remove the deck from its case, fan it keeping the duplicate Aces at the top together in a closed group. Remove the four regular Aces from the lower part of the deck and place them one at a time, and face outwards, on the display stand. The first Ace being placed on the left end of the stand, and the others to the right of it in the usual 2, 3, 4, order. The deck is now given a dovetail shuffle without disturbing the twelve extra Aces on top, and the statement is made that each Ace being displayed will be given three cards for company. Do this by dealing three cards (Aces) from the top of the deck onto each of the four Aces on the stand, leaving the top portion of each Ace visible, as already explained.

Now invite any spectator to call out the name of any Ace, allowing him to change his mind as often as he likes until he is perfectly satisfied. Take the Ace packet selected and, without reversing the Ace so that it is facing the same way as the three odd cards, place it in one of the envelopes. Seal it and mark it with a large numeral "1." Hand this to the assisting spectator, who is asked to initial it and place it in his pocket.

The remaining Ace heaps are now gathered up and placed in the second envelopes on which you write a large numeral "2", saying, "I will place this envelope in my pocket as you have done. Oh! I beg your pardon, I forgot to have you initial my envelope." As you say this, you are placing your envelope into your inside coat pocket, so bring it out again immediately and have the spectator initial it. Actually, you switch envelopes and bring forth the duplicate bearing the numeral "2" which you had there before the trick began. There should be no hestitation; the action should be timed perfectly with your patter, so that it appears as though you were just placing the envelope in your inside coat pocket but changed your mind and brought it out again immediately.

After the spectator initials your envelope, you have another thought and place the envelope in your outside breast pocket, and ask the spectator to do the same with his envelope, "so that everyone may see the flight of the cards." As the working of th etrick is already done, the climax depends upon the individual performer's ability to build it up. When the magic words are spoken, the performer's envelope is torn open and twelve indifferent cards are found, four of which are reversed in the packet as they should be. Now the spectator opens his envelope and finds the four Aces!

Everything is clean. The envelopes may be tossed out, and the deck is again a complete one of 52 cards. A trial will convince you of the effectiveness of this routine, for there is no forcing, no indirect action, and no sleights.

A QUESTION OF POWER

L. VOSBURGH LYONS

Methods of revealing a number of chosen cards are legion, but here is a new and different way that lends itself to an interesting line of patter.

Three cards are selected and returned to the pack you hold, as you explain that tricksters usually locate cards by exercising a strange power which enables them to make cards appear at any position in the deck. The most common position, of course, being the top of the deck.

However, you turn over the top card to prove that is is not one of those chosen. It is then turned face down on the deck as you ask one of the spectators to name his card. When he does so, you snap the top of the deck, turn the card face up once more — and it's now the selected card just named!

Turning it face down on top of the deck again, you explain that had you asked one of the other two spectators to name his card first, the result would have been the same. To prove your point, the second spectator now names his card which is immediately found on top of the deck after you have snapped it and turned the top card face up. The same action is again repeated with the third spectator, whereupon the third chosen card appears at the top of the deck. As a finale, you mention that had no one named a card then the original card shown would have remained on top of the deck . . . . . . and so it has, as you prove by turning the top card up for all to see. As an example of pseudo mass hypnotism, this effect is in a class by itself.

The only preparation consists in having an extra duplicate of any card in the deck. I prefer to use duplicate Jokers, and one of these has been trimmed to make it a short card. Both of these are on top of the deck at the start, with the short Joker as the top card.

To present: — Introduce the deck, shuffle it retaining the two Jokers on top, and have three cards freely selected by as many spectators. Under cut about half of the deck, have the first card replaced on top of the two Jokers, and then drop the lower or under cut half on top, and square the deck. In approaching the next spectator, riffle cut to the short card and have the second selected card returned on top of it. Square up the deck which brings the second selected card just below the first one. Repeat the same maneuver with the third card. Thus you have the three selected cards under your control while to the audience they seem to be hopelessly lost. As you return to the platform, cut the deck several times; then at the short Joker, and finally cut three cards from the bottom to the top. This leaves you with the three selected cards on top in the order of their replacement, and directly below them the two Jokers. Now cut off about fifteen of the top cards, lay aside the rest of the deck, and explain that you will need only a few cards to make clear your example of power.

As you say this, you are holding the packet of fifteen cards squared up in your left hand as if for dealing. It is, of course, held face down. Now the right hand comes over and covers the packet with its palm just as though you were going to transfer the cards to the right hand. The left hand tilts the packet a bit towards the right and, at the same

time, the left thumb pushes the four top cards off to the right where
the left fingers grasp them and pull them around onto the bottom of

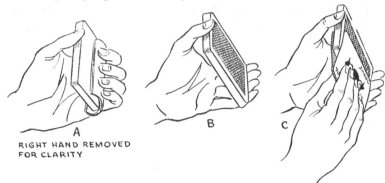

A
RIGHT HAND REMOVED
FOR CLARITY

B

C

the packet. See illustration A. Sliding around the right edge of the
packet under cover of the right palm, they end up on the bottom in a
reversed position, face to face with the bottom card of the packet. (The
action is a sort of half-pass, and is easily discovered by testing it with
the cards in your hand.) With these four cards face up on the bottom
you are left with the regular Joker on top of the deck.

Now change the position of the packet in the left hand so that it is
still held with its real back to the audience, but with the left thumb
at one of the narrow ends and the left fingers at the opposite narrow
end. The packet is tilted somewhat to the left, so that from the audience
point of view it is in a diagonal position, just short of being upright. See
illustration B. The right fingers now slide the top card off the right
(towards you) about a quarter of an inch where it is grasped between
the fingers and thumb (the latter behind the right edge of the card,)
and turned over towards the audience as you replace it face out on the
packet of cards. Everyone sees it's the Joker.

The Joker is now slid off the deck and replaced face down in a
repetition of the moves just explained with this difference. As the card is
slid off to the right with the right fingers, the right thumb goes behind
the packet and draws off the bottom card in alignment with and behind
the Joker. Illustration C. Thus the two cards, held as one, are turned
face down on the front of the packet. The top card is now the first
selected card. To the audience you have merely turned the Joker face
down. Now ask the first person to name his card, snap the deck with
your right second finger, and turn the top card only face up. It is
the first person's card.

As you patter along as to how it would have been the second person's card had you asked him first, you repeat the moves described in the above paragraph and thus steal and bring the second person's card from the bottom to the top of the packet as you turn the first person's card face down. Tap the deck again, and show the second person's card on top. Repeat again to show the third person's card.

Finally, in turning the third card face down on the deck, you secretly bring the last reversed card, the short Joker) from the bottom of the packet to the top. Now you say that if no one had named a card, the original Joker would have remained there, and so it has apparently as you turn it over to prove your statement. The deck is all one way again for anything else you want to do, and the short Joker may be palmed off or not as you like. You will find that the three changes are psychologically correct for this routine, the repetition actually heightening the effect.

SIMPLEX TORN CARD IN BALLOON

LU BRENT

Versions of the card in a balloon are many, but the majority of them are accomplished by mechanical means. The following was designed as an emergency method, and its simplicity will be appreciated by all club performers.

The effect is that the performer exhibits four colored balloons on a small tray. A spectator who will act as an assistant is requested to select one of the balloons after which it is inflated. A ribbon is tied secretly bring the last reversed card, (the short Joker) from the bottom spectator now selects a card. A corner is torn from it and he is asked to retain it temporarily. The remainder of the card now vanishes, only to make its reappearance as the balloon bursts. The torn corner is fitted to the card and it is the very one selected.

The preparation consists of the following: A regular deck of cards with one duplicate, four colored opaque balloons, a straight pin or two, a piece of ribbon and a little tray complete the list of articles required. Tear a corner from one of your duplicate cards and place the corner in one of your side pockets where it may easily be obtained during the trick. The torn card is now rolled up and inserted through the neck of one of the balloons, after which it is straightened out inside. The other three balloons are unprepared. Set the balloons in a line across the tray so that the balloon containing the card is second from your left as you hold the tray in front of you. Place the tray on your table or on a nearby chair, and you're ready to perform.

Force the balloon containing the card with this subtle method. State that you have four toy balloons and that one will be selected for the trick. Ask a spectator for a number from one to four. (Don't say, "between one and four.") He will generally say, "two," or "three" regardless, and it sounds more logical. Let us assume he has chosen "three," Step to your table, pick up the tray, walk to the spectator and have him count to the third one in the usual fashion from left to right. If he says, "two," it is there also depending on how you pick up the tray. Remember, the tray is always picked up after the number is mentioned, so there is no reason for the force to fail. Just pick up the tray either from front or back as required. The forced balloon is now inflated by blowing it up in the usual fashion, and the spectator ties the ribbon around its neck. He holds the ends of the ribbon so that the balloon dangles for all to see.

Now force the duplicate card, and drop the pack in your pocket. Secure the torn corner as you bring your hand out. Take the selected card, tear off the proper corner, switch it for the palmed corner and drop the latter into the spectator's hand. Fold the torn card over, incidentally folding up the genuine corner with it, and vanish it with your cigarette vanisher, or a double handkerchief. Pull one of the pins from your lapel and explode the balloon. The selected card makes its appearance, minus the corner, and it's given to the person who selected it to match it with the corner he is holding. After the applause, throw out the remaining three balloons as souvenirs.

(Editor's note: — Another simple method of performing the card in the balloon is to have the card backpalmed. Hold the inflated balloon with the same hand, nipping the neck of the balloon between the tips of first and second fingers and the thumb, and with the palm of the hand facing the audience. To cause the card to appear, just touch the balloon with the lighted end of a cigarette and, as it bursts, produce the back-palmed card at the finger tips! Credit for this streamlined version belongs I believe, to Albnice, one of America's most meticulous and ingenious club performers.)

CARD FINESSE

THE GREAT MAURICE

The following effect together with the method described has been used over a period of years by Maurice with outstanding success. It is a fine example of professional showmanship, and has the further advantage of using subterfuge rather than difficult sleights.

The effect: — Two cards are chosen by as many members of the audience, whereupon you hand the deck to each in turn and have them shuffle their cards back into the deck. It is very important to impress upon everyone that nothing of a "tricky" nature takes place. This you do by your actions in handling the deck as you take it back from the second spectator. Hold it high and in view of everyone as you step back to your table. With the other hand pick up a long strip of newspaper about 3½ inches wide (equal to the length of a playing card) and wrap up the deck by rolling it over and over so that the paper completely encircles the pack several times. The ends are left open. A rubber band is snapped around the package to hold it secure.

"It happens in the air!" you say, as you toss the deck to the first person who chose a card. He tosses it to the second person, who in turn tosses it back to you. Holding the wrapped deck flatwise to the audience you ask for the name of the first card selected. Remove the elastic band and deliberately tear into the wrapped package until the back of top card of the deck shows. Pick it out, turn it over showing it to be the first selected card, and then throw it out to the first assistant. Now turn the deck over and ask for the name of the second card chosen. Tear away the wrapping on this side of the package and reveal the second chosen card face outwards on the bottom of the deck. Remove it and throw it out to the person who selected it!

Remarkable as this appears to the audience, it has been pure showmanship throughout and little else. The newspaper strip used is about sixteen inches long, and three and a half inches wide, and has been provided with a double pocket of newspaper about four inches from one end of the strip. This pocket is open on both ends where they adjoin the edges of the paper strip. See illustration. Now insert a face down card in this pocket. About three quarters of an inch below this first pocket make a second pocket, and insert in this a second card, but face upwards.

The duplicates of these cards in the deck you use may be cut or trimmed to make them easy to locate. At any rate it is essential to have

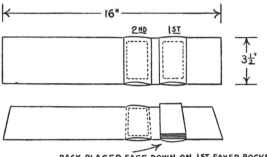

PACK PLACED FACE DOWN ON 1ST FAKED POCKET

them quickly accessible. These are forced upon the two spectators while you patter along about a new and strange way you have of locating the two cards touched by the two spectators. Now force the two duplicate short cards in a quick and direct manner. Either use the classical fan force, or riffle the deck to a point designated by the spectators and slip the force card from the top to the cut. I insist that it makes no difference how the force is made, as you only come under suspicion after the spectators shuffle their two cards back into the deck and then hand the deck to you. Actually, at this point you become blameless!

Hold the deck in your right hand well above your head, so that everyone may see that you make no effort to fool with the cards. Pick up the strip of paper with your left hand, show it on both sides, and place the deck face down on top of the first faked pocket on the strip. Try not to let the bottom card of the deck be seen any more than possible. The end of the strip is now turned over the deck, and then the deck is turned over and over wrapping it up completely in the strip of paper. Naturally the first turn brings the top of the deck in alignment with the second faked pocket, so that everything is now correctly placed for the production of the two cards as described. Encircle the package thus formed with an elastic band before tossing it out into the audience.

The rest of the presentation is pure showmanship — the tossing back and forth of the deck, the subsequent tearing away of the newspaper, and the production of the two chosen cards. The cards produced being, of course, the two previously hidden in the two faked pockets. Experience proves that the first card should be produced back outwards; the second face outwards.

THE RED AND BLUE BACK COLOR CHANGE

TED ANNEMANN

This trick is a fast favorite of mine, and I have fooled well versed card men with it because of its subtle working points.

The exact effect is as follows: A pack of cards is held face up in the left hand as though for dealing. Taking the two face cards openly with the right hand, you show both faces and backs of them calling particular attention to the fact that one card has a red back, the other a blue. Replacing these face up on the deck again, you slowly turn over the first card showing its blue back, and then drop it face up on the floor. The next card is shown to have a red back, and this likewise is dropped face up on the floor a few feet from the first card. Stressing once again which has a blue back and which has a red back, any spectator is allowed to turn the two cards face down. When he does so, the color of the backs of the two cards has changed. The one that was blue backed is now red; the one that was red backed is now blue!

No faked cards are needed for this unique effect, just your own deck and two extra cards from another deck with opposite colored backs. These may be any cards. The subtle part of the effect is that in turning the top card each time to show its back, the face of the card underneath it is seen. After the top card has been dropped onto the floor, the card remaining on the face up deck is the one noticed but a moment before, thus giving the lie to any possibility of you having turned more than one card . . . which is exactly what you do!

Arrange your face up pack as follows, the numbers indicating the position of the cards from the face of the pack.

     1. Any red backed card
     2. Any blue backed card
     3. Any blue backed card
     4. A duplicate of No. 2, but with a red back
     5. A duplicate of No. 3, but with red back
     The remainder of the deck is red backed

At the start, you hold the deck face upwards in your left hand and remove the two face cards with the right hand. Holding these fanned in your right hand you show them stating that you will use these two cards which are (name them.) Now carelessly show the backs of the two cards calling attention to the fact that one is blue backed, the other red. As you display the cards turn them back to front a couple of times so that no one has a chance of seeing just which card is red, and which is blue backed. Now replace the two cards face up on the face up deck, being careful to close the two card fan so that the cards go back in the same order they originally had.

Now explain that you will show the two cards slowly so there will be no mistake as to which is which. The right thumb, which is at the rear of the pack, lifts up the rear right corner of the top three cards so that the left little finger may hold a break. Calling attention to the face up card showing, the right thumb and fingers lift off the three top cards as one and turn them face down on the face up pack. The three cards are grasped by the lower right corner to turn them over, and they are not placed square with the rest of the pack, but are pulled back about half the length of the deck and left protruding over the rear end. Attention is called to the back of the card, which is blue, whereupon the right hand takes the three cards as one, exactly as before, and turns them face up on the deck once more. This time, however, they are squared even with the deck. Thus you have apparently shown both the face and back of the top card. The left thumb now slides the top (face) card about half way over the right side of the deck where it is taken by the edge with the right fingers and dropped perfectly flatwise onto the floor. You will find that it will not turn over as it descends, but will drop straight to the floor from any height. The card now face up on the deck will be seen to be the one formerly occupying that position, although you do not call attention to it specifically. Unknown to the spectators, however, it is actually the duplicate of the one originally seen.

As matters now stand, you have placed a blue backed card on the floor in a face up position. Now call attention to the new card on the face of the deck, show its back to be red by using the triple lift, then turn it face up again on the deck, exactly as you did with the first card, and finally drop this one on the floor in a face up position a few feet to the side of the first card. The card remaining face up on the face of the deck will be noted by everyone to be the card that should be there, thanks to your original set up. And don't think they won't notice it, for they most assuredly will.

It only remains now to have one of the spectators name the back colors of the two face cards on the floor, and then have him turn them over. To everyone's surprise the backs of the cards have changed color!

A point that makes the presentation easy to follow is to use a black spot card for the blue backed one; and a red spot card for the red backed one. This helps the spectators remember the colors, and makes the change really surprising.

(If presenting the effect for an audience which is seated, hold the face up deck in the left hand in approximately the first position of the Charlier Pass, but tilt the hand so that the face of the cards may be seen by everyone. The routine may just as easily be performed with the cards in this position, and the effect can be followed quite readily by the audience.)

THE FINDERS

ORVILLE MEYER

This effect differs with the size of the audience, but in each case the performer appears to have perfect control of the cards.

A deck of cards is riffled, and a spectator inserts his finger or a knife into the pack and removes the card under his finger. This is a free selection, and is not forced. The selected card is replaced upon the deck, and you withdraw two odd cards and show them as you set the deck on the table and cut it to bury the selected card. Explaining that these two odd cards are your "Finder Cards" which you intend to reverse and thrust back into the deck, you ask everyone to note particularly the names of the two cards. To make the feat you are about to perform even more remarkable, you offer to locate the selected card with your "Finders" while the deck is behind your back. Pick up the deck with one hand and place it behind your back, as the other hand with the two "Finder Cards" also goes behind your back for merely a second. The deck is now brought forward and either fanned or ribbon spread on the table. In the center of the spread your two "Finder Cards" are seen to be face up with a face down card between them. Withdrawing these three cards from the deck, you ask the name of the selected card. Upon it being named, you turn over the three cards and the center card is found to be the one selected. Thus in a matter of a second you have managed to insert your two cards into the deck and locate the chosen card!

The effect can be made even more miraculous by having the spectator himself thrust the two cards into the deck while it is behind his back, and thus locate his own selected card. If you are doing the effect for only one or two spectators, we recommend that you follow this latter procedure.

Now for the secret which is really quite simple. You use two duplicate cards, for instance two Four of Diamonds and two Three of Spades. One Four of Diamonds is reversed on top of the deck, and one Three of Spades is reversed on the bottom. Now the duplicate Four of

Diamonds is placed face down on top of the deck, and the duplicate Three of Spades is placed face down on the bottom. Thus both of the reversed cards(the second and fifty-first) are effectively hidden, and you are ready to perform the feat.

Riffle shuffle the deck without exposing the two reversed cards, and then riffle one end of it for the insertion of either the spectator's forefinger or a knife. He withdraws the card thus selected, looks at it and replaces it on top of the deck. Hold the deck with its back slightly tilted and facing the spectator and lift up the inner end of the top card so that you can withdraw the second card from the top. This is your first duplicate "Finder" and it should be removed without exposing the face up card under it. Also remove the bottom card of the deck (your second "Finder" card) and throw them face up on the table as you cut the deck bringing the selected card to the center. Square it up carefully and set it on the table. Thus the selected card is now already sandwiched between the two face up cards unknown to the specator. Pick up the two "Finder Cards," explain what you intend to do, and place both the deck and the "Finder Cards" behind your back. As soon as both hands are out of sight, slip the two "Finder Cards" into your hip pocket and bring forth the deck. Upon it being spread on the table or fanned, the reversed cards show up with the selected card between them.

For the second method where the spectator inserts the "Finder Cards" and locates his chosen card, you use the same set up as in the first method, with the addition that you have removed any two cards from the deck and have them hidden in some available place on your person, such as your lower vest pocket. Have a card selected, remove your "Finders," and explain to the spectator what he is to do. Hand him the pack (which of course, has already been cut to bring his selected card to the center) but keeping the two "Finders" in your own hand. Have him turn around, and the moment his back is turned change the two "Finders" for the two odd cards in your vest pocket. Give these two cards to him behind his back warning him to keep them face up. Actually, however, you hand them to him face down. He follows through, inserts them into the deck, and then brings the deck to the front and finds that he has located his selected card as already explained. While this method is only good for one or two people at the most, it is a stunner in its place.

(Editor's note: — The trick can be done impromptu without any duplicates, at the same time eliminating the pocketing or switching of the "Finder Cards". Just use two sets of cards instead of the duplicates, such as the Seven of Diamonds and the Eight of Clubs, and the Seven of Clubs and the Eight of Diamonds. Use these exactly as described in the routine. Show the Seven of Diamonds and the Eight of Clubs as your "Finder Cards," place them behind your back, turn them face down and insert one near the top and one near the bottom of the deck, and then bring the deck forward. The two reversed cards showing up in the spread will be the Seven of Clubs and the Eight of Diamonds, but it will have to be a very astute spectator who can detect the swindle.)

THREE CHANCES
LU BRENT

Easy and practical is this method of performing the popular "Here, There and Everywhere" effect, which heretofore depended largely upon the execution of top and bottom changes. In the present version I have eliminated these so that the average card worker may present this classic for close-up table work with a minimum of skill. Its presentation however, still requires good patter and timing.

The effect is that a card is selected from a pack, replaced and the deck shuffled. The performer asks that he be given three chances to locate the chosen card. Showing card number 1, the spectator is asked if it is his selected card. He denies it, and it is dropped face down on the table. Twice more a card is shown, yet neither prove to be the chosen card. These in turn are placed side by side and face down on the table. A second person now chooses one of the three cards on the table, and when turned over it proves to be the chosen card; a second choice is made and this, too, is the selected card; and finally the third card is turned over and it's the selected card also. The climax is reached when it is shown that only one of the three cards on the table is the selected one, the other two being indifferent cards. Everything may now be examined.

You'll need three Queens of Spades for this trick, one of which may well be a short card for ease in working. They are distributed in the deck as follows — two on top with the short Queen being the top card, and the third Queen second from the bottom of the deck.

Riffle shuffle the deck without disturbing the three Queens. Now force the top short Queen by using the well-known "Tell me when to stop" riffle force, slipping the top card to the top of the lower half as the deck is cut at the point indicated by the spectator. This Queen is replaced in the pack at any spot desired and, being a short card, you can forget it entirely for the time being. The pack is again shuffled, keeping the top Queen and the one second from the bottom in place.

Now offer to locate the chosen card in three chances. Turn the deck face up and show the bottom card as your first guess. This is denied, so turn the deck face down in the left hand, glide back the bottom card with the left third finger, and withdraw the second card (Queen) from the bottom with the right fingers. Lay this face down on the table.

For your second guess, double lift the top two cards showing the face of the second card. This is denied, so turn it face down again, and deal off the top card (Queen) face down on the table beside the first one.

For your third guess state that you will try a card from the middle of the deck. Hold the pack face down in the left hand with thumb and fingers at the sides, and riffle the rear edge of the deck with the right thumb. At the point where the short card snaps by, cut the deck bringing the short Queen to the top. (A short card made by trimming the upper left and lower right corners is the best type to use. With it you can riffle the upper left edge of the deck with the left thumb, as the pack is held up near your left ear, stop at the short, and cut the deck at this point bringing the short Queen to the top.) Now double lift the two top cards again, show an indifferent card, turn them face down and deal off the short Queen onto the table beside the first two cards. Thus you have a row of three cards on the table, none of which the spectator claims.

At this point, ask the spectator if he is positive that none of the three cards was his selected card. The answer, of course, is "No." From this point on a second person is asked to assist. This person points to any one of the three cards on the table, and you turn it over to show that it really is the selected Queen. After everyone has seen it, turn it face down and drop it to the right of the other two cards but near the edge of the table.

Now state that everyone is wondering what would have happened had the assistant happened to point out one of the remaining two cards. As you mention this, you are still holding the deck in your left hand and have brought the right hand over the deck. Riffle count the two bottom cards of the deck with your right thumb and hold a break between them and the rest of the deck with your left little finger. Now ask the assistant to select another of the two remaining cards. This is turned face up and found to be the Queen of Spades also. After showing it, turn it face down and drop it on top of the first Queen which was previously shown and placed near the edge of the table.

At this moment, you square up the two queens near the edge of the table and pick them up between your right thumb at the rear and your fingers at the front edge. As you do so, look at the assistant and ask him to see what would have happened had he selected the last card on the table. While he turns this over and finds the Queen of Spades again, you reach over and take the pack out of the left hand with the right and place it on the table, leaving the two indifferent bottom cards (those retained by the little finger below the break) in the left hand. The two Queens in the right hand remained palmed. The left hand throws its two indifferent cards face down on the table as you say, "Most people think that all one needs is three cards all alike, but I can assure you that it is just an illusion." As this is said, carefully place your right hand in your trousers' pocket, while your left hand points to the two odd cards just dropped on the table. The spectators will always pick these up to examine them, and the deck, too, only to find everything in order.

A trial or two to smooth out the action is all that is needed to make this a well liked stunt. Surely, it makes an ancient classic much easier to do, and the man who cannot make a good top or bottom change will find this a welcome addition to his repertoire.

HERE OR THERE

R. M. JAMISON

This effect is quite different from the usual run of card tricks, mainly because of the unusual presentation. A spectator names aloud any card in the deck. The performer removes it, shows it and proceeds to punch a hole in the top of the card. It is shown both front and back and then hung back outwards, by the hole on the head of a pin stuck in the performer's lapel.

The performer now selects another card as his own, shows it first and then punches two holes in the top of the card. This card is then hung in like manner on the head of pin stuck in the opposite lapel.

Upon command, the two cards change places, for now the spectator's freely named card is on the opposite lapel with two holes punched in it, while the performer's card has moved over to the opposite lapel and has but one punch hole in it! The spectator may remove the two cards and examine them.

The novelty of this effect is very striking. One extra card is needed, and the two duplicates are on top of the deck at the start. Stick a common pin into each lapel in such a fashion that the heads projects sufficiently for the cards to be hung on them.

Present the trick by having a spectator name any card he likes. Fan the deck face towards you, locate the card and slip it to the top of the deck between the two duplicate cards reposing there. Now close up the fan and hold it face down. Remove the top two cards as one, and show the face of the selected card. Replace it (two cards) face up on top of the deck, but extending about a half inch over the front of the deck. Now hold the deck up vertically so that the reversed card on top of the deck is facing you, and remark that you will mark it beyond all question of doubt. Pick up a ticket punch and punch a hole in the card (two cards) near the center of the top edge. To avoid difficulty in lining up the holes

later on, hold your punch parallel with the card and the deck, and pushed in as far as the jaws of the punch allow. The side of the punch lays along the top edge of the deck, and the top of the projecting card (s) does not project beyond the side edge of the ticket punch. See illustration. Thus you have set a gauge to be followed later which prevents you from enlarging this hole when you punch it a second time.

After punching the card (s) and showing the face of the selected card once more, turn the two cards face down and in alignment with the top of the deck by grasping the protruding end and turning them over towards you. Then the left thumb slides off the top card (one of the duplicates) and the right hand takes it and, holding it with its back to the audience, hangs it back out on the left lapel.

Now the next two cards are lifted a little at the rear end and are pushed forward as one card. The right fingers move forward to the front of the deck, lift up the two cards as one and turn them face up on top of the deck, but projecting about a half inch over the front of the deck. The card face up is one of your duplicates, and you show it as your selection. Remark that you will mark this one with two punch holes. Gauging the first punch exactly as before lines it up with the hole already in the card underneath the face up one. The second punch is made alongside of it, and through the two cards, and this punch hole need not be measured at all. Just make it to the right of the first hole.

The two cards, as one, are now turned face down on the deck, and the top one (the spectator's card) slid off and hung back outwards on the right lapel. Now palm off the top card of the deck and set the deck aside. Explain what you intend to do, ie: have the two plainly marked cards change places, and then after a bit of hocus pocus show that they have done so in spite of the identifying punch holes.

This is a nice stunt to be shown anywhere; an extra card, a punch, and two straight pins being all that is necessary. Hanging the cards on the coat lapels is cute and very effective.

HIDDEN MYSTERY

HERB. RUNGIE

This trick is one of the most baffling effects with a borrowed pack you will ever do, and when used in combination with the trick described at the end you'll find it a very acceptable addition to your repertoire.

You remove a card, say the Five of Diamonds, from a borrowed deck and place it face up on the table. The deck is now shuffled and cut, as you ask one spectator to mention any number. Suppose he calls out the number "16." You deal sixteen cards, one at a time, into a packet on the table and ask him to look at and remember the top card of the packet dealt. He replaces it on the packet, and you drop the remainder of the deck on top of it.

You pick up the deck once more, ask a second spectator to mention another number (we'll suppose he calls out 14,) and you proceed to deal a second packet of fourteen cards. The second spectator looks at the top card of the packet, remembers it, replaces it on top of the packet, and finally the remainder of the deck is dropped on top of the selected card.

The deck is now given a cut, after which you pick it up with one hand and place it behind your back. You also pick up the Five of Diamonds, which has been laying face up on the table, and place it behind your back with your other hand. You say that you will place the Fve of Diamonds into the deck so that it will be next to one of the chosen cards. This you do, for when you bring the deck forward and ribbon spread it across the table top, the Five of Diamonds shows face up in the spread. The card to the left of it, when turned face up, proves to be the first card chosen. The Five of Diamonds is removed and the deck is cut again, once or twice. The same procedure is gone through a second time, and you succeed in locating the second card in the same manner. And, as the ads say, everything may now be examined!

This trick is a varation of an Annemann effect wherein the spectator locates a chosen card behind his back by inserting an indicator card into the deck.

However in the trick just described, a subterfuge is employed which makes its working incomprehensible. You actually introduce into the borrowed deck two stranger cards. In this case, two Five of Diamonds. As their backs are never seen, they can be from any odd decks.

During the course of some other tricks you add your two extra Five of Diamonds to the borrowed deck, one going face up on the bottom, the other face down in the middle of the deck. The top card of the deck is now slipped to the bottom and effectively hides the face up Five. Now the regular Five of Diamonds belonging to the deck is brought to the top of the pack, and you're set to perform the double location.

Turn the deck face upwards, fan it, remove the "stranger" Five of Diamonds from the center, and place it, face up, on the table. Dove-tail shuffle the deck, keeping the top and bottom cards in place, and finally slip the bottom card to the center during a cut or an overhand shuffle. This leaves the deck with your other Five of Diamonds face up on the bottom, and the deck's regular Five of Diamonds on top.

Ask for the first number. Deal the cards one at a time from the top of the deck into a pile on the table, and have the last one dealt noted and replaced. Drop the rest of the deck on top of the pile which puts your face up Five of Diamonds on top of the first noted card. The above maneuver also brings the deck's Five of Diamonds to the bottom. Have a second number called out and again deal a pile of cards to that number. Have the top card of the pile noted and returned, and then drop the remainder of the deck on top of it. This action brings the deck's Five of Diamonds on top of the second selected card. Now you are all set.

Cut the deck once or twice, being careful not to let the reversed card show during this action. Pick up the face up Five of Diamonds from the table, and place it and the deck behind your back. Explain that you will attempt to place the face up Five of Diamonds next to one of the chosen cards. Actually, however, you slip the Five of Diamonds you are holding into your hip pocket, and then bring the deck forward and ribbon spread it across the top of the table. A face up Five of Diamonds is seen (your duplicate "stranger" card.) Pull out the card to the left of it, and it's the first person's card.

Now take out the face up Five of Diamonds, and ask someone to cut the deck once or twice, completing the cut each time. While this is being done be sure to hold your Five of Diamonds face up and not let it's back be seen, for it's your duplicate card. Pick up the deck with the other hand, place both hands behind your back and say you'll try and locate the second selected card in the same way. As before, slip the duplicate Five of Diamonds you're holding into your hip pocket, and bring the deck forward once again. Ribbon spread it across the table top face down, but this time no revealed card shows up. Apologize, saying that you must have made a mistake and put the Five of Diamonds in upside down. Catch hold of the end card of the spread, and using it as a lever, cause the ribbon of cards to turn themselves over face up. Locate the Five of Diamonds, and next to it will be found the second person's card. The deck may be examined, if anyone is so minded, but you are in the clear for you have gotten away with the two duplicate "Stranger" cards, and no clues are left.

Note by Annemann: This is an excellent trick to do before showing my "one-hand cutting" trick mentioned earlier. Follow up the trick just described by saying that perhaps one of the spectators would like to try it. Have him stand at your left or right, depending upon which hand you use for making a Charlier pass. He takes a card, notes it and puts it back in the deck. You control it and shuffle it to the top, adding one more card on top of it. Now turn up the top card of the deck saying you'll use it as a "locator" card. Leave it face up on top of the deck, and put your hand with the deck behind the spectator's back. (You are both facing front.) As your hand goes out of sight behind his back, make the Charlier pass which brings the reversed top card, and the selected card under it, to the center of the deck. Have him take the deck in one hand and with his other hand remove the top card, but keep it "face up," and stab it into the center of the deck. This he does, and then brings the deck forward and spreads it face down on the table. The face up "locator" card, which was used apparently, is staring upwards in the middle of the spread, and directly under it to its left is found the selected card. Thus he has supposedly done the trick himself, although actually he only pushed an odd, face down card somewhere into the deck thinking he was pushing in the face up "locator."

Thus by using Mr. Rungie's trick first and following with mine, you have brought an interesting routine to a successful finish with definite audience participation. And best of all, you end up with a wholly unprepared deck!

TRICKS WITH FAKED & DOUBLE FACED CARDS

CARD IN HIGH

TED ANNEMANN

This effect is about as dramatic a presentation of the card in the wallet as it is possible to do. You have a card selected and lay the deck aside as the spectator initials the chosen card. He then gives you the card which you fold very openly and fairly, inside of a square of newspaper. The folded package is now lighted with a match and is held while the flames consume it until but a tiny corner is left which is dropped onto an ashtray to burn to a crisp. You say, "Your marked card is gone, sir, and it would take a real magician to put together the ashes, let alone make them resume the appearance of the card as it formerly was. I am not a magician in that sense, for to actually restore it would be an impossibility. Your card was not burned — I kidnapped it! I might, were I a true magican, have put it behind that drapery, within that chandelier, under the table — but, before your eyes, I hid it close to myself — in my wallet."

"You see? Inside my pocket —safe with my money. What was that card you selected and marked?" As you say this, you have taken your wallet from your inside pocket. "Look," you continue, "a rubber band to keep out the moths, and under the glassine window in the middle of the wallet is — your card, sir! Put there by the latest of magical chicanery — from the burning paper to the wallet without a visible singe. Pick it up please; check your signature on it. Right? Thank you. You may keep it as a souvenir," you say as you shake the card out of the wallet onto a tray, or onto the table.

The method of accomplishing this effect is of the utmost simplicity. There are two definite parts to the trick — the burning of the card, and its reproduction from the wallet.

As you are well aware, no playing card will burn up completely inside a piece of paper. Its thickness causes it to burn much slower, so it should be obvious that you must employ some subterfuge to accomplish the illusion. And here's the secret. The card that is apparently burned has been printed in offset on a reproduction of a sheet of newspaper.

This is easily arranged as follows:

Cut out a section of the classified advertising page exactly 8½" by 11" in size. Paste a playing card face up on the center of this page. Use an Ace, 2, 3 or 4 of Clubs, or the same values in Spades with the exception of the Ace of Spades. Outline this card with black ink, and then ink in the shadow lines across the top and on the left side of the card, as illustrated. Next paste onto the back of this sheet another section from the classified advertising page, providing, of course, that the opposite side hasn't already such a set up. Take your paste up job to any good offset house (or your printer can arrange the reproduction for you) and have them make a hundred reproductions, both sides, for you. The cost will be but a few dollars, and you'll have a perfect replica of a playing card resting on a sheet of newspaper.

Take such a prepared sheet and tear about a half inch strip off the four edges of it. Fold the sheet roughly into thirds each way in order to form a packet with the imprinted card on the inside of the middle square. Then open it out to make a regular No. 10 envelope size one-third

letter fold, and place it in your inside coat pocket with the folds against your body when the coat is closed.

Now as to the wallet. This is in the same pocket. It's one of the usual three-fold type having a center glassine section, which normally is used for your license or identification cards. Slip a duplicate of the card pictured on the newspaper under the glassine, face up, so that it will be visible immediately upon the wallet being opened. Encircle the wallet with a heavy and very noticeable rubber band, and place it in your pocket behind the newspaper square. See to it that the folds of the wallet face your body when your coat is closed.

Thus prepared, and I offer no excuses for the modus operandi as I work purely for "effect," you are ready to present this club item at any point in your program using an unprepared deck of cards.

Force the duplicate of the card already in your wallet. We'll say it's the Two of Clubs. I have always used the following force for this particular trick, and you may like it, too. While shuffling the deck just prior to the force, bring the Two of Clubs to the top. As you approach the person who is to select a card, you cut fourteen or fifteen cards from the bottom of the deck to the top, square the deck, and hold a small flesh break above the Two of Clubs with the left little finger at the right rear corner of the pack. Extend your left hand towards the spectator and riffle the outer left edge of the deck (from the top down) with your left thumb, asking him to say "stop" whenever he likes. In proffering the deck it should be held with the left arm outstretched and at a backward angle from the shoulder, and with the thumb edge of the deck directed to the spectator.

When the spectator says "Stop," your left thumb stops riffling and holds an obvious break at that point. Swing your left hand in front of your body, about waist high, and immediately bring your right hand over the deck. In this position, the right fingers grasp the front of the deck, and the thumb the rear. Apparently your right hand picks off all the cards above the break being held by the left thumb at the front edge of the deck. However, the right thumb actually picks off only those cards above the break being held by the left little finger **at the rear** of the deck, the right fingers meanwhile assisting at the front end of the deck.

RIGHT HAND PICKS UP TOP PACKET "A" FROM ABOVE BREAK HELD BY LEFT LITTLE FINGER

As the upper packet is taken in the right hand, the left thumb releases the break it holds at the front of the deck (this action is covered by the right fingers to a great extent) and the left hand immediately proffers the lower half of the deck to the spectator for the withdrawal of the top card (the Two of Clubs.) All this should be done in one continuous move and as a matter of course. Fair choice is prevalent in demeanor, if not in action! (Editors note: The illustration herewith is not quite accurate — for the left thumb should be holding a decided break on the side of the pack, while the left little finger should be holding a tiny flesh break on the right rear corner.)

The spectator now has his card and is asked to initial it, or mark it in such a manner that he cannot but fail to identify it later. It is very important to the effect that this marking procedure be emphasized. The deck is laid aside at this point, for it is not used again during the trick.

And now it is best to follow the rest of these instructions with a wallet in your pocket, a folded paper in front(near the body) of it, and a single playing card in your hands.

Take the marked card from the spectator with your right hand. Keep it in view. Step back to the front and reach into your inside coat pocket with your left hand and bring out the faked square of newspaper. As the folds of the paper are towards your body, and thus on the thumb side, the paper is easily flipped open. The card is placed into the semi-folded newspaper, but when it is behind it (from the audience's point of view) the right hand tilts the card to conform with the left palm and shoves the end of the card, as far as possible, under the left thumb.

The right hand is grasping the paper with fingers on the outside nearest the audience, and it is important that the right thumb, which is on the inside, be upon the edge of the pictured card as though it is holding it in place against the paper. The right hand now pulls the newspaper away from the left hand and turns the newspaper around to let the audience see the Two of Clubs apparently being held against the paper. The left hand simultaneously drops with its back toward the audience, and with the real Two of Clubs palmed, and without any hestitation goes immediately into your left trousers pocket and brings out a paper of matches. The palmed card, of course, being left in the pocket.

Toss the paper of matches to a nearby spectator with the request "Please light a match — any one." While he does so, you deliberately and openly fold the newspaper in all directions around the pictured card. As the spectator proffers you the lighted match, turn the paper package over several times between the fingers of both hands to let it be seen that everything is fair, and incidentally to allow your hands to be seen empty otherwise.

The package is lighted and burns quickly to the accompaniment of the patter as already outlined. It is held with the right hand, as the left, which is not otherwise being employed, is casually inserted into your left trousers pocket and palms the marked Two of Clubs. Do not be in any hurry to move the left hand from the pocket, just let it rest there until the moment the right hand is forced to drop the last bit of burning newspaper. As this occurs, withdraw the left hand from the trousers pocket, with the Two of Clubs palmed, and reach into your inside coat pocket. Grasp the wallet with the fingers behind it and bring it out into view. The palmed card is held against the back of the wallet, and is thus hidden as the left hand is turned over to exhibit the wallet resting lengthwise on its palm. The left hand is held somewhat to the left of the body. Peel the rubber band off the wallet with the right hand, and toss it out into the audience to the accompaniment of the patter suggested.

The right hand now opens out the wallet and the Two of Clubs is seen under the glassine section inside the wallet. The bottom edge of the wallet should, at this point, be towards the floor. Grasp this bottom edge with the right hand (the top edge of the wallet is still being held by the left thumb resting on the glassine section, while the left fingers are behind the case) and allow the two outer sections of the wallet to close automatically onto the center section. This is intentional, although not obviously so, and serves to hide the enclosed card for a second. Both hands now swing towards the center of your body and, at this point, the right hand pulls the wallet away from the left hand and leaves the palmed and marked Two of Clubs in view in the left hand. Apparently the left hand has pulled the card out of the wallet. This action takes place as you start toward the person who chose the card, and you now hand him his originally marked card. If timed properly there need be no suspicion of trickery.

That's the trick as I do it. There is no trying to load a card into a wallet, no fumbling, and no jerky pulls trying to get the wallet off of a clip as happens with other methods. Just reach into your pocket and remove the wallet in one smooth, continuous move perfectly synchronized with your patter. It's natural, and there are no interruptions or unnecessary movements. The effect is clean and deliberate throughout, so toss away your sleight-of-hand methods and devote your thoughts and actions to showmanship!

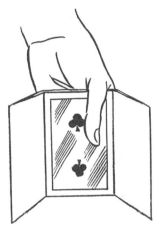

AUDIENCE VIEW — PALMED DUPLICATE HELD BEHIND WALLET

A final thought. Some may be tempted to peel a card down to its final thickness, and to try to use this with a real piece of newspaper. Don't. You will find that the newspaper still burns quicker than the layer of card, and this will spoil the effect. The patter and intent of the whole effect is that the card **disappears**. It must not, under any circumstances, appear that the selected card is taking time to burn.

A CARD IN FLIGHT

LES GILBERT

This is an exceptionally clever version of causing a chosen and marked card to vanish from the deck only to be found by the spectator in the performer's pocket. The fact that the card is marked and seen in the pack up to the very last minute makes it a superb piece of card conjuring.

The preparation required takes but a few minutes, and consists of converting the pips at one end of the Jack of Spades with india ink. See illustration A. Such a card may be shown either as the Jack of Clubs or the Jack of Spades depending upon which end of the card is hidden by the fingers. This prepared card plus the regular Jack of Spades are

used, and both are on the bottom of the deck at the start. The regular
Jack of Spades is the bottom card, and the prepared Jack is second from
the bottom with the Club end outward. The regular Jack of Clubs is
removed from the deck entirely. Now follow the following routine.

Hand the Joker, or any indifferent card, to the spectator to use as
an indicator card with which to select a card. Riffle shuffle the deck
leaving the two bottom cards in place, and then undercut about twenty
cards and place them on top of the deck, holding a break between the
halves at the right rear corner with the left little finger. The Jack of
Spades is now directly above the little finger .

Ask the spectator to push the Joker into the deck at the squared
front end, but see to it that he pushes it in below the upper portion. Hold

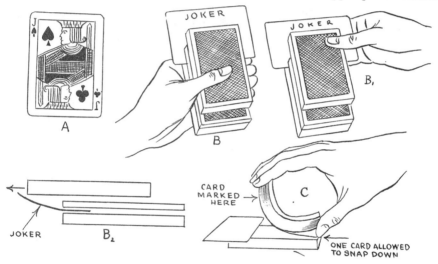

the deck face down and parallel with the floor as this is done. Have the
Joker pushed in sidewise, and raise the deck so that it faces the spectator.
The right thumb lifts the upper portion above the break, and pushes this
portion up about an inch behind the protruding Joker. See illustration B.
Now the right fingers press against the face of the Joker while the right
thumb presses against the rear of the upper portion, squeeses them
together, and pulls them entirely free of the pack. Illustrations B1,
and B2 shows this action. Thus the Joker is brought against the face
of the Jack of Spades, and you've forced the Jack in a clean cut manner.

Hold the packet with the right hand for a moment so that the
spectator may see the card at which he apparently cut and, of course, he
sees the lower half of the real Jack of Spades. Immediately replace the right

hand packet on top of the deck, leaving the Joker protruding, and hold a break between the packets as before. Now reach for your pencil and hand it to the spectator with the request that he initial his selected card so that there can be no mistake as to its identity.

The left hand, which is holding the pack, is raised a bit so that the right fingers may bend back the packet above the Joker for the spectator to initial the Jack of Spades, which is the bottom card of this upper packet. As the Jack is being marked, the right thumb at the rear end of the pack lifts up the rear of the upper packet above the break, and allows one card (the Jack of Spades) to drop onto the lower portion of the pack, illustration C. As this card snaps down, the left finger which has been holding the break moves out of the way. Now the right fingers allow the front end of the upper portion to snap back onto the Joker, and the right thumb, which is now holding the break, pushes the upper packet forward a bit onto the back of the Joker. As you do so, both hands are lowered so that the deck is once again parallel with the floor. (This is the same maneuver as used in the force.) The left little finger, or the third finger, now presses on the top card of the lower packet to anchor it, while the right fingers and thumb pull the upper packet and Joker off the deck exactly as before. The top card of the left hand (lower) packet is now the regular Jack of Spades which has been initialed.

The right hand packet is raised facing the spectator, and so far as he is concerned things are exactly as before, for he still sees the lower half of the Jack of Spades (the fake card) protruding below the Joker. Now the right hand places its packet face up on the table for a moment, while you look directly at the spectator and ask to have your pencil returned. As you make this request, bring your two hands together and palm off the regular Jack of Spades with the right hand. Lay the packet of cards on the table, take back the pencil, transfer it to the right hand and put it in your side coat pocket together with the palmed card.

Now pick up the Joker packet with its fake Jack of Spades still visible, and keeping this at the inner end, turn the packet over sidewise and proceed to give it a good overhand shuffle. Remark that impossible as it may seem the marked Jack will vanish. Turn the packet face upwards once more, being careful to turn it over sidewise as before, and fan the cards slowly. The Jack of Spades has disappeared! The reason being, of course, that the faked card now shows as the Jack of Clubs in the fan. The spectator now reaches into your pocket and finds his initialed Jack of Spades. For a stunning close-up trick, and one giving the appearance of exceptional sleight-of-hand ability, it's a hard one to beat!

Editor's note:—If you can do a good, one hand top palm with the left hand, the working of the trick may be made even smoother. At the point where you ask for the return of the pencil, lay the packet of cards on the table with the left hand, palming the top card —the Jack of Spades—as you do so. Now take back the pencil with the right hand, transfer it to the left and return the pencil to your upper right vest pocket. As you do this, drop the palmed card into your inside coat pocket, and at the same time reach forward with the right hand to pick up the Joker packet. All the movements blend into one, making the pocketing of the card entirely unnoticeable. Later when the spectator finds the card in your inside coat pocket, it seems even more remarkable.

THE SUPER EYE POPPER

JESS E. MILLS

Here's a smart "Ambitious Card" routine with the faked Jack of Clubs-Spades card used in the foregoing trick. Have this card on the bottom of the deck with the Spades end at the inner end of the deck, and have the regular Jack of Spades on top of the deck. As in the preceeding trick, the regular Jack of Clubs has been left out of the deck.

Turn the deck face up, hiding the faked Spade pips under your right thumb, so that the face card appears to be the Jack of Clubs. Now run through the deck slowly showing each card, and reversing their order, so that as you finish the deck the regular Jack of Spades becomes the face card. Remove this card and lay it face up on the table.

Now turn the deck face down in the left hand, turning it end for end, which brings the Spade pips of the faked Jack to the front end of the deck. Pick up the regular Jack of Spades and place it face down on top of the deck. Show it once more by lifting up the front end of it and bending it back. Slide it off the deck, take it with the right hand and place it, face down, second from the top. Riffle the edge of the deck with the left thumb, and then lift up the outer end of the top card and show the fake Jack of Spades by bending back the card. The Jack has apparently climbed back to the top!

Let it snap back onto the deck, slide it off with the left thumb, take it face down with the right hand and replace it under the top card once again. Riffle the deck as before, lift back the outer end of the top card and show the Jack of Spades once more on top. Slide it off with the left thumb, take it with the right hand, show it freely and then place it face down in the center of the deck. Riffle the deck once more and bend back the fake Spade end of the top card showing the Jack apparently on top again.

Pick off this fake card with the right hand and, holding it so that the Club end is hidden by the fingers, place it on the bottom of the deck by sliding it face down under the deck with the Club end nearest you. Riffle the deck once again and then turn it face up, turning it end for end and immediately covering the Spade end of the faked card nearest you with your left thumb. The bottom card now shows as the Jack of Clubs. Bring your hands together immediately, place your right thumb over your left, withdraw the latter, and push the deck well down into the crotch of the right thumb so that the fake Spade pips are hidden. Now fan the deck slowly face upwards and locate the real Jack of Spades somewhere near the center. Casually cut the deck and complete the cut, and then hand it to the spectator so that the Jack of Clubs end of the fake card will be at the outer end of the pack as he holds it. He may then fan through the deck, as he probably will, with little likelihood of spotting the faked card.

CARD ON THE WING

This is another variation of Mr. Mills using the same faked Jack. As before, the real Jack of Clubs is left out of the deck. The Jack of Spades is used, but has been removed and placed in your pocket. The fake card, showing as the Jack of Spades at the outer end of the deck, is placed 10 or 15 cards from the bottom. All other face cards are removed from below it, and placed further up in the deck.

To present, introduce the deck and give it a false shuffle and cut, retaining the bottom stock of cards in place. The deck is now held in an upright or vertical position by the left hand, while the right fingers get ready to riffle the top of the deck. A spectator is asked to make a mental note of the first picture card he sees and, of course, he notes the Jack of Spades. You now cut the deck and give it a good shuffle. Now turn the deck face up in your left hand, by turning it over end for end, hand it to the spectator to fan through and pick out his selected card. He cannot find it; and the mystery is solved, so far as you are concerned, when you nonchalantly produce it from your pocket. If you feature the "Card in the Wallet" trick, then try the above. It's clean, snappy and sure-fire!

UNIFLIGHT

ORVILLE MEYER

Effect:—A card is chosen by a spectator and the pack is then separated into two halves which are secured by rubber bands. Each half contains 26 cards, and the spectator notes carefully in which half his card is located. The chosen card now passes from one packet to the other, where it is discovered reversed. The packets are counted again and are found to consist of 25 and 27 cards respectively, proving that one card actually did travel from packet to packet.

This is a most convincing effect and depends upon a cleverly faked card. Get one extra duplicate of any card in the pack, say the Two of Clubs. This is glued, at one end only, to the back of any other card in the pack. (Editor's note: Rather than glue, use a strip of Scotch Tape and make a hinged card, as illustrated. Such a card will give much more latitude in working.) With such a card in the deck, the cards may be fanned or counted, and only 52 will be seen with no duplicates visible. However, with this faked card on top, the rear one — the Two of Clubs — may be raised at the free end by the right fingers and shown, as the pack is held in the left hand.

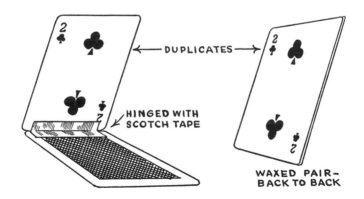

Now to the back of any other card in the deck affix a bit of wax or diachylon at two opposite corners, and to this card — but back to back with it — press the regular Two of Clubs, as illustrated. Have this double card about thirteenth from the bottom of the face down deck with the Two of Clubs facing upwards, ie: reversed in the deck. The hinged fake card is on top of the deck.

Introduce the effect by having a spectator insert his finger into the end of the deck as you riffle it. Slip force the top faked card by slipping it down onto the top of the lower half of the deck, as you separate the cards at the point indicated by the spectator. Lay the upper half of the deck to one side. Holding the lower half of the deck in your left hand, raise the outer free end of the faked card with your right fingers, so that the spectator notes the Two of Clubs. Let the Two of Clubs fall back on top, and then push the faked card off the right side of the packet with the left thumb. Take it with your right hand and place it on top of the heap just laid aside.

You are still holding the bottom half of the deck in your left hand, so turn it face up and slowly and fairly count off twenty-six cards face up on the table. The waxed double card, with the duplicate Two of Clubs on its back, goes through the count unnoticed. These 26 cards (really 27) are now secured with a rubber band. If there are not twenty-six cards, take a few from the bottom of other heap, showing each one as you do so. If on the other hand there are more than twenty-six, place the extra ones on the bottom of the opposite heap. Lay this packet of 26 cards aside temporarily.

Now pick up the other heap and show the Two of Clubs still on top by lifting up the free end of the faked card. After showing it, push it into the center of the packet, or cut it to the center, and then secure the packet with a second rubber band, saying, "We will also secure this remaining half (really only 25 cards) with another band."

You're all set now for the transposition, for after a magic hocus pocus or two, you slowly count this second packet face up on the table, one card at a time, and the Two of Clubs has disappeared! And in keeping with its disappearance, there are only 25 cards to be seen, the faked card, of course, showing up as an indifferent card. Picking up the first packet, you slip off the elastic and fan through it face down. Near its center is found the face up Two of Clubs. Remove this, separating it from the card to which it was stuck and lay it face up on the table. Turn the packet face upwards, and count the cards one at a time onto the face up Two of Clubs. There are 27 cards in all, proving conclusively that one actually did pass across to the other packet.

LOST AND FOUND

J. E. WHEELER

Many card effects have a sound beginning and a weak ending, while others are built in just the opposite manner. For that reason this pair of tricks should be found welcome. Together they make a clean and complete discovery with a novel climax. Separately they may be used either as a force, or as a finale in conjunction with other card effects.

You have a card selected quite fairly and then the spectator shuffles it back into the deck himself. The deck is now dropped into a goblet with the back of the deck towards the audience. A silk handkerchief is thrown over the deck in the glass, and a spectator is requested to grasp the deck by its sides through the silk and lift it clear of the glass. He does so, but one card remains back outwards in the goblet. When the spectator names the card he selected (which he could have marked) it is seen to be the one left in the goblet, as the latter is turned around. Nothing is used in this effect but the goblet, the cards, a silk handkerchief and a knife.

The working of the effect depends on a narrow card. Just trim one-sixteenth off one side of any black Ace, two, three, four or five spot. With such a card in the deck and the latter held in your left hand face down, the left thumb can instantly locate it while riffling down the side of the deck. Upon locating it, as it snaps past, cut the deck at this point and bring the narrow card to the bottom.

The deck is now held face down in the left hand from above, with the fingers curving around the left side of the pack and the thumb in a like position on the right side. The left third finger tip is underneath in such a position as to make drawing back the bottom card about half an inch very easy and, at the same time, unnoticed. (This is known as the "Glide.")

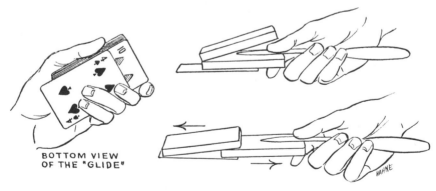

BOTTOM VIEW
OF THE "GLIDE"

With the deck held as described, the spectator is handed a knife and asked to insert it anywhere he pleases into the front end of the deck. As he does so, you glide back the bottom card. Now the right thumb presses down on the top of the knife blade, with the tip of the thumb near and almost touching the front end of the deck, while the right first finger curls under the deck and presses upwards against the packet of cards below the knife. With the bottom packet and the knife thus clamped between the right thumb and first finger, both are removed by pulling them forward and out of the left hand. See illustration. The bottom card of the lower packet, which had been pulled back with the left third finger, now automatically becomes the bottom card of the upper packet as the left fingers close tightening their hold on the cards. This card can now easily be squared with the deck, either by pushing it forward with the left third finger, or with the left little finger which will naturally be free behind the rear edge of the deck.

"Remember the card you have cut at," you say, as you tip up this left hand packet, so that the spectator may see the bottom (narrow force) card. Do not make any attempt to look at it yourself, in fact it's best to turn your head to one side as the spectator looks at the card. "Here, take them all and mix them up yourself," you say handing him both packets of cards. While he does this, pick up the goblet and exhibit it in an off-hand manner, and then replace it on your table.

Take back the deck, give it one or two cuts, riffling to the short card and bringing it to the bottom once again. Place the deck, back outwards, in the goblet and cover it with the silk handkerchief.

The goblet should be one that does not bind the deck, and also allows it to protrude about an inch above the brim so that the spectator can get a good hold on the edges of the cards through the handkerchief when he lifts out the deck. Have the spectator stand facing the audience and to the left of the table when lifting out the deck. The selected card being narrower than the others, and being the rear card of the deck, remains in the glass as the deck is removed. It is then revealed as already explained. The entire effect seems to have been accomplished by the assisting spectator himself so far as the audience is concerned, which only adds to the mystery.

RENOVATED SPHINX CARD TRICK

EDDIE CLEVER

Old and well known card tricks which make use of specially printed faked cards can often be improved and modernized to make present day miracles. Here is an up-to-the-minute version of the old "Sphinx Card Trick" which has graced so many magic catalogues through the years.

The effect is as follows for those who may have forgotten it. Any three spectators select as many cards from a shuffled deck and initial the face of the cards. These are dropped into a hat and the performer asks

one spectator for the name of his card.   This is removed from the hat
and replaced in the deck.   Now the two remaining spectators name their
cards, but when they look in the hat these two cards have vanished, and
the card they had seen the performer place in the deck
has returned to the hat in some unaccountable manner.
Upon spreading the deck, the two missing cards are
found reposing in the center. The three selected cards
may now be shown one by one.

Faked cards are employed, of course, but they
are natural and unsuspected. One is the familiar double
backed card to match the deck being used; the other
is made as per the illustration. This card has had the
7 index at one end erased, and an 8 index drawn in.
This faked card is placed on top of the deck, and the
double backed card is placed on top of it. The real Eight of Clubs is in
a position to be forced, and as you have three chances to do this it should
offer no problem.

When the three cards have been selected (one of which is the forced
Eight of Clubs) they are returned face up on top of the deck after being
initialed. The Eight of Clubs being returned first so that it occupies the
third position from the top. Now the 5 top cards are turned over face down
onto the deck. In as much as the spectators realize you are turning over
three cards, the addition of the other two will go unnoticed. Now the
three top cards are openly thumbed off into the hat. Thus, in the fairest
way possible you have placed into the hat the real Eight of Clubs, plus
the double backed card and the faked Seven of Clubs. The remaining
two selected cards are now on top of the deck, so you cut the deck burying them in the center, and place the deck on the table.

Turn to the three people assisting in the trick and, as if by chance,
look at the one who selected the Eight of Clubs and ask him to name his
card.   When he does, you reach into the hat and bring out the double
backed card and the faked 7 of Clubs as one card, holding your finger over
the 7 index and allowing the 8 index to show. Thus the two cards appear
to be the Eight of Clubs, so replace it face up on top of the deck which
is held in the left hand. Now tilt the deck so that everyone may get another
look at the fake Eight of Clubs, keeping your left thumb over the 7 index,
and then pick up the card with your right hand and turn it face down
on top of the deck. Slip cut this faked card to the center, which leaves
the double backed card on top of the pack.

Now finish as outlined in the effect. On looking into the hat the two
spectators find only the genuine, initialed Eight of Clubs. The deck is

run through face up with the 7 end of the fake card showing, and the other two spectator's cards are found in the deck. The pack may even be handed to a spectator, after you have palmed off the double backed card, and he may search through the deck himself just as long as you see to it that the 7 index of the faked card is upwards. This is an excellent close-up item and provides the maximum of effect with a minimum of skill. It can be used anytime simply by carrying the two necessary extra cards in your wallet, and the deck to match in your pocket. Just as a precaution, it might be well to ask the spectators to initial their cards in the index corners. Thus there will be little chance of the person selecting the Eight of Clubs challenging you when you show the faked card, for he will presume that your thumb is covering his initials as you hold the card by one index corner.

THE MUTILATED CARD

RUSSELL PRUNIER

Here's a torn and restored card trick that, from an audience standpoint, really has rhyme and reason. The card is restored with the sections taped together, which is a lot more logical than the fallacious method wherein the torn pieces unite into a completely restored card. Modern audiences know that a magician is clever rather than supernatural, so why not perform the trick with a natural climax and get credit for being clever. The following, up-to-the-minute version by Russell Prunier is the perfect answer.

The effect is as follows. One card is selected from a shuffled deck and the spectator is asked to tear the card into quarters. An elastic band is now furnished and the spectator snaps it around the torn pieces. You take this packet and hand it to another spectator together with a piece of paper and ask him to wrap up the torn packet. As he starts to do so, you slip out one of the torn pieces and return it to the person who selected the card asking him to hold it for later identification. At this point, and with very little comment, you show a roll of adhesive tape. Just make the remark that the only way to mend torn pieces is with tape, and set the roll down on your table in view of all. Now approach the person holding the tissue wrapped packet and hand him an ashtray or plate. Have him place the packet on the plate and touch a lighted match to it. There is a blinding flash of flame following which the assistant is asked to show everyone what he finds on the plate. He picks up the three pieces of card, but they are now joined together in proper fashion with adhesive tape. These are passed along to the original selector of the card, who matches up the odd corner he is holding and finds that the mended card is actually the one he selected at the start of the trick!!!

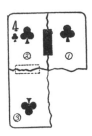

The preparation consists of taking a duplicate card and tearing it into quarters. Now take three of these, as in the illustration, and fasten them together with quarter inch tape, one piece on the front and one piece on the back. Fold number 1 over on top of number 2, and bend number 3 underneath. The separate piece is now laid face out on top of side number 3. (See second illustration.) Snap a rubber band around all, and place the packet in your left trousers' pocket. Have a piece of flash paper about four inches square in your right coat pocket, and some matches, elastic band, and a roll of adhesive tape handy. Now you're all set.

Force the duplicate of the torn card on a spectator, and ask him to tear it into quarters, and to secure them in a packet with the rubber band you furnish. While this is being done, palm the duplicate, taped packet from your trousers' pocket with your left hand. Take the packet of torn pieces from the spectator with your right hand, turn slightly to your left, and pretend to place the spectator's packet into your left hand. Actually, you palm the spectator's packet in your right hand, and simultaneously open your left hand letting the duplicate packet be seen. Hand this to another spectator, while your right hand reaches into your side coat pocket, disposes of the spectator's pieces,.and brings forth the piece of flash paper. Hand this to the second spectator who is holding the elastic bound packet and then, merely as an afterthought, slide the loose index corner out of the packet and hand it to the first spectator. You now introduce the roll of adhesive, as already mentioned, and set it on the table. The second spectator wraps up the packet in the piece of flash paper, sets it on the ashtray and ignites it. There is a resultant flash as the paper disappears, leaving the packet of torn pieces on the ashtray. He picks up the packet, unwraps the elastic band and finds — the torn pieces joined together with the pieces of adhesive. The first spectator now matches up the corner piece he is holding which completes the card, and you get credit for really doing a clever bit of conjuring!

COLOROTO

DR. ROTHBART

This trick is one which is far superior to most closing tricks and, because of its apparent frankness, has the distinct advantage of making friends with the audience, even though you turn the tables on them at the finish.

The effect consists of explaining to the audience that tricks with playing cards can be traced back to books of some 300 years ago. Indeed one of the first of these was the then miraculous feat of making one card change into another.

You proceed to demonstrate this as you patter along, color changing the face card of the pack once or twice. You then explain how magic has improved through the ages, and state that the changing of one card's face, or denomination, is today considered of little moment by the modern magician. Today is the age of mass production and effort, and magicians have had to keep up with the times. For example, you call attention to the fact that the deck you have been using is blue backed. This you hand to a spectator with the request that he remove four cards of the same value, suggesting that he take out the Jacks, as they are knaves and shouldn't be left at large anyway. The remainder of the deck is then returned to you and laid aside. You now pick up another deck with red backs, fan it, and pick out four cards before setting this deck aside also.

You fan the four cards thus removed and show them as four Sevens. You also show the backs of them to be red, as they should be. The fan of four cards is now closed, and the packet held in your left hand face out as in the regular color change. Passing your right hand over the face card of the packet it is seen to change to a Jack of the same suit. The packet is immediately fanned again and the four cards are all seen to be Jacks. When the fan is turned over,, the backs have changed to blue! To conclude the little story, you close up the fan, drop the packet on top of the blue backed deck and remark, "And that's how a magician takes care of difficulties today. No matter how many cards are involved, he can make both the faces and backs of the cards all change at one and the same time. Thus he keeps his deck complete."

The answer to this beautiful bit of deception is roughened cards. The preparation of the cards is shown in the accompanying illustration, which indicates how and where the roughing fluid is applied. Note that both the backs and faces are treated at either ends in the order designated in the diagram.

These eight cards appear to be but four due to the adhesive quality of the roughing fluid and are, of course, the "four" cards removed from the red deck for the trick. Before fanning them, they are squared face down in your left hand. The right hand then picks them up with the thumb on the face side and the index finger at the back. In this position the four are fanned and shown as four Sevens while the backs show as red. You need have no worry about fanning them, for treated as described they will fan perfectly when spread with one hand in the manner explained. However, it is a help, when learning where to grasp them for the first fan, to mark the proper end with a pencil.

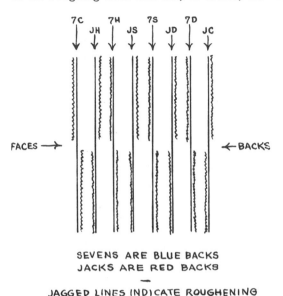

SEVENS ARE BLUE BACKS
JACKS ARE RED BACKS
—
JAGGED LINES INDICATE ROUGHENING

Thus four Sevens are shown in the first fan and, when turned around, the backs are seen to be red, as they should be. Everything then is in order, so far as the audience is concerned. The fan is now closed and held face outwards in the left hand ready for the regular color change sleight. The face card, a Seven, is changed into a Jack by palming off the rear Jack in the right hand and depositing it on the face card of the packet, as the right hand passes in front of it. This is the elementary color change.

Now the face card is a Jack. The right hand takes the packet from the left by grasping it at the far left side and thus reversing the packet (turning it end for end) as it is exhibited. The packet is now fanned once again, with thumb in front and fingers behind, and all the four cards are seen to be Jacks. The roughing treatment plus the change of one card from the back of the packet to the front takes care of this problem. And when the fan is turned around the backs of the cards are seen to be blue!

You can easily obtain roughing fluid from your magic dealer today, and if you do not care to prepare the cards yourself the dealer will be glad to do it for you. One word of caution though. In using the fluid be sure to apply it with a small wad of cotton in a single stroke across the surface of the card. Try not to deposit more than a very thin layer of fluid on any one spot. Then let the cards dry for a day or so before using them. Do not, under any circumstances, try to match up the pairs until all the cards are perfectly dry.

Editor's Note: About the time the above effect appeared in "The Jinx," Dr. Rothbart sent a similar trick to Max Holden. The effect, as I remember it, was most effective and depended upon the principle just explained. You counted off two packets of four cards each, one from a red deck and one from a blue deck. Both of these were fanned, one in each hand, and showed four Aces in the right hand fan, and four Kings in the left hand fan. The fans were closed for a moment, and when refanned, the Aces and Kings had changed places as well as the colors of the backs of the cards. The effect, as you can well appreciate, was truly magical although effortless on your part. Knowing the principle employed, you can easily figure it out. You will, of course, have to lay one packet down temporarily under some pretext or another so that you can turn the packets end for end. Dr. Rothbart claimed that he had been using roughing fluid for a great many years, and it may well be that he was one of the first persons, if not the first, to employ it.

VICE—VERSA

DR. DALEY

This effect is a tricky transposition of two cards that's very thought provoking. It is far from difficult even though it employs the Mexican Turnover, for it makes good use of this sleight as a trick rather than as a Monte effect. The fact that it may be done with any borrowed pack of cards is a definite asset, even though a double faced card is worked into the effect. Its use is never suspected, and you easily get rid of it so as to finish with just the original, borrowed deck.

We will suppose that this double faced card has the Ace of Clubs on one side, and the Two of Diamonds on the other. The slight preparation consists of removing the regular Ace of Clubs and placing it secretly in your right trousers' pocket, face outwards. The Two of Diamonds is brought to the bottom of the deck, and finally the double face card, with the Ace side outwards, is palmed onto the bottom of the deck completing it.

After a riffle shuffle, which leaves the two bottom cards in place, turn the deck face upwards and say you will need a couple of cards for your next effect. Throw out the Ace of Clubs (double faced card) face up on the table. Then take off the Two of Diamonds, and lay the deck aside. Now request everyone to pay strict attention so as not to miss what happens.

Pick up the Ace and hold it a few inches above the table to emphasize it, and then lay it down again with the Ace side showing. Hold the Two of Diamonds in your right hand. Remark that you will leave the Ace on the table, but face down. Accompany this remark by apparently flipping the Ace over with the Two of Diamonds you are holding. Actually, however, you employ the well known Mexican Turnover moves but with the following variation which carries it a step further. Push the Two spot under the right side of the Ace, flip the Ace over exchanging the two cards, and retain the double faced card in your right hand with the Two of Diamonds side upwards. In short, both cards are turned completely over during the exchange. The result being that the Ace is apparently face down on the table, while your right hand still holds the Two of Diamonds. The illusion is perfect, even with a not too good Mexican Turnover, and no one has any reason to suspect that the face down card is not the Ace of Clubs.

At this point say, "Watch everything closely," and slowly place the Two spot in your trousers' pocket. Actually, however, you push it into the very top of the pocket, while your hand continues downward to the bottom bulging out the pocket. Remove your empty hand saying, "Now, which card is which? Do you remember?"

They'll swear that the Ace is on the table and the Two spot is in your pocket which, of course, is what you want them to say. Pretend to be surprised and accuse them of not paying attention. Reach into your pocket, bring out the Ace of Clubs and, at the same time, pull the pocket inside out. The card in the upper corner remains hidden. Drop the Ace face upwards on the table and ask anyone to turn over the other card. It's the Two spot! Everything may now be checked. The trick is complete, the deck is complete, and the double faced card is safely out of the way.

SYMPATHETIC CLUBS

HERBERT MILTON

This exceptional club effect was one of Nate Leipzing's favorites, and should receive careful consideration by all those who want practical and well conceived material.

Two packs of cards are at hand, and a spectator selects one. You remove your pack from its case, hold it with the faces of the cards towards the audience, and openly remove all thirteen of the Club suit. The remainder of the deck is tossed aside, and the thirteen cards are deliberately arranged — with faces still towards the audience — from Ace to King, and with the Ace on the face of the packet. Two wide elastic bands are now used to secure the packet at top and bottom. These are made from three-quarter inch garter elastic and of a size to just fit the packet snugly without binding. The packet, thus secured, is set on your table, or in a glass, with the Ace of Clubs in view and facing the audience.

You now take the spectator's pack and give it several genuine shuffles. The spectator runs through the cards himself and removes the Club suit as each card is reached. You take these, show that they are well mixed, and then fan them face down for the spectator to select one. He shows it around for all to see, and then replaces it in the fan of thirteen — but face up. The fan is closed up, and two elastic bands are slipped around it exactly as was done with the first packet. This packet is given to the spectator to hold.

Now you explain the sympathy which exists between the two Club packets and how, because of this, your packet, which was arranged from Ace to King, will invisibly shuffle itself into the same arrangement as the group being held by the spectator. He removes the bands from his packet, and holds the latter squared and with the bottom face card, the Five of Clubs, towards the audience. You pick up the first packet, hold it face towards the spectators, remove the two elastic bands, and the Ace of Clubs, which has been in view throughout, is seen to have become a Five of Clubs. Thus it matches the spectator's first card!

The spectator removes his face card to reveal the next one, you follow suit, and your second card is seen to match his. As the action continues, of a sudden the spectator reveals a card back outwards on the face of his packet — the chosen and reversed card. You show that your next card is also reversed, and both cards are shown to be the same.

And the remainder of the cards in both packets match up, card for card, to a successful conclusion.

The preparation consists of making 12 double face cards in the following combinations. All suits are Clubs. (An excellent description of how to make these double face cards will be found on page 409 of Hugard's "Expert Card Technique.")

The combinations:

Ace-Ten	Two-Six	Three-Four
Four-Three	Five-King	Six-Two
Eight-Jack	Nine-Queen	Ten-Ace
Jack-Eight	Queen-Nine	King-Five

The 7 of Clubs is left unprepared, but is included with the packet. To set the deck you will use, arrange the double faced cards, including the unprepared 7 of Clubs, before you from Ace to King. Hold the remainder of the deck (minus the Club suit) before you face up, and distribute the thirteen Clubs haphazardly throughout the deck so as to mix them up in value order. Replace this deck in its case.

Now take the deck the spectator will use and from it remove the thirteen Clubs. Set them, from back to face: 5-9-8-A-Q-J-7-2-K-3-4-6-10. In order to save memorizing this arrangement, I mark the backs of these cards so that the entire suit can be set from 1 to 13 quickly. Mark the back of the 5 of Clubs as 1; the 9 of Clubs as 2, etc. Use any simple system of little dots for this. Put these thirteen cards on top of the deck and replace the pack in its case, face down. Have your four elastic bands at hand.

Show the decks and ask a spectator to point to either one. If he selects the double faced faked pack, thank him, lay the other deck aside,

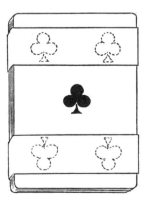

and proceed. If he takes the other, say that is his and ask him to hold it for the time being. Remove the cards from your case and hold them with the face of the bottom card towards the audience. Run through them and remove the Club suit. Then openly arrange them from Ace to King, with the Ace on the face of the packet. Now slip two of the elastic bands around the packet, as illustrated. The rear card of this packet facing you is the Five of Clubs, and the wide elastics are used to cover the upper and lower Club spots leaving only the center one showing. Thus the rear card appears to be an Ace of Clubs and matches the face card of the packet.

In putting this packet on the table, just turn it over so that the five spot side is up. That's all! The Ace, which the audience has seen, is apparently still at the face of the packet. (If you use a glass to exhibit your packet, be sure that when the spectator comes up to assist you he cannot get a view of the rear card of the packet. Just keep him well in front of the glass.)

Now ask the spectator for his pack, remove it from its case, and give it two or three genuine riffle shuffles. The 13 arranged Clubs on top of this pack are thus distributed through the pack without disturbing their order. Hand the deck face up to the spectator. He deals through the deck, one at a time, and lays aside each Club as he comes to it. (He can deposit them on your outstretched palm, or onto a small tray or plate.) This packet of 13 Clubs is still in the same order in which you previously stacked it, but simply reversed.

Now ask the spectator to step up beside you, as you show the 13 Clubs well mixed, and then fan them face down for him to select one. Actually you force the 7 of Clubs, which is the center card of the fan. He shows it around, while you hold a break at the point in the fan from where he withdrew it. Have him return the 7 of Clubs to the same spot in the fan — but face up. Now square up the fan, the face card of which is the Five of Clubs, and encircle it with the two remaining elastic bands in the same manner as you secured the first packet. Be open about this, allowing the Five of Clubs on the face of the packet to be seen by the audience, although not making an obvious point of it.

For the finish, the spectator removes the elastic bands from his packet, and holds it with the Five of Clubs full face to the audience. You pick up your packet, remove the elastic bands, and what was originally the Ace of Clubs on the face of your packet is now seen to be the Five of Clubs. The effect continues, are described, until the chosen 7 of Clubs is found reversed in the spectator's packet. As you remove the previous card from the face of your packet—you always let him remove his face card first—a back out card is seen on your packet. This, too, is the 7 of Clubs, and it shows automatically in your packet because it was the only regular card in your set up, and is, of course, the middle card of the original stack. Continue on to the finish with its climax!

TRICKS WITH SIMPLE SET-UPS

CARD VOICE

TED ANNEMANN

The following effect is one I have used for years as a finale to a routine of tricks using a stacked deck.

As you shuffle a deck of cards you ask three spectators to step forward to assist you. They stand in line to your left and facing the audience. The deck is now ribbon spread face down across the table, and the man on the far end of the line is requested to come over to the table, and pick out any card he likes and place it in his right side coat pocket. He is asked not to look at the card selected for the time being, and to step back and take his place in line.

You scoop up the deck, give it another shuffle and ribbon spread it across the table top again. The middle spectator now makes a selection, places his card in his right side coat pocket without looking at it, and steps back to his place in the line. The last spectator, the one nearest to you, does likewise.

At this point you explain, "No one living could know the identity of those cards you have in your pockets, nor do I pretend that I could name them either. However, I am going to try to name them with the assistance of one card in the deck, the 'tattle tale' card. I'm lucky enough to have discovered the language used by cards, as I shall show you. You know that in a small town everyone knows everything about everyone else. There is always one person who has little to do except keep watch on her neighbors. This applies to a pack of cards as well because they live so close together. You are skeptical?"

"In my deck the _____ of _____ is what some people call a snoopy person. It knows all about those who come and go." As you say this, look through the deck and remove the card you named. Place the deck on the table and, holding the "tattle tale" card in your left hand, put it into the nearest person's side coat pocket and hold it there for a moment. Then withdraw it and hold it up to your ear. Pretend to listen and then name the card in that person's pocket. Ask him to remember the card you name for the time being.

Pass along to the middle person and repeat the same moves. When you name his card, ask him, "to remember that card!" Do the same with the last, or farthest person on the line, ending up by asking him to remember his card. Now turn to the audience, still with the "tattle tale" card in your hand and give it to another spectator as you say, "Keep this as a souvenir. The _____ of _____ can tell you many things if you treat it right." Now turn back and ask the first person in line, "What did I tell you I heard from the _____ of _____?" He names a card, and is then asked to reach into his pocket and produce it, which he does. Each of the other two persons respond to your question in the same way and produce the very cards you named!

The general effect of this trick was invented by Charles T. Jordan who called it "The Sagacious Joker". There have been a number of variations of the trick as the years went by, but they all depended upon a force of one card, a top change, etc., and none of the variations made any pretense of routining the trick for presentation to fair to large size audiences.

Now my version, as described, was built primarily for audience participation and for club work. On parties I use it as a finale to a routine of stacked deck tricks (any arrangement you are accustomed to use.) The important part being that you line up the three spectators facing the audience, and standing to your **left** so that you can use their **right** side coat pockets. And while the first, or farthest man makes the first card selection, the middle man the next and the nearest man the last selection, you work back in reverse along the line using your left hand for the in-and-out-of-pocket operations. Thus there is no lost motion or confusion.

You shuffle the deck at all times. The first time it necessarily must be a false shuffle. When the first card is removed from the ribbon spread, you pick up the cards in groups, scoop them up so to speak, cutting the deck at the point where the selected card was removed. A glance at the bottom card of the pack as you start to overhand shuffle it will, of couse, give you the name of the first selected card automatically. Just count one ahead in the arranged setup you are using, and you know his card.

The last two selections are fair, and you really give the deck an authentic overhand shuffle each time. Now go into your patter story and mention as your snoopy "tattle tale" card the one you know the farthest man in line has in his pocket. Look through the deck as you are talking, and make a real pretense of searching for it. Finally remove any card, memorize it, but don't show its face. Hold this card face down in your right hand, lay the deck aside with your left hand, and finally transfer the "tattle tale" card face down to your left hand.

Now turn to the nearest assistant, saying, "You don't know your card, do you?" Then plunge your left hand with the "tattle tale" card into his right side coat pocket. As you stand, your fingers must go between the card in his pocket and his body. Release the card you are holding, and take hold of the one which is in his pocket. Lift your head, concentrate for a mental count of three, and then tell him the name of the card you just inserted in his pocket—its actual name, not the one you were pretending to hold. Withdraw the card you now have hold of without letting its face be seen. Step to the second person and plunge your left hand with this card into his right coat pocket. In this slight interval and short trip you glimpse the card you have just stolen from the first spectator's pocket. That one is named and left in the second person's pocket as you steal out the card he originally placed there. Repeat the same moves with the last and farthest fellow in line, finally bringing your hand out of his pocket with his originally selected card (the one you pretended to be using all along). Because of your maneuvering and acting you haven't shown the face of this card at all up to this point. Now, however, you turn it face up and hand it to one of the nearby spectators in the audience.

As a finale, the three men in line name the cards you told them they had, and they produce them one at a time!

A FUTILE LESSON

PAUL ROSINI

One of my favorite card tricks for many years is a spelling effect which uses a person from the audience without the usual "take a card" angle. It brings many laughs and makes the audience think you are an expert manipulator.

Only thirteen cards are used, Ace to King, all of them black except the 9 spot which is red. These are arranged from back to face as follows: 3,5,K,A,Q,10,9,2,8,7,J,6,4. Have these on top of your face down deck with the 3 spot as the top card. For ease in handling the packet may be bridged.

Ask a spectator up to assist you, and when he arrives give the deck a fancy shuffle and cut or two, pick off the top 13 set-up cards, toss the deck aside and say that you need only a few to teach him how to become an expert magician. Tell him that the cards respond to their spelled out names. Spell out A-C-E by putting a card from the top to the bottom of the packet for each letter. Turn up the next card. It's the Ace. Toss it away. Repeat the same moves for T-W-O, and then T-H-R-E-E.

Hand the packet to the spectator and he spells F-O-U-R, but turns up the red 9 spot. Take the cards from him, return the 9 spot to the bottom, and proceed to spell out F-O-U-R and turn up the next card which is the 4 spot. He then tries to spell F-I-V-E, but turns up the red 9 spot again. You take the cards again, place the 9 spot on the bottom, and successfully spell out the five. He tries S-I-X, and gets the 9 spot again. You try it and get the six. Then you spell out S-E-V-E-N and, of course, you get it.

Now ask the lady to come up and help. Hand her the packet and she tries E-I-G-H-T and gets it. She also spells out N-I-N-E and T-E-N. As the nine spot goes out, you remark that you're glad that card won't bother anyone any more. The man now is allowed to try to spell out J-A-C-K but he misses, as usual, getting the King. Place the King on the bottom. You try J-A-C-K and get it. You give up now as you start to have him try the Queen, shake your head and say that it's of no use. Then you spell out Q-U-E-E-N and K-I-N-G. Excuse your helpers with a sad smile. "It just isn't in the cards, I guess, to make expert magicians out of you in one lesson." (Note: As each card is spelled out correctly, discard it.)

THE SCARNE THOUGHT CARD

In most versions of the trick of finding a thought-of card, it is necessary to employ some adroit pumping and elimination. This version by the inimitable John Scarne is simplicity itself, and is accomplished quickly and surely with but little, if any, questioning. Try it a few times and see for yourself how perfect the effect is for laymen.

Prepare any deck by arranging ten cards of mixed suits, from Ace to ten spot, on top of the deck. The ten spot should be the tenth card from the top; and the top card, the Ace, should be a short card for ease of presentation.

Introduce the deck, and give it several dovetail shuffles without disturbing the ten cards stacked on top. Now undercut about half of the deck and throw on top. The left hand holds the pack up vertically and facing the audience, while the right fingers riffle the top edge of the deck from face towards back, asking the spectator to watch the cards and "think of one." However, you actually force him to think of one of the stacked ten cards as follows:

When you cut the deck after shuffling it, you brought the ten stacked cards to a position approximately about fifteenth to twenty-fifth from the face of the deck. Thus when you now riffle them as described, you let the first fifteen cards snap by rapidly as you ask the spectator to watch the cards. Just as you tell him to "think of one," you reach the stacked packet, so at this point you let the cards snap by slowly and deliberately so that each may readily be seen. After these ten are run through, let the remainder of the cards snap by more rapidly as you ask if he has made a mental note of one of the cards he's seen. It's purely a matter of timing, and after a few trials you should have no difficulty in gauging the location of the ten stacked cards and the comparative speed in riffling through the deck from face to back.

Now lower your hands with the deck to about waist high, and ask him to be sure and keep his card in mind. As you ask this, cut the deck at the short card bringing the ten stacked cards to the top. and shuffle the deck retaining the stack on top. Place the deck on the table, and cut it into two piles. Offer the spectator a choice of one half, and interpret his selection so that you pick up the half with the ten stacked cards on top.

Now ask him to think of the number of spots on his mentally selected card and, as you deal cards one at a time onto the table, to count mentally along with your deal until that number is reached. At this point he is to stop you. When he stops you, lay that card to one side and ask him the name of his card. As he names it, turn over that card and it is the selected one! It has to be, of course, for as long as he thinks of one of the ten stacked cards—and he will without fail, if you work it with assurance —the trick must work, because the cards are stacked from one to ten.

RESTLESS CARDS

TED ANNEMANN

In this effect, you show two decks of cards—one has red backs, the other blue. From the red pack, a card is freely selected. You now take a bunch of about a dozen cards from this pack and have the selected card returned to this packet. A rubber band is placed around the packet and it is set in full view in a clip stand on the table.

The same procedure is then adopted with the blue backed pack. A card is chosen and replaced among a small group of a dozen cards from the blue pack. This blue packet is also fastened with a rubber band, and is then displayed in a second clip stand on the table, some distance from the red packet.

Taking the red packet, you remove a card and set it in front of the stand with its back to the audience. See illustration. This acts as a marker to identify the red packet. Another elastic is snapped about the packet lengthwise, so that now an elastic band encircles it in both directions. and it is replaced face outwards in its stand. The same procedure is now gone through with the blue packet. An identifying blue card is set in front of the stand, and the blue packet is doubly secured with a second elastic and set back in its stand. Thus it is impossible for you to remove another card from either packet.

Now comes the mystery. The two packets are taken, one in each hand, and are tapped together just prior to being tossed into the air. Each is caught as it descends and replaced in its proper stand. The red packet is now taken and handed to the person who chose the red card, and the blue packet is given to the person who selected the blue card. When they look through their packets they find one card with an opposite colored back. Thus the person with the red packet finds the selected blue card in his group; and the person with the blue packet finds the chosen red card in his!

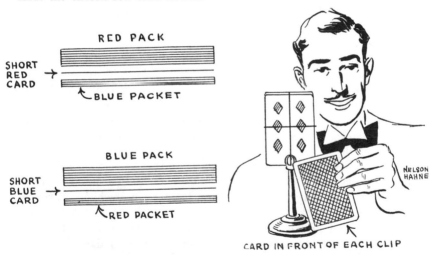

The method is both subtle and simple. The packs are arranged before hand as follows:—take a dozen red cards and add them to the bottom of the blue pack; and then add a dozen blue cards to the bottom of the red packet. Just above the packet of red cards have a "short" blue card; also have a "short" red card in the red deck just about the packet of blue cards. The bottom card of each bottom group of cards should be the same, say the Six of Diamonds. The two stands used are of the clip type as illustrated.

To present, the red backed deck is fanned without the bottom stock of blue cards being spread. A card is now selected. While it is being noted, riffle the rear of the pack with your right thumb until you reach the short card and take these thirteen cards as a group in your left hand. The top card of this group is the red card, while al lthe remainder, unknown to the audience, are blue backed. Lay the red deck to one side and have the chosen red card returned to the packet of cards you are holding. Just slide it into the center of this packet without exposing the backs of any of the cards below the top red card. Snap an elastic band around this packet and insert it, backs outwards, in one of the clip stands.

Now do exactly the same with the blue pack. Have a card selected, cut off the bottom group of red cards with the blue short on top, have the chosen card returned to this packet, snap an elastic band around it and place this packet, backs outwards, in the second clip stand.

Now turn both stands around so that the face cards are to the audience. Remove the first packet and, holding it with its face to the audience, slip out the red short card from the rear, and rest it back outwards against the first stand as a marker. Snap a second band around the packet, and set the packet, face outwards, back in its stand. Do exactly the same with the second packet, using the blue short card at the rear of this packet as your marker. Place this packet back in its stand with its face card to the audience. Thus, although everything appears fair to the audience, you actually have a blue backed packet identified by a red card; and a red backed packet identified by a blue card.

Now take both heaps, one in each hand and with their faces towards the audience, tap them together and toss them in the air simultaneously. This unexpected action prevents anyone from noting which packet is which. When the packets are caught, they are turned backs to the audience, the color of their backs supposedly identifying them. The one with the red back is now placed in the stand with the red marker; and the one with the blue back goes back into the stand with the blue marker. Actually, however, the switch has been accomplished, and so far as you are concerned the mechanics of the trick are over.

It simply remains for you to give the red packet to the man who chose the red card; and the blue packet to the man who chose the blue card. They take off the elastic bands and each finds a stranger card in his packet; and both of these cards prove to be the ones chosen by the opposite party.

THE CARD PHENOMENON

AUDLEY WALSH

Here's a neat variation of the card spelling trick with a neat twist that makes it completely baffling. The spectator is given a deck of cards and is instructed to count off a small packet of cards and place them in his pocket. You turn your back so as not to see the number of cards counted off. Now while your back is still turned, he counts off a second packet of a like number of cards, looks at the bottom card of this packet, shuffles it, and replaces the packet on top of the deck. You now turn around, ask him to replace the packet of cards he has in his pocket on top of the deck and then to name his selected card. When he does so, you have him spell out the name of his card by dealing off one card for each letter from the deck. He then turns over the next card . . . and it's the chosen one! And the best part of the trick, so far as you are concerned, is that it works entirely automatically.

A simple set-up is arranged in advance. Select all the cards that spell with twelve letters and place them on top of the deck. There are only fourteen of these in all—the 4-5-9-J-K of Hearts and Spades, and the 3-7-8-Q of Clubs. Mix these up a bit before placing them on the deck, remember the top card as a key card, and finally top the deck with four indifferent cards.

To perform, hand the deck to a spectator with the request that while your back is turned he is to count of any number of cards, from 5 to 10, into one pile on the table. You direct him to place these in his pocket for a moment, and then deal another pile of cards of the same amount. He is to pick up this second pile, look at and remember the bottom card, shuffle this packet and replace it on top of the deck. At this point you turn around, and pick up the deck by way of illustrating what you want him to do. Point out how impossible it is for you know either the number of cards he has in his pocket, or the number counted. Explain that when you hand the deck back to him, he is to replace the packet of cards he has in his pocket on top of the deck, and then spell out the name of his card. dealing off one card for each letter. To make this perfectly clear, you illustrate by spelling out the name of the key card (the original top card of the stack) which you memorized. You deal one card at a time into a pile for each letter of your key card, and then turn over the next card on top of the deck as an example of what he is to do. (Spelling out the key card is a cute angle, for it cannot be the selected card yet it enables you to reverse the order of 12 cards quickly and with certainty.) Having thus shown the spectator what he is to do, you replace your counted off packet on top of the deck and step aside. He picks up the deck and adds the packet of cards from his pocket to the top of the deck. He now names the card he selected, spells it out, and then turns over the next card—and it's his selected card!

As already mentioned the climax is entirely automatic as long as you follow the above routine. You never know the name of the selected card, nor the number of cards he has in his pocket; and the more the spectator tries to figure it out, the more baffled he becomes.

THE ULTRA FIND

TED ANNEMANN

I honestly believe that this is the most perfect and genuine of all locations. It is based upon the endless chain principle of a dovetail shuffle first introduced by Charles Jordan about 1919, although I believe the discovery of the principle really belonged to Arthur Finley. I'm sure all my readers are familiar with the principle which, to explain it briefly, operates as follows. Suppose you have one suit stacked from Ace to King on top of your deck. Now cutting the deck in half and dovetail shuffling the top half into the lower half results in your stacked suit retaining its original order in the shuffled deck, although each card in the stack may be separated from the next card in sequence by several odd cards. In other words, the chain or sequence of the cards is maintained. (For a full description of this principle and its many ramifications, see Jordan's booklet, "Thirty Card Mysteries".)

The location which I have named "The Ultra Find" is a simplification of the Jordan method. Take a deck now and separate the suits, arranging each from Ace to King reading from the face of the packets. Now assemble the packets so that they read from the face of the pack— Clubs, Hearts, Spades and Diamonds.

Now cut the deck a couple of times, and complete the cuts.

Next cut the deck in two parts (about even) and dovetail shuffle them together.

Give the deck a couple of more cuts, completing the cuts.

Cut into two parts, and dovetail shuffle again.

Complete another cut or two.

Now cut the deck into two piles.

Look at the top card of **either** pile. Put this card back into the **center of its own pile.**

Now dovetail shuffle the two piles.

And finish by cutting the deck, and completing the cut, once or twice more.

Could anyone expect you to find a card after that procedure? Well, Charlie Jordan did it by starting at the right hand card of the pack after it was spread face up on the table, and following the endless chain over and over, time after time, through the deck until he found one card out of place in relation to its original stacked position.

In my method, you need only to go through the deck once, starting at the right hand end of the spread, or fan. Put your finger on the first card at the right end. Whatever that may be, let your eyes move to the left along the spread and look for the card of the same suit next in order (one higher.) It shouldn't be far away. If you are pointing at the 4H, look for the 5H. If the KD, look for the Ace of the next suit in order, and then, after finding it, move your finger to the second card from the right end of the spread. Now look for the next card (one higher) of this suit. Continue in this manner, never missing a card as you continue moving your finger to the left. To the onlooker you are touching each card in order. A little practice and you can move along quite rapidly.

All at once you'll touch a card, and in looking further on you'll see, not the next card in the chain, but the one after that. You may be touching the 10S. Before you reach the JS you'll hit the QS. Something is undoubtedly askew. First, glance back to the right a bit and look for the Jack. If it is there, **it is the selected card.** If it isn't there, glance back to the left again until you find it. If it is found to the left beyond the Queen (and it must be beyond or it wouldn't be out of place) then the Queen is the right card.

This rule applies to any card in the deck that may be out of place. The best way to finish, after noting the right card, is to close up the deck, run through it and toss the card face down on the table. The spectator names his card, and then turns it up! The best way to practice, incidentally, is to pencil mark the back of the "selected" card but do not look at it during the shuffling and cutting. Later when you find the face up card you can verify it by the pencil mark on its back.

Those who try this out will swear by it. To the onlooker there is no answer, for he does all the mixing, cutting, selecting, and added mixing while your back is turned. There is no visible trickery! If you know

the factory arrangement of any certain brand of playing cards, you can
have a new deck opened while your back is turned and the selection
made. The method is sure fire, clean and decisive, and it has fooled some
of the best brains in card magic. Try it!

TRICKS WITH SPECIAL DECKS

CRISS-CROSS

STEVE SIMPSON

In this cleverly routined effect you write a number and the name of
a card on a piece of paper, without allowing anyone to see what you
write, and then fold the paper and lay it in the center of the table.
A spectator also secretly writes a number and the name of a card on
a second slip, which is likewise folded and laid on the table. The deck
of cards being used is dealt into two piles. Upon counting down in
the two piles to the numbers chosen, your card is found to occupy a
position corresponding to the spectator's freely chosen number in one
pile, while the spectator's card is found in the other pile at the number
you designated.

While most effects of this nature require a switch of the prediction
slips, this one does not. And while some readers may stand aghast at
the implement used to insure success, we can emphatically state that
the presentation completely eliminates any thought of the weapon being
used to bludgeon the senses of those watching. A most important point
to lovers of subtleties is that after the trick is over one may proceed
with any card problems you like that call for an ordinary pack of cards.

Method: A Svengali deck of 52 cards is used, the duplicate short
cards being at positions 1, 3, 5, 7, etc. from the top of the deck. The
alternate unprepared cards at the even numbers are, of course, all different.
Such a pack may be cut indefinitely yet always leaves a short card
on top.

You begin the presentation by announcing that you will write
down a number between 1 and 26, and do so. (It is best to take one
somewhere around 13.) You then say that you will note a card in the
deck, so pick up the Svengali deck and riffle through it with the faces
towards yourself. Stop anywhere, and note a card apparently. Then
write on your prediction slip the name of the duplicate short cards in
the deck. Now either fold your slip and lay it on the table, or just
turn it over face down. The spectator is asked to write on his paper
a number from 1 to 26. After he does this you pick up the deck. Hold
it face towards the spectator in a vertical position, and riffle through

it a couple of times to show the cards all different—(but without saying so.) Then lower it to a horizontal position and ask the spectator to insert his finger in the deck as you riffle it once more. As he does this, you raise the upper part of the deck to a vertical position facing the spectator, and he is asked to note the card he sees and to write it on his paper below his written number. (Please note that the spectator gets a free choice of a card, and that no force is employed. He notes, of course, one of the indifferent cards.)

As he notes his card, you drop your left hand, which is holding the lower half of the deck, and secretly mark the short card on the top of this half with your finger nail, a crimp, or with daub. The top portion held in the right hand is now dropped on top of those in the left hand, and the cards are squared.

Now deal the deck into two piles, silently counting the cards in the "short" pile and noting the number at which the marked card falls. Subtracting this number from 28 will give you the position of the spectator's card in the other pile, counting from the top down. For instance, say that the position of the spectator's card is found to be 16th from the top. If you predicted the number 13 on your paper, you know that 3 cards must be transferred from the top to the bottom of the pile of ordinary cards in order to bring the spectator's card into place.

Stating that you do not know into which pile the spectator's card has fallen, you pick up the ordinary card pile, fan it in a vertical position facing the spectator, and ask him to state if his card is present. This gives you an opportunity to make a slight break below the top three cards (or whatever number is necessary to bring the chosen card to its proper place) and on closing the fan, make a simple cut transposing those cards to the bottom. Set the pile on the table.

Now pick up the other "short" pile, fan it towards yourself and say that your card is in this pile. Square it up and set the pile down again on the table.

The two papers are now opened and read, and the cards and numbers are noted. Pick up the pile of "short" cards and count down in that pile, from the top, to the number decided upon by the spectator. Lay this card to one side, face down. Now pick up the other pile and slowly count down to the number you have written, and lay the card occupying this position to one side. The remaining cards are gathered up and the two cards are turned face up. They are found to be the two chosen ones!

If you desire to continue with some other card effects, then let the spectator count down in the "regular" pile and lay the card arrived at to one side. This is all the misdirection you need to switch the "short" pile of cards for another packet of 26 cards complimenting the ones the spectator is handling, so as to have a complete deck—except for one short card—at the completion of the trick. Needless to say the short card can then be put to good use.

THE FUTURE DECK

JACK VOSBURGH

In this stunning effect, the performer says he will write a prediction for any spectator present. Not having a piece of paper handy, he jots down a few words upon the face of one of the cards from his deck. This is tossed into the spectator's hat and is not touched again by the performer. The remainder of the deck is ribbon spread face down across the top of the table, or floor, so that every card is exposed. The spectator points to any card, and this is a perfectly free choice. This card is picked up and dropped into the hat with the first card. When the spectator dumps the two cards out onto the table, it is found that the prediction written by the performer correctly names the card freely selected. The performer then proceeds with any other card tricks in his repertoire.

This trick is as near perfect as any card trick can be. Its secret is simplicity itself, and it would almost seem that everyone seeing it would immediately spot the method used. However, they don't. A prepared deck is used, making the trick an excellent one for those who do but one or two card tricks in their routine.

Take the Ten of Clubs, for instance, and lay it aside temporarily. Now write "Ten of Clubs" on the face of each of the other 51 cards in the deck, writing in the upper left corner near the index, as illustrated. Place the Joker on the face of the deck, and the real Ten of Clubs on the top. Place the deck in its case and you are ready.

Take the cards from the case, fan them slightly with faces towards you, and remove the Joker saying you will not need it. Replace it in the card case. Give the deck an overhand shuffle, keeping the faces of the cards tilted away from the audience, and bring the Ten of Clubs from the top of the deck to the bottom. Now pretend to write a prediction on the upper left corner of this card with your pencil, not allowing the spectators to either see the face of the Ten of Clubs or what you are pretending to write. Pick this card up and drop it, back outwards, into the spectator's hat.

Hold the deck face down in the left hand so that the written on ends are nearest your body. Fan the cards and let the spectators see the faces of them, indicating in this manner that the deck is well mixed. The writing on the cards is concealed at the lower and almost unfanned end by the left fingers. The illustration shows how the deck is fanned.

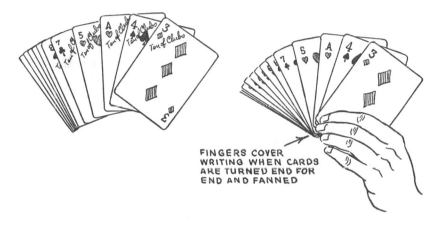

FINGERS COVER WRITING WHEN CARDS ARE TURNED END FOR END AND FANNED

Next ribbon spread the deck face down in a semi-circle so that the back of each card is visible. Ask one of the spectators to point to any card, impressing on him that it is a perfectly free choice, and that he may change his mind if he likes. Pick up the card he points to and, without showing its face, drop it into the hat with your prediction card.

Scoop up the deck, fan it as before to show they are all different and remark that but one was selected. Have one of the spectators pick up the hat and dump out the two cards it contains. Have him read the prediction written on one of the two cards which, of course, reads "Ten of Clubs". The other card is the Ten of Clubs!

As the spectator reads the prediction and shows the Ten of Clubs, you drop the deck in your pocket and switch it for another matching deck which is minus the Ten of Clubs. This leaves you with a deck containing but one duplicate (the written on card) and this card may be left with the spectator as a souvenir. You're set now to carry on with your card tricks, watching out that the duplicate of the written on card does not show up prominently at any point in your later routine.

THE OMEGA CARD ACT

TED ANNEMANN

The card routine given herewith is one which I honestly believe can revolutionize the presentation of card effects. Followed by many, such a practice undoubtedly would wreck havoc with tricks of classic origin. It's a case of condensing into a few minutes the various card effects which past masters have made separate features, and which lasted from five to fifteen minutes each. This presentation should not run over twelve minutes, and I sincerely offer it as a routine worthwhile.

When I titled this a "card act," I meant it in every sense of the word. It was conceived for the purpose of routining into ten minutes the classic card locations with each having its own presentation. Another objective was to build a complete and showy card act suitable for night clubs, and especially for those performers who have their half hour or hour of magic and want to introduce one trick with cards. It may well be termed an effort to produce an item which can be shown as a card location presentation to end all card locations—that is, as far as the audience in front is concerned.

Frankly only the tips, hints, wrinkles and asides are original, the five basic tricks having been picked up from here and there. However, my whole aim has been to combine the effects into one smooth and continuous working routine which, to any audience, will appear as something far different and mysterious than anything they have previously seen. The lack of apparatus is a vastly important feature. The audience sees you step forward with but a new pack of cards. The few outside objects used are obviously ordinary and can be borrowed. The rest of the apparatus, if it can be called that, is on your person without any discomfiture.

THE ROUTINE: The deck is given someone for a shuffle, and five people around the room are asked to choose cards in succession. Upon the return of these cards, you stand at the front of the stage and shuffle the deck. You now explain that to find the cards you must resort to different and varied methods, "for like people no two cards are of the same temperament nor do they excell in the same branches of business or hobbies. It is, therefore, necessary to locate them according to their own pursuits of happiness."

The deck is now placed into a stemmed goblet, following which you show a small embroidery hoop which you pass over the glass of cards several times, and finally toss aside. Incidentally, the hoop may be made of rope like a quoit ring, and thus may be more easily carried in your pocket. However, you now pick up the goblet, set it on your outstretched hand, and ask the first person to name his card. Slowly and deliberately the named card rises. It is tossed out into the audience and the glass set aside.

You next insert the deck into its case and wrap it in your pocket handkerchief. The name of the second card is requested, and it is seen to penetrate both the handkerchief and the case. This card also is tossed into the audience, after which you unwrap the pack and remove it from its case.

The third person is asked to stand. As he does so you approach him, shuffling the cards, and ask him if he is certain that he knows his card. You then hand him the deck and request that he look through it and remove his card. As he does so, remove a double banded wallet from your pocket and toy with it, taking care to keep it well in view and at the very tips of your fingers. The spectator admits that he cannot find his card. He is asked to name it. You then very deliberately remove the elastic from around your wallet, and it is seen to be a three-fold type. The flaps open outwards, and inside, under the glassine card holder, is seen the chosen card. It is likewise removed and thrown out.

You now take back the deck and ask the fourth person to stand. He is given the deck and asked to shuffle it, while you remove from your pocket an ornamental dagger. This can be a decorative envelope opener, preferably in a sheath for appearance sake. You take back the deck in one hand, and ask him to accompany you to the stage where you place the deck face down on the table and have him spread them about. You now tie a handkerchief around your head, covering your eyes, and proceed to stab a card, although you don't show it immediately. Ask him to name his card, and then dramatically raise the dagger to show the selected card with one hand, while you whip off the blindfold with the other.

Now assemble the cards and ask the fifth person to stand. Explain that ordinarily two decks would be used for the final effect, but that tonight one will have to suffice. As you say this, tear the deck into two halves and lay one half on the table. The other half you shuffle, after which you begin to deal them by dropping one piece at a time on the floor. The spectator is requested to call "Stop" at any time, and the half card at that point is placed, back outwards, and protruding from your breast pocket. The second half of the deck is handled in the same fashion and another half card is stopped at, as the spectator commands. The two half cards are held together so that the torn ends match, but with their backs to the audience. The spectator names his card, and the two halves are turned over facing the audience, and are found to match and make the chosen card!

The routine is over, and the cards are gone! There has been no stalling, no duplication of effects, and each revelation has been a decisive one. I honestly believe this to be just about the best possible card routine for showmen who believe as I do, that the effect upon the audience is the thing.

As for the patter, people are different, and each reader will no doubt think of some pet effect he would rather substitute for each one in the routine as given. Whether this can be done with safety or not, I cannot say. It depends upon the individual performer's ability and his selection of tricks. Herein, I have made single use of the classic locations, none of which are complicated in their unfolding, and all of which appeal to the eye of the spectator. In short, my selections are elemental, and as such can be depended upon to entertain without confusion or boredom.

INITIAL PREPARATION: This consists of making a "short card" of one of the Aces, preferably the Ace of Clubs or Spades. Either can be seen and recognized instantly from a good distance. This card is made into a "short" by trimming a thin half moon from each narrow end. The cutting should start one-quarter inch from each side, and the half moon should not be more than one-sixteenth of an inch deep at the very center. Such a "short card" does not require tapping the deck to locate it, a mere squaring of the deck with the fingers being sufficient. It is easily located, too, by riffling the deck.

The other requisites will be mentioned as the separate effects are described and, after all is said and done, the necessary bits of preparations and adjuncts will be tabulated as a whole.

START OF THE ROUTINE: The deck is removed from its case and pretense is made of opening a new deck. The cards are fanned to show them in very uniform order, as usually received from the manufacturer, and the deck is handed to a spectator for a thorough mixing. After this, five people are approached for the selections. I suggest that it be done from left to right around the room. The revelations later will be in reverse order, that is, from right to left from your point of view, but these climaxes will be from the left to the right of the audience which is natural from their viewpoint.

Nearing the first person you riffle and cut the deck a time or two, and bring the "short card" to the top. The first and second spectators have free choices of any cards from the center of the pack. Upon the third person, though, is forced the top "short" card. I suggest for the force, and the technique of controlling the returned cards, the information contained in "Light on the Hindu Shuffle," which appeared in "The Jinx" No. 56, page 398. This article covers forcing and the control of cards after their return by a method unsurpassed in modern cardology.

The fourth and fifth persons have a perfectly free selection of cards. Each in turn retains his selected card until after the fifth one has been chosen. Then you start back and have the five cards returned to the deck starting again with spectator number 1. If you use the aforementioned Hindu Shuffle method, the first person's card is brought to the top on the shuffle and the near left hand corner is bent upwards and broken by the right thumb. This acts as a key card for easy location later.

The second and third cards are returned on top of the key card during the next shuffle through. Then the fourth and fifth cards are returned during the third shuffle through. This leaves the cards, from top of deck downwards, 5, 4, 3, 2, 1, as replaced, and card No. 1 has the broken corner. Should you use any other method of control, just remember to bring the five cards to the top of the pack in the order designated. All the revelations will take place in that order from the top of the deck downward, the broken corner card being for the last effect. The forced "short" card upon its return is in the middle of the five, or third from the top. Naturally, you must know to whom each card belongs, and that is the reason we have emphasized the business of working from one side to the other in a regular order.

With the cards all under control on top of the deck, you step back to the stage all ready for the successive denouements.

No. 1 — THE RISING CARD

For this effect the audience may be as close as you like while the card is rising from the glass, for although a thread is used it is impossible for anyone to see it. Simplicity is paramount, especially since but one card is required to rise. A piece of black thread about six inches long is used, and two or three hard knots are tied at each end. One end, is coated with a small piece of wax. See illustration.

Stick the waxed end of the thread to the top right hand button of your evening coat, or to the most easily reached button of a single or double breasted suit. Let the other end hang down.

Hand the goblet to someone to examine (in the night club the spectator blows into the glass. A strong breath helps the subsequent occurrence!) and, while he does so, you secure the waxed end of the thread from the button and press it against the center of one end of the top card of the deck. Upon receiving the goblet drop the pack, with the waxed end of thread downwards, into the glass. The other end of the thread lies outside the goblet and is hidden by the cards. Set the glass on the table and pick up your hoop. To make the card rise, pick up the glass and, with the other hand, pass the hoop around it several times from different angles. Now hold the goblet between two fingers of one hand with the bowl of the goblet resting on your upturned palm, and pull down on the knotted end of the thread with the thumb of that hand. This move-

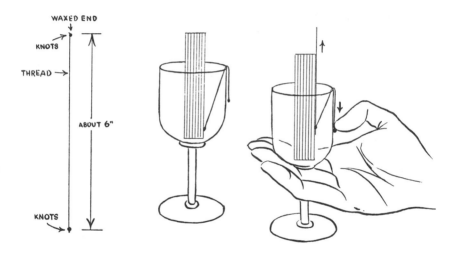

ment draws the card upwards. When nearly out of the pack, take the card with your free hand and toss it out into the audience, after the thumb digs off the waxed thread. Just drop the thread on the floor and everything remaining is unprepared. The illustration shows the necessary action.

No. 2 — THE PENETRATING CARD

The next top card belongs to the second spectator. When the cards are removed from the glass, the top card is slipped to the bottom or face of the deck. The case introduced and shown. It is of the flap variety and the deck is inserted with its back to the flap, as illustrated. Upon replacing the flap, it must be inserted **between** the bottom card and the outside of the case. See Figure 1. In this condition the case is thrown onto the table with the notched side undermost, as the pocket handkerchief is removed and shown.

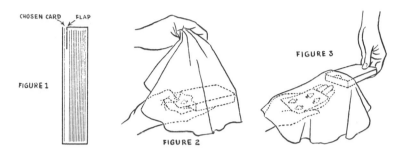

CHOSEN CARD   FLAP

FIGURE 1

FIGURE 2

FIGURE 3

With the handkerchief held in your left hand, pick up the pack with your right hand so that the thumb hides the tell-tale portion of the

bottom card visible through the notch. As soon as the handkerchief is thrown over the pack, the right thumb, which should be slightly moistened, draws the selected card three-quarters of its length out of the case, see Figure 2, while the left hand simultaneously lifts up the handkerchief from the bottom end of the case to show that the case is still there. The left hand then takes the case and withdraws it from under the handkerchief, Figure 3. The fold of the handkerchief which had been drawn back is allowed to fall down again, and the left hand places the case on the handkerchief on top of the upturned palm. This, of course, places the case directly above the palmed card, separated from it only by the thickness of the handkerchief.

The trick is now done. The part of the handkerchief nearest the audience is drawn back over the case, and the whole is lifted by the left hand with the left fingers pressing the palmed card through the cloth against the enclosed case. The palmed card, of course, being kept to the rear. If now the hanging portion of the handkerchief is slightly screwed up and held in the right hand, as illustrated, the case will hang down enclosed in the handkerchief, and the selected card will be behind the handkerchief and gripped in its rear folds. A slight shake imparted to the bundle will cause the card apparently to force its way through both the case and the handkerchief, and make its appearance at the bottom of the bundle. By having the card at the bottom when placed into the case, it makes its appearance with its face towards the audience.

No. 3 — THE POCKETBOOK CARD

After tossing the second person's card out into the audience following its appearance as above, remove the case from the folds of the handkerchief and offhandedly show the handkerchief free of any holes or trap doors. Now remove the cards from the case, but leave the top card in the case and toss the latter onto the table. The card it contains is the third person's selection.

You have a three-fold wallet in your right coat pocket, and the center section of the wallet has a glassine window pocket usually used for identification cards. In this pocket, and facing outwards, is a duplicate of the forced "short" card. The flaps have been closed, and a heavy rubber band has been put around the wallet in each direction.

The third person stands, as have the others, and after admitting that he remembers his card he is given the deck and asked to find it by fanning the cards. Naturally, it isn't there! While he's looking, you reach into your pocket and bring out the wallet which you keep in full view, turning it over and over with your fingers. When the spectator says that his card is not in the deck, you ask the name of it, and then say it just had to be missing because you had that card in your possession all the time. Strip the rubber band off of the wallet with as much showmanship as possible, open the wallet towards the audience and let the card be seen under its protective transparent covering. The spectator who selected it removes his card himself.

No. 4 — THE IMPALED CARD

While the third spectator withdraws his card (the duplicate, of course) from your wallet, you take back the deck he has been holding. His looking through it while fanned does not disarrange the cards in any way, and the fourth person's card is still on top. The fourth person is now asked to stand, and you hand him a dagger which you take from your inside coat pocket. The left hand removes the dagger from your pocket, and while under the coat and out of sight takes the opportunity of getting a good smear of daub, from a daub pot attached to the edge of the pocket, on your thumb. After giving the dagger to the spectator, you bring your hands together and daub the center of each side edge of the top card of the pack which your right hand has been holding.

You now reclaim the dagger, and give the deck to the spectator for a thorough shuffling. Take the deck back from him and, holding it high above your head, return to the stage with the spectator and spread the cards face down on the table. The daubed card, turned either way, will show up immediately among the others. The cards are not spread evenly from left to right, but pushed in all directions to make a truly mixed up mess. After the first spread, when the daubed card is spotted, it is kept in view and left somewhere about the middle of the spread. Now ostentatiously tie a handkerchief over your eyes in the usual manner which, of course, does not prevent you from seeing down the sides of your nose. Then perform the card tsabbing feat, building it up for all it's worth. Take off the blindfold with your left hand, ask for the name of the card. After it is acknowledged, it is either tossed away, or taken off by its selector.

No. 5 — THE TORN CARD

The cards are now gathered up, squared, and the deck handed to the fifth spectator who is asked to stand and shuffle them once more. This spectator's card was the first one returned, and has the bent corner. Therefore a thorough mixing of the deck has little affect upon its subsequent location.

Take back the deck and face everyone. Cut the deck a time or two, stating that you have but one deck and should have two. This interval allows cutting the broken corner card to the top, after which you tear the deck into two halves.

You had better take an old deck in hand while reading this. Square it as perfectly as possible, and grip it by one end with the right hand. The four fingers are all on the outside and within an inch of the end. The heel of the hand is on the opposite side of the same end of the deck. Now the left hand fingers are placed on the inside surface of the deck (side nearest your body) and next to the heel of the right hand, which is on the same side.

This position is attained by twisting the left hand over towards the body and **not** under towards the body. The heel of the left hand is therefore on the outside of the deck together with the right hand fingers.

The tearing of the deck is begun from the inside, the side nearest the body, and the pressure is on the heels of both hands which make the tearing effort against each other. Keep the deck squared by not releasing the pressure of the fingers. Don't let it slip. A firm and increasing pressure will start the separation. It may be necessary to regrip the deck for better leverage after tearing half way, but this only serves to make it easier from there on.

Contrary to belief, the tearing of a deck does **not** require strength at all. Merely a bit of leverage, properly used, does the trick for the weakest person.

Torn in half, one part of the deck is laid aside for the moment. The other half-pack is held outwards along the curved fingers and given an overhand shuffle. The curved fingers around and against the back of the cards holds the top card (selected one) in place while the others are shuffled fairly onto the face of the packet. The half-pack is turned face down and held in the left hand in dealing position. The left hand is now raised so that the cards are vertical, and the left thumb draws the top card down about a quarter of an inch where it is hidden by the fingers. The right fingers "second deal" the remaining cards of the packet right into the air, so to speak, so that they fall onto the floor. The spectator has been asked to call out "Stop" at any time, and you continue your dealing until he halts you. The left thumb immediately pushes up the top half-card until it is in alignment with the rest of the half-pack, and the left hand is lowered so that all may see that you take only the top half-card off the packet and place it, back outwards, in your breast coat .pocket. Leave about 50% or more of it protruding. What is left of the undealt half-pack is tossed into the air to fall in a shower on the floor.

The other half of the deck is now picked up, and the same action is repeated, resulting in the forcing of the remaining half of the selected card. Discard the undealt portion of the half-pack as before, remove the half-card from your pocket, and match it up with the half-card you are holding in your right hand — backs outwards ,of course. The last spectator is asked to name his card, and the two pieces are turned around to reveal the card for your grand climax. Thus ends this twelve minute super routine with a deck of cards.

REQUISITES: A table at center stage.

One stemmed goblet.

An embroidery hoop, or a rope quoit hoop.

A new deck in a case of the flap type, with one card a "short card" cut to specifications.

One duplicate of this "short card" incased in a three-fold wallet under the center glassine section, and facing outwards. The wallet bound with one or more rubber bands.

A length of six inch thread knotted at both ends and waxed at one. The waxed end is attached to a convenient coat button.

A breast pocket handkerchief at least 18" square.

An ornamental dagger, or flashy envelope opener in your inside coat pocket.

Either one container of card daub pinned to the top of your inside coat pocket, or powdered graphite rubbed into the edge of the left coat sleeve where a smear of it may easily be gotten onto the right thumb, or vice versa on the right sleeve for use by the left thumb.

FIVE FINDO

TED ANNEMANN

I evolved the following routine some years ago and it has stood me in good stead. There is the desired clean cut difference between each of the five locations, plus valuable audience participation.

In effect, a deck, which may be a borrowed one, is used. Five persons each select cards, note them and return them to the deck. You can patter to the effect that different personalities require different technicalities of mystery, and that the modern card sharp must be prepared to analyse his opponents and be able to put to instant use that particular system which will insure success. Now each of the five assistants step up from the audience, one at a time, and his or her card is found in an entirely different and novel manner. That's all there is to it, but it's a winner!

It would be well at this point if you will take your deck in hand and follow the moves as I outline them.

The cards are selected, noted, and returned to the deck where you get them on top, and mentally designate them from the top card down as 1, 2, 3, 4, and 5. They will be located in that order, and it is preferable that the top card, or number 1, be one that was selected by a lady. Use any method you like to get the five cards on top of the deck. I have found the Hindu Shuffle excellent for this. At other times I would merely nail nick the upper left edge of the top card after the selections were made, cut it near to the center of the pack, and then fan the deck at this point for the return of each card under the edge nicked key card. The remark, "Just drop it in the deck somewhere, it doesn't really matter where for I'm not going to find them. Your own personalities will do the trick," always seemed to keep people from getting fancy on returning the cards. Now step back to the stage, and cut the key card to the bottom, which automatically leaves the five chosen cards on top of the deck. The locations now start with the last person who returned a card, and follow in sequence down to the first card selected.

No. 1 — CARD AT ANY NUMBER

At this point you dovetail shuffle the deck a couple of times, and during the riffling add seven cards on top of the deck above the set of five. Ask the lady (she was the last person selecting a card) to step up beside you and name a number from 1 to 10. You are holding the deck face down on your outstretched left hand, but as she takes her place you secure a finger break with the left little finger under the top two cards. This sets you for numbers 5,6,7, and 8. If 5, you deal and count cards onto her hand. The first two go on as 1, followed by single cards as 2, 3, 4 and 5. You then point at the top card of the deck and ask her to name her selected card. She does so, and you double lift the top two cards and show her card. Thank her at this point and, as she returns to her seat, you turn the two cards face down on the deck and then shift them to the bottom. The cards she had been holding are also placed on the bottom of the deck.

(For the other numbers she might have named, proceed as follows: If the number is 6, make the first count a double deal as already mentioned, then count off the cards onto her hand, one at a time, and allow her to turn up the top card remaining on the deck herself. If 7, do it fairly throughout, and she turns over the next card. If 8, it is a fair count throughout and the 8th card is turned up. You may have perfect confidence in these four numbers because when 4 or less is called you merely say, "It should be a more difficult one", and say nothing more. You'll get a good number.)

No. 2 — "YOU COUNT 'EM"

Finishing this, the four remaining selected cards are on top of the deck. The next person steps forward as the lady returns to her seat. He stands at your left side. Hand the deck to him and ask him to deal the cards face down, one at a time, onto your left hand. When he gets to the fourth card, add, "And you may stop dealing at any time you like. It's entirely up to you." You hold the cards counted in your left hand as though for dealing. He stops! Your left thumb pushes the last card dealt (the top one) off the right edge of the packet you are holding, your right hand picks it up by its right side and, without showing the card it is shaken a bit to draw attention to it as you say, "This is as far as you want to go?" At the tail end of this query the card is carelessly dropped back on top of the left hand packet; you are looking directly at the spectator as you do so, and your left thumb goes across the top of the packet to meet the second finger of the same hand on the right side of the cards. This second finger pushes out the bottom card a trifle and as spectator replies, and while you still are looking at him, the right hand comes over and takes the bottom card, as illustrated, while the left hand

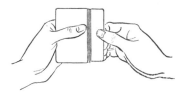

moves away in an open gesture to the spectator as you say, "Then tell everybody what card you looked at." The right hand moves to an outstretched position to your right and, as he names his card, you turn your head to look at the card you are holding while the right fingers

slowly turn the card to face the audience. Let the fingers do all the work, do not move either your hand or your right arm. Every move given is important, and the timing will make or break the trick. Remember, you are not trying to be clever. You are fooling an audience!

All cards dealt on your left hand are now replaced on the bottom of the deck. This leaves the three remaining selections in reverse order on the bottom of the deck, with the third person's card on the very bottom.

No. 3 — CARD FINDER

Ask the third person to step forward and hand him the top card of the deck saying, "Is this the card you took, sir?" He says it is not, so you continue, "I'm glad it isn't for if it were right you might think I was deceiving you with card tricks. You appear to be a difficult person to judge or figure out. I'm afraid to contend with a perfect poker face, so we'll leave it all to chance this time. Use the card you are holding as an indicator and just push it into the deck anywhere you like. Keep its back towards you."

While talking, you have cut the deck at about 15 cards from the bottom, completed the cut, and now hold a little finger break at that spot. As the spectator inserts the indicator card, see to it that it only goes into the deck about half way, and also that it goes below the break you are holding. With your right fingers move the indicator card around so that it is at right angles to the pack, and at one end, if it is not already in this position. Say, "You admit this is a chance guess, but that you will abide by it?" As you set the indicator card in position, tilt the deck so that it is upright, and retain that position. Simultaneously your right thumb pushes all the cards above the break, as a group, up about a half inch onto the back of the indicator card. (This is the same move as described elsewhere in this book in the trick entitled

" A Card In Flight".) The spectator now names his card. Your right hand grasps the indicator card and the packet of cards resting on it, the fingers resting against the face of the indicator and the right thumb pressing on the top edge of the packet of cards, and the hands are separated slowly. The indicator card now rests against the face of the bottom card of the right hand packet which, of course, is the third selected card! Show it, have it acknowledged, and dismiss the third spectator with thanks.

No. 4 — "STOP"

Now invite the fourth spectator to step forward. As he does so, replace the right hand packet of cards onto the bottom of the deck, slip off the indicator card and the third person's card and casually replace these on top of the deck. Thus you again have the last two selected cards on the bottom of the deck, the very bottom one of which is the fourth person's card.

This spectator is asked to stand at your right as you cut the deck, this time at the center, complete the cut and once more hold a break. (You had better follow this with the cards in your hands.) Hold the break at the lower right corner with the left little finger, the left thumb being free to riffle, from back to face, the upper left corners. The left forefinger should be bent in and supporting the deck from below. Now hold your left hand to your left at arm's length and as high as possible, turning your hand so that the corner being riffled faces the audience.

Tell the spectator that you will use no numbers or guesses. He is merely to think of his card, watch you riffle slowly through the pack several times and, when he feels an uncomfortable urge, say, "Stop". Now you riffle the deck several times and stop at the point he indicates. Without any further movement of arm or hand, you turn your head towards him saying, "Are you sure that was a real urge? You may try again if you wish. It's up to you." When he is satisfied, the left hand comes down in front of you with a swing and tipped forward so that the backs of the cards are facing the audience. Bring your right hand over and lift off the top packet, thumb at rear and fingers at front, and carry it back to the right again immediately so that you are holding it in front of the spectator. He now names his card and you slowly turn the pack over face up and reveal his card on the bottom of the packet. Simple? Terrifically so. Everything is fair except the pick off at the finish. The right thumb actually picks off the packet **above the break held by the left little finger,** regardless of the break

being held at the front of the deck by the left thumb. The position of
the pack and the handling absolutely prevents even one "in the know"
from seeing what goes on. (This is the same force as used in "Card in
High.")

No. 5 — "THE SPELLER"

As the fourth gentleman takes his place, the cut off packet in the
right hand is replaced on the bottom of the deck, and the card just
located is removed and pushed into the center of the pack. The last
person's card is now on the bottom of the deck, but do not allow this
to be seen. While the fifth spectator is coming up to join you, overhand
shuffle the deck, noting the bottom card, and shuffling it to the top.
Hold a little finger break below the second card from the top of the deck.

Say to the spectator, "I am sorry, but it's necessary to ask a question.
Was your card a black one?" You name the opposite color to what you
know it to be. The answer, of course, is "No." Continue, "In fact I'm
against a stone wall. It will be necessary to let the card find itself, for
my not knowing it prevents a psychological discovery such as I would
like to show. Will you see that your card is still among the others as
I fan through the deck?" The break below the second card allows these
two to be kept together as you fan through the pack with the faces
of the cards towards the spectator. He does not see his card, but, silently
spelling the first (really two) card with two letters, you slowly fan the
cards spelling out the top card's name as you do so. When you arrive
at the last letter, let the right forefinger rest on this card in front, and
keep on fanning against the forefinger. And, as you continue through
the deck, the right thumb behind the deck pushes the top card over
towards the left behind the fan. As you near the end of the deck, ask
if he has seen his card. You know the answer will be "No," but as
you ask the question, the right forefinger pushes back a little to open
the fan, the left thumb reaches over and pulls the selected card further
to the left, and the portion above the first finger is dropped back onto
the chosen card. Thus the chosen card is now in position to be spelled out.

Square up the deck at this point and hand it directly to the spectator
with the request that he fan through it and look for his card again.
He does so, and announces that he has found it. Ask him to square up
the deck, hold it face down, and name his card aloud. He then is asked
to deal one card at a time from the top of the deck as you spell out
the name of the card, letter by letter. On the last letter you stop him,
and have him turn over his own card for the climax!

An alternate finish is to use the spectator's first and last names for the spelling location rather than the name of the chosen card. This subtle way of building for the spelling is open to many variations. It is my application of a principle used in an old Jordan effect for an entirely different purpose.

So there you have it. I dislike long explanations but in this case it couldn't be helped were I to do justice to the routine. I haven't padded with a single word unless this last paragraph might be construed as unnecessary. I do know that John Hilliard wanted this routine for his book, "Greater Magic," but over the years we just never got around to making the necessary notes.

FORCES AND IMPROVEMENTS

ONE HAND CARD FORCE

TED ANNEMANN

This force is an honest to goodness pet of mine and one that I have used constantly for several years. It's a combination of two well known principles, but I have eliminated the faults of each as I think you'll agree when you try it. You'll find it particularly useful when you are standing in front of an audience and have a volunteer assisting you. You are both facing the audience, and the assistant is standing on your right. The card to be forced is either on top of the deck, or on the bottom.

Bring forth the deck and give it a thorough shuffle, controlling the force card so that at the completion of the shuffle you have brought it to the bottom, and face to face with the bottom card. There are various methods for accomplishing this, one or more of which I'm sure you know. However, the force card is now reversed on the bottom of the deck, and you are holding the deck face down in your left hand. You can give it a dovetail shuffle at this point without revealing the reversed card.

Tell the spectator that a card is to be selected but that neither he nor you will see anything that is done. Put your left hand behind your back, and ask him to reach behind your back with his left hand and cut a bunch of cards off the deck. He can't see what he is doing, but he feels the deck and cuts off any number of cards as requested. As he brings them forward you say, "You know how impossible it is for me to know how many cards you have cut off. Now kindly reach back again and take the next card for yourself." While saying this, you simply turn over the packet of cards behind your back so that the reversed bottom card is now the top card of the packet, and he reaches behind your back and draws this card. As soon as he takes it, you turn the packet over again, bring it forward and toss it on the table. The whole maneuver is excuted with one hand, and there isn't any elbow motion to give you away, nor is there any time lost. The turning of the packet with one hand is very simple. The left thumb merely tilts the packet over onto the fingers, whereupon the thumb and fingers take a new hold on it and the feat is accomplished.

FORCING WITH A DIE
TED ANNEMANN and CLEMENT DeLION

In my book, "202 Methods of Forcing," I described a method of forcing the second card in a row of four cards by casting a die, and using the number turned up by counting to the force card in the row. It is easy for you to end your count on the second card from the left of the row whenever a 2, 3, 5 or 6 turns up on the die. Just start your count from one end of the row, or the other, counting through the row and back again as required. Thus for 2 you would start your count at the left end; for 3, from the right end, etc.

However, the numbers 1 and 4 were stumbling blocks, and it was recommended that when either of these numbers turned up you tell the spectator to cast again just to prove to everyone that the die is not loaded. This was a lame excuse at best, and there was always the chance that the 1 or 4 might turn up again on the second roll.

To overcome this weak point, Mr. Clement de Lion has found the answer. When the 1 or 4 turns up merely say, "We will use the hidden number. Please lift up the die and see what is on the under side." It has to be a 6 or a 3.

If you use this once, you'll use it a lot. The novelty of it appeals to men particularly, and, in so far as the die may be any unprepared one, use one furnished by the audience whenever possible.

ADDENDA
IT GOES THIS WAY
ANNEMANN'S IMPROVEMENT ON THE ONE-WAY
BACK PRINCIPLE

CENTER DIP LENGTHENED

SEPARATION LINE

SEPARATION LINE

BOTTOM POINT CUT
OFF A TRIFLE

Performing with a one-way deck has a drawback that doesn't seem to have occurred to many performers, but which is apparent to the watchers after a trick or two. When a performer makes use of the one-way back principle he must always maneuver so that the backs can be watched. That's elementary! But I have yet to find a card man using this principle who doesn't make apparent his scrutiny of the backs in watching for a card to show up. This undue scrutiny is what registers every time, and don't think it doesn't! Although the spectator may not know anything about it all before or after, he does know or realize that the backs of the cards have been watched. There are several well known reverse back decks on the market, the League Backs being probably the easiest and fastest to work with.

To get away from depending entirely on the backs themselves, I have devised a method for marking the face of the cards so that the cards are one-way faces in combination with the one-way backs. Consequently you can use the back design at will, but whenever it is necessary to pick out a single chosen card you can fan through the face up deck and find it as easily as from the back. Thus you have a double-barrelled asset at hand that may be used for dozens of tricks.

A needle or pin is the only tool necessary, and with it you scratch mark the suit indicators as illustrated. The Spades and Clubs are separated from their standards as shown. The center dip of the Heart is lengthened, and the bottom point of the Diamond is scraped off a trifle. Thus it should be obvious that any one card reversed end for end when being put back in the deck is bound to show up like a sore thumb. Always hold the deck face towards you with the unprepared indices at the top, and simply fan the cards. The one reversed scratched card will show up immediately. That's the entire secret of this face and back one-way deck, and I'm revealing it for a good reason. My aim in writing it up is to help improve where I can, and to point out faults that others seem to be unaware of. If I can fool magicians with a subtle principle like this, you can do the same. And if you can fool magicians you won't have much trouble fooling laymen as long as you don't lose yourself in technicalities and get away from simplicity and direct action.

Editor's note: — Paul Curry in a recent issue of "The Phoenix" made reference to the above Annemann idea of scratch marking the pip in the index corner so as to distinguish it from the unmarked index pip at the opposite end. He suggested that its use was particularly valuable in tricks of a mental nature wherein you should be looking at the face of the cards. He recommended carrying the idea further and using one of the current bridge decks having a very obvious one way back. With such a deck in hand, turn half of the cards so that their backs are in opposite directions, and then go to work with your needle on the faces of all the cards. The resulting mixed condition of the backs will then rule out any possibility of "one way" to those in the know.

THE END

A CATALOG OF SELECTED
DOVER BOOKS
IN ALL FIELDS OF INTEREST

A CATALOG OF SELECTED DOVER
BOOKS IN ALL FIELDS OF INTEREST

CONCERNING THE SPIRITUAL IN ART, Wassily Kandinsky. Pioneering work by father of abstract art. Thoughts on color theory, nature of art. Analysis of earlier masters. 12 illustrations. 80pp. of text. 5⅜ x 8½.   23411-8 Pa. $3.95

ANIMALS: 1,419 Copyright-Free Illustrations of Mammals, Birds, Fish, Insects, etc., Jim Harter (ed.). Clear wood engravings present, in extremely lifelike poses, over 1,000 species of animals. One of the most extensive pictorial sourcebooks of its kind. Captions. Index. 284pp. 9 x 12.   23766-4 Pa. $12.95

CELTIC ART: The Methods of Construction, George Bain. Simple geometric techniques for making Celtic interlacements, spirals, Kells-type initials, animals, humans, etc. Over 500 illustrations. 160pp. 9 x 12. (USO)   22923-8 Pa. $9.95

AN ATLAS OF ANATOMY FOR ARTISTS, Fritz Schider. Most thorough reference work on art anatomy in the world. Hundreds of illustrations, including selections from works by Vesalius, Leonardo, Goya, Ingres, Michelangelo, others. 593 illustrations. 192pp. 7⅛ x 10¼.   20241-0 Pa. $9.95

CELTIC HAND STROKE-BY-STROKE (Irish Half-Uncial from "The Book of Kells"): An Arthur Baker Calligraphy Manual, Arthur Baker. Complete guide to creating each letter of the alphabet in distinctive Celtic manner. Covers hand position, strokes, pens, inks, paper, more. Illustrated. 48pp. 8¼ x 11.   24336-2 Pa. $3.95

EASY ORIGAMI, John Montroll. Charming collection of 32 projects (hat, cup, pelican, piano, swan, many more) specially designed for the novice origami hobbyist. Clearly illustrated easy-to-follow instructions insure that even beginning papercrafters will achieve successful results. 48pp. 8¼ x 11.   27298-2 Pa. $3.50

THE COMPLETE BOOK OF BIRDHOUSE CONSTRUCTION FOR WOOD-WORKERS, Scott D. Campbell. Detailed instructions, illustrations, tables. Also data on bird habitat and instinct patterns. Bibliography. 3 tables. 63 illustrations in 15 figures. 48pp. 5¼ x 8½.   24407-5 Pa. $2.50

BLOOMINGDALE'S ILLUSTRATED 1886 CATALOG: Fashions, Dry Goods and Housewares, Bloomingdale Brothers. Famed merchants' extremely rare catalog depicting about 1,700 products: clothing, housewares, firearms, dry goods, jewelry, more. Invaluable for dating, identifying vintage items. Also, copyright-free graphics for artists, designers. Co-published with Henry Ford Museum & Greenfield Village. 160pp. 8¼ x 11.   25780-0 Pa. $10.95

HISTORIC COSTUME IN PICTURES, Braun & Schneider. Over 1,450 costumed figures in clearly detailed engravings–from dawn of civilization to end of 19th century. Captions. Many folk costumes. 256pp. 8⅜ x 11¾.   23150-X Pa. $12.95

STICKLEY CRAFTSMAN FURNITURE CATALOGS, Gustav Stickley and L. & J. G. Stickley. Beautiful, functional furniture in two authentic catalogs from 1910. 594 illustrations, including 277 photos, show settles, rockers, armchairs, reclining chairs, bookcases, desks, tables. 183pp. 6½ x 9¼. 23838-5 Pa. $9.95

AMERICAN LOCOMOTIVES IN HISTORIC PHOTOGRAPHS: 1858 to 1949, Ron Ziel (ed.). A rare collection of 126 meticulously detailed official photographs, called "builder portraits," of American locomotives that majestically chronicle the rise of steam locomotive power in America. Introduction. Detailed captions. xi + 129pp. 9 x 12. 27393-8 Pa. $12.95

AMERICA'S LIGHTHOUSES: An Illustrated History, Francis Ross Holland, Jr. Delightfully written, profusely illustrated fact-filled survey of over 200 American lighthouses since 1716. History, anecdotes, technological advances, more. 240pp. 8 x 10¾. 25576-X Pa. $12.95

TOWARDS A NEW ARCHITECTURE, Le Corbusier. Pioneering manifesto by founder of "International School." Technical and aesthetic theories, views of industry, economics, relation of form to function, "mass-production split" and much more. Profusely illustrated. 320pp. 6⅛ x 9¼. (USO) 25023-7 Pa. $9.95

HOW THE OTHER HALF LIVES, Jacob Riis. Famous journalistic record, exposing poverty and degradation of New York slums around 1900, by major social reformer. 100 striking and influential photographs. 233pp. 10 x 7⅞. 22012-5 Pa. $10.95

FRUIT KEY AND TWIG KEY TO TREES AND SHRUBS, William M. Harlow. One of the handiest and most widely used identification aids. Fruit key covers 120 deciduous and evergreen species; twig key 160 deciduous species. Easily used. Over 300 photographs. 126pp. 5⅜ x 8½. 20511-8 Pa. $3.95

COMMON BIRD SONGS, Dr. Donald J. Borror. Songs of 60 most common U.S. birds: robins, sparrows, cardinals, bluejays, finches, more—arranged in order of increasing complexity. Up to 9 variations of songs of each species.
Cassette and manual 99911-4 $8.95

ORCHIDS AS HOUSE PLANTS, Rebecca Tyson Northen. Grow cattleyas and many other kinds of orchids—in a window, in a case, or under artificial light. 63 illustrations. 148pp. 5⅜ x 8½. 23261-1 Pa. $4.95

MONSTER MAZES, Dave Phillips. Masterful mazes at four levels of difficulty. Avoid deadly perils and evil creatures to find magical treasures. Solutions for all 32 exciting illustrated puzzles. 48pp. 8¼ x 11. 26005-4 Pa. $2.95

MOZART'S DON GIOVANNI (DOVER OPERA LIBRETTO SERIES), Wolfgang Amadeus Mozart. Introduced and translated by Ellen H. Bleiler. Standard Italian libretto, with complete English translation. Convenient and thoroughly portable—an ideal companion for reading along with a recording or the performance itself. Introduction. List of characters. Plot summary. 121pp. 5¼ x 8½. 24944-1 Pa. $2.95

TECHNICAL MANUAL AND DICTIONARY OF CLASSICAL BALLET, Gail Grant. Defines, explains, comments on steps, movements, poses and concepts. 15-page pictorial section. Basic book for student, viewer. 127pp. 5⅜ x 8½. 21843-0 Pa. $4.95

CATALOG OF DOVER BOOKS

BRASS INSTRUMENTS: Their History and Development, Anthony Baines. Authoritative, updated survey of the evolution of trumpets, trombones, bugles, cornets, French horns, tubas and other brass wind instruments. Over 140 illustrations and 48 music examples. Corrected and updated by author. New preface. Bibliography. 320pp. 5⅜ x 8½. 27574-4 Pa. $9.95

HOLLYWOOD GLAMOR PORTRAITS, John Kobal (ed.). 145 photos from 1926-49. Harlow, Gable, Bogart, Bacall; 94 stars in all. Full background on photographers, technical aspects. 160pp. 8⅜ x 11¼. 23352-9 Pa. $12.95

MAX AND MORITZ, Wilhelm Busch. Great humor classic in both German and English. Also 10 other works: "Cat and Mouse," "Plisch and Plumm," etc. 216pp. 5⅜ x 8½. 20181-3 Pa. $6.95

THE RAVEN AND OTHER FAVORITE POEMS, Edgar Allan Poe. Over 40 of the author's most memorable poems: "The Bells," "Ulalume," "Israfel," "To Helen," "The Conqueror Worm," "Eldorado," "Annabel Lee," many more. Alphabetic lists of titles and first lines. 64pp. 5³⁄₁₆ x 8¼. 26685-0 Pa. $1.00

PERSONAL MEMOIRS OF U. S. GRANT, Ulysses Simpson Grant. Intelligent, deeply moving firsthand account of Civil War campaigns, considered by many the finest military memoirs ever written. Includes letters, historic photographs, maps and more. 528pp. 6⅛ x 9¼. 28587-1 Pa. $11.95

AMULETS AND SUPERSTITIONS, E. A. Wallis Budge. Comprehensive discourse on origin, powers of amulets in many ancient cultures: Arab, Persian Babylonian, Assyrian, Egyptian, Gnostic, Hebrew, Phoenician, Syriac, etc. Covers cross, swastika, crucifix, seals, rings, stones, etc. 584pp. 5⅜ x 8½. 23573-4 Pa. $12.95

RUSSIAN STORIES/PYCCKNE PACCKA3bl: A Dual-Language Book, edited by Gleb Struve. Twelve tales by such masters as Chekhov, Tolstoy, Dostoevsky, Pushkin, others. Excellent word-for-word English translations on facing pages, plus teaching and study aids, Russian/English vocabulary, biographical/critical introductions, more. 416pp. 5⅜ x 8½. 26244-8 Pa. $8.95

PHILADELPHIA THEN AND NOW: 60 Sites Photographed in the Past and Present, Kenneth Finkel and Susan Oyama. Rare photographs of City Hall, Logan Square, Independence Hall, Betsy Ross House, other landmarks juxtaposed with contemporary views. Captures changing face of historic city. Introduction. Captions. 128pp. 8¼ x 11. 25790-8 Pa. $9.95

AIA ARCHITECTURAL GUIDE TO NASSAU AND SUFFOLK COUNTIES, LONG ISLAND, The American Institute of Architects, Long Island Chapter, and the Society for the Preservation of Long Island Antiquities. Comprehensive, well-researched and generously illustrated volume brings to life over three centuries of Long Island's great architectural heritage. More than 240 photographs with authoritative, extensively detailed captions. 176pp. 8¼ x 11. 26946-9 Pa. $14.95

NORTH AMERICAN INDIAN LIFE: Customs and Traditions of 23 Tribes, Elsie Clews Parsons (ed.). 27 fictionalized essays by noted anthropologists examine religion, customs, government, additional facets of life among the Winnebago, Crow, Zuni, Eskimo, other tribes. 480pp. 6⅛ x 9¼. 27377-6 Pa. $10.95

FRANK LLOYD WRIGHT'S HOLLYHOCK HOUSE, Donald Hoffmann. Lavishly illustrated, carefully documented study of one of Wright's most controversial residential designs. Over 120 photographs, floor plans, elevations, etc. Detailed perceptive text by noted Wright scholar. Index. 128pp. 9¼ x 10¾. 27133-1 Pa. $11.95

THE MALE AND FEMALE FIGURE IN MOTION: 60 Classic Photographic Sequences, Eadweard Muybridge. 60 true-action photographs of men and women walking, running, climbing, bending, turning, etc., reproduced from rare 19th-century masterpiece. vi + 121pp. 9 x 12. 24745-7 Pa. $10.95

1001 QUESTIONS ANSWERED ABOUT THE SEASHORE, N. J. Berrill and Jacquelyn Berrill. Queries answered about dolphins, sea snails, sponges, starfish, fishes, shore birds, many others. Covers appearance, breeding, growth, feeding, much more. 305pp. 5¼ x 8¼. 23366-9 Pa. $8.95

GUIDE TO OWL WATCHING IN NORTH AMERICA, Donald S. Heintzelman. Superb guide offers complete data and descriptions of 19 species: barn owl, screech owl, snowy owl, many more. Expert coverage of owl-watching equipment, conservation, migrations and invasions, etc. Guide to observing sites. 84 illustrations. xiii + 193pp. 5⅜ x 8½. 27344-X Pa. $8.95

MEDICINAL AND OTHER USES OF NORTH AMERICAN PLANTS: A Historical Survey with Special Reference to the Eastern Indian Tribes, Charlotte Erichsen-Brown. Chronological historical citations document 500 years of usage of plants, trees, shrubs native to eastern Canada, northeastern U.S. Also complete identifying information. 343 illustrations. 544pp. 6½ x 9¼. 25951-X Pa. $12.95

STORYBOOK MAZES, Dave Phillips. 23 stories and mazes on two-page spreads: Wizard of Oz, Treasure Island, Robin Hood, etc. Solutions. 64pp. 8¼ x 11. 23628-5 Pa. $2.95

NEGRO FOLK MUSIC, U.S.A., Harold Courlander. Noted folklorist's scholarly yet readable analysis of rich and varied musical tradition. Includes authentic versions of over 40 folk songs. Valuable bibliography and discography. xi + 324pp. 5⅜ x 8½. 27350-4 Pa. $9.95

MOVIE-STAR PORTRAITS OF THE FORTIES, John Kobal (ed.). 163 glamor, studio photos of 106 stars of the 1940s: Rita Hayworth, Ava Gardner, Marlon Brando, Clark Gable, many more. 176pp. 8⅜ x 11¼. 23546-7 Pa. $12.95

BENCHLEY LOST AND FOUND, Robert Benchley. Finest humor from early 30s, about pet peeves, child psychologists, post office and others. Mostly unavailable elsewhere. 73 illustrations by Peter Arno and others. 183pp. 5⅜ x 8½. 22410-4 Pa. $6.95

YEKL and THE IMPORTED BRIDEGROOM AND OTHER STORIES OF YIDDISH NEW YORK, Abraham Cahan. Film Hester Street based on Yekl (1896). Novel, other stories among first about Jewish immigrants on N.Y.'s East Side. 240pp. 5⅜ x 8½. 22427-9 Pa. $6.95

SELECTED POEMS, Walt Whitman. Generous sampling from *Leaves of Grass*. Twenty-four poems include "I Hear America Singing," "Song of the Open Road," "I Sing the Body Electric," "When Lilacs Last in the Dooryard Bloom'd," "O Captain! My Captain!"–all reprinted from an authoritative edition. Lists of titles and first lines. 128pp. 5$\frac{3}{16}$ x 8¼. 26878-0 Pa. $1.00

THE BEST TALES OF HOFFMANN, E. T. A. Hoffmann. 10 of Hoffmann's most important stories: "Nutcracker and the King of Mice," "The Golden Flowerpot," etc. 458pp. 5⅜ x 8½. 21793-0 Pa. $9.95

FROM FETISH TO GOD IN ANCIENT EGYPT, E. A. Wallis Budge. Rich detailed survey of Egyptian conception of "God" and gods, magic, cult of animals, Osiris, more. Also, superb English translations of hymns and legends. 240 illustrations. 545pp. 5⅜ x 8½. 25803-3 Pa. $13.95

FRENCH STORIES/CONTES FRANÇAIS: A Dual-Language Book, Wallace Fowlie. Ten stories by French masters, Voltaire to Camus: "Micromegas" by Voltaire; "The Atheist's Mass" by Balzac; "Minuet" by de Maupassant; "The Guest" by Camus, six more. Excellent English translations on facing pages. Also French-English vocabulary list, exercises, more. 352pp. 5⅜ x 8½. 26443-2 Pa. $8.95

CHICAGO AT THE TURN OF THE CENTURY IN PHOTOGRAPHS: 122 Historic Views from the Collections of the Chicago Historical Society, Larry A. Viskochil. Rare large-format prints offer detailed views of City Hall, State Street, the Loop, Hull House, Union Station, many other landmarks, circa 1904-1913. Introduction. Captions. Maps. 144pp. 9⅜ x 12¼. 24656-6 Pa. $12.95

OLD BROOKLYN IN EARLY PHOTOGRAPHS, 1865-1929, William Lee Younger. Luna Park, Gravesend race track, construction of Grand Army Plaza, moving of Hotel Brighton, etc. 157 previously unpublished photographs. 165pp. 8⅞ x 11¾. 23587-4 Pa. $13.95

THE MYTHS OF THE NORTH AMERICAN INDIANS, Lewis Spence. Rich anthology of the myths and legends of the Algonquins, Iroquois, Pawnees and Sioux, prefaced by an extensive historical and ethnological commentary. 36 illustrations. 480pp. 5⅜ x 8½. 25967-6 Pa. $8.95

AN ENCYCLOPEDIA OF BATTLES: Accounts of Over 1,560 Battles from 1479 B.C. to the Present, David Eggenberger. Essential details of every major battle in recorded history from the first battle of Megiddo in 1479 B.C. to Grenada in 1984. List of Battle Maps. New Appendix covering the years 1967-1984. Index. 99 illustrations. 544pp. 6½ x 9¼. 24913-1 Pa. $14.95

SAILING ALONE AROUND THE WORLD, Captain Joshua Slocum. First man to sail around the world, alone, in small boat. One of great feats of seamanship told in delightful manner. 67 illustrations. 294pp. 5⅜ x 8½. 20326-3 Pa. $5.95

ANARCHISM AND OTHER ESSAYS, Emma Goldman. Powerful, penetrating, prophetic essays on direct action, role of minorities, prison reform, puritan hypocrisy, violence, etc. 271pp. 5⅜ x 8½. 22484-8 Pa. $6.95

MYTHS OF THE HINDUS AND BUDDHISTS, Ananda K. Coomaraswamy and Sister Nivedita. Great stories of the epics; deeds of Krishna, Shiva, taken from puranas, Vedas, folk tales; etc. 32 illustrations. 400pp. 5⅜ x 8½. 21759-0 Pa. $10.95

BEYOND PSYCHOLOGY, Otto Rank. Fear of death, desire of immortality, nature of sexuality, social organization, creativity, according to Rankian system. 291pp. 5⅜ x 8½. 20485-5 Pa. $8.95

A THEOLOGICO-POLITICAL TREATISE, Benedict Spinoza. Also contains unfinished Political Treatise. Great classic on religious liberty, theory of government on common consent. R. Elwes translation. Total of 421pp. 5⅜ x 8½. 20249-6 Pa. $9.95

MY BONDAGE AND MY FREEDOM, Frederick Douglass. Born a slave, Douglass became outspoken force in antislavery movement. The best of Douglass' autobiographies. Graphic description of slave life. 464pp. 5⅜ x 8½. 22457-0 Pa. $8.95

FOLLOWING THE EQUATOR: A Journey Around the World, Mark Twain. Fascinating humorous account of 1897 voyage to Hawaii, Australia, India, New Zealand, etc. Ironic, bemused reports on peoples, customs, climate, flora and fauna, politics, much more. 197 illustrations. 720pp. 5⅜ x 8½. 26113-1 Pa. $15.95

THE PEOPLE CALLED SHAKERS, Edward D. Andrews. Definitive study of Shakers: origins, beliefs, practices, dances, social organization, furniture and crafts, etc. 33 illustrations. 351pp. 5⅜ x 8½. 21081-2 Pa. $8.95

THE MYTHS OF GREECE AND ROME, H. A. Guerber. A classic of mythology, generously illustrated, long prized for its simple, graphic, accurate retelling of the principal myths of Greece and Rome, and for its commentary on their origins and significance. With 64 illustrations by Michelangelo, Raphael, Titian, Rubens, Canova, Bernini and others. 480pp. 5⅜ x 8½. 27584-1 Pa. $9.95

PSYCHOLOGY OF MUSIC, Carl E. Seashore. Classic work discusses music as a medium from psychological viewpoint. Clear treatment of physical acoustics, auditory apparatus, sound perception, development of musical skills, nature of musical feeling, host of other topics. 88 figures. 408pp. 5⅜ x 8½. 21851-1 Pa. $10.95

THE PHILOSOPHY OF HISTORY, Georg W. Hegel. Great classic of Western thought develops concept that history is not chance but rational process, the evolution of freedom. 457pp. 5⅜ x 8½. 20112-0 Pa. $9.95

THE BOOK OF TEA, Kakuzo Okakura. Minor classic of the Orient: entertaining, charming explanation, interpretation of traditional Japanese culture in terms of tea ceremony. 94pp. 5⅜ x 8½. 20070-1 Pa. $3.95

LIFE IN ANCIENT EGYPT, Adolf Erman. Fullest, most thorough, detailed older account with much not in more recent books, domestic life, religion, magic, medicine, commerce, much more. Many illustrations reproduce tomb paintings, carvings, hieroglyphs, etc. 597pp. 5⅜ x 8½. 22632-8 Pa. $11.95

SUNDIALS, Their Theory and Construction, Albert Waugh. Far and away the best, most thorough coverage of ideas, mathematics concerned, types, construction, adjusting anywhere. Simple, nontechnical treatment allows even children to build several of these dials. Over 100 illustrations. 230pp. 5⅜ x 8½. 22947-5 Pa. $7.95

DYNAMICS OF FLUIDS IN POROUS MEDIA, Jacob Bear. For advanced students of ground water hydrology, soil mechanics and physics, drainage and irrigation engineering, and more. 335 illustrations. Exercises, with answers. 784pp. 6⅛ x 9¼. 65675-6 Pa. $19.95

SONGS OF EXPERIENCE: Facsimile Reproduction with 26 Plates in Full Color, William Blake. 26 full-color plates from a rare 1826 edition. Includes "The Tyger," "London," "Holy Thursday," and other poems. Printed text of poems. 48pp. 5¼ x 7. 24636-1 Pa. $4.95

OLD-TIME VIGNETTES IN FULL COLOR, Carol Belanger Grafton (ed.). Over 390 charming, often sentimental illustrations, selected from archives of Victorian graphics—pretty women posing, children playing, food, flowers, kittens and puppies, smiling cherubs, birds and butterflies, much more. All copyright-free. 48pp. 9¼ x 12¼. 27269-9 Pa. $7.95

PERSPECTIVE FOR ARTISTS, Rex Vicat Cole. Depth, perspective of sky and sea, shadows, much more, not usually covered. 391 diagrams, 81 reproductions of drawings and paintings. 279pp. 5⅜ x 8½. 22487-2 Pa. $7.95

DRAWING THE LIVING FIGURE, Joseph Sheppard. Innovative approach to artistic anatomy focuses on specifics of surface anatomy, rather than muscles and bones. Over 170 drawings of live models in front, back and side views, and in widely varying poses. Accompanying diagrams. 177 illustrations. Introduction. Index. 144pp. 8⅜ x11¼. 26723-7 Pa. $8.95

GOTHIC AND OLD ENGLISH ALPHABETS: 100 Complete Fonts, Dan X. Solo. Add power, elegance to posters, signs, other graphics with 100 stunning copyright-free alphabets: Blackstone, Dolbey, Germania, 97 more—including many lower-case, numerals, punctuation marks. 104pp. 8⅛ x 11. 24695-7 Pa. $8.95

HOW TO DO BEADWORK, Mary White. Fundamental book on craft from simple projects to five-bead chains and woven works. 106 illustrations. 142pp. 5⅜ x 8. 20697-1 Pa. $4.95

THE BOOK OF WOOD CARVING, Charles Marshall Sayers. Finest book for beginners discusses fundamentals and offers 34 designs. "Absolutely first rate . . . well thought out and well executed."—E. J. Tangerman. 118pp. 7¾ x 10⅝. 23654-4 Pa. $6.95

ILLUSTRATED CATALOG OF CIVIL WAR MILITARY GOODS: Union Army Weapons, Insignia, Uniform Accessories, and Other Equipment, Schuyler, Hartley, and Graham. Rare, profusely illustrated 1846 catalog includes Union Army uniform and dress regulations, arms and ammunition, coats, insignia, flags, swords, rifles, etc. 226 illustrations. 160pp. 9 x 12. 24939-5 Pa. $10.95

WOMEN'S FASHIONS OF THE EARLY 1900s: An Unabridged Republication of "New York Fashions, 1909," National Cloak & Suit Co. Rare catalog of mail-order fashions documents women's and children's clothing styles shortly after the turn of the century. Captions offer full descriptions, prices. Invaluable resource for fashion, costume historians. Approximately 725 illustrations. 128pp. 8⅜ x 11¼. 27276-1 Pa. $11.95

THE 1912 AND 1915 GUSTAV STICKLEY FURNITURE CATALOGS, Gustav Stickley. With over 200 detailed illustrations and descriptions, these two catalogs are essential reading and reference materials and identification guides for Stickley furniture. Captions cite materials, dimensions and prices. 112pp. 6½ x 9¼. 26676-1 Pa. $9.95

EARLY AMERICAN LOCOMOTIVES, John H. White, Jr. Finest locomotive engravings from early 19th century: historical (1804–74), main-line (after 1870), special, foreign, etc. 147 plates. 142pp. 11⅜ x 8¼. 22772-3 Pa. $10.95

THE TALL SHIPS OF TODAY IN PHOTOGRAPHS, Frank O. Braynard. Lavishly illustrated tribute to nearly 100 majestic contemporary sailing vessels: Amerigo Vespucci, Clearwater, Constitution, Eagle, Mayflower, Sea Cloud, Victory, many more. Authoritative captions provide statistics, background on each ship. 190 black-and-white photographs and illustrations. Introduction. 128pp. 8⅞ x 11¾. 27163-3 Pa. $13.95

EARLY NINETEENTH-CENTURY CRAFTS AND TRADES, Peter Stockham (ed.). Extremely rare 1807 volume describes to youngsters the crafts and trades of the day: brickmaker, weaver, dressmaker, bookbinder, ropemaker, saddler, many more. Quaint prose, charming illustrations for each craft. 20 black-and-white line illustrations. 192pp. 4⅝ x 6. 27293-1 Pa. $4.95

VICTORIAN FASHIONS AND COSTUMES FROM HARPER'S BAZAR, 1867–1898, Stella Blum (ed.). Day costumes, evening wear, sports clothes, shoes, hats, other accessories in over 1,000 detailed engravings. 320pp. 9⅜ x 12¼. 22990-4 Pa. $14.95

GUSTAV STICKLEY, THE CRAFTSMAN, Mary Ann Smith. Superb study surveys broad scope of Stickley's achievement, especially in architecture. Design philosophy, rise and fall of the Craftsman empire, descriptions and floor plans for many Craftsman houses, more. 86 black-and-white halftones. 31 line illustrations. Introduction 208pp. 6½ x 9¼. 27210-9 Pa. $9.95

THE LONG ISLAND RAIL ROAD IN EARLY PHOTOGRAPHS, Ron Ziel. Over 220 rare photos, informative text document origin (1844) and development of rail service on Long Island. Vintage views of early trains, locomotives, stations, passengers, crews, much more. Captions. 8⅞ x 11¾. 26301 0 Pa. $13.95

THE BOOK OF OLD SHIPS: From Egyptian Galleys to Clipper Ships, Henry B. Culver. Superb, authoritative history of sailing vessels, with 80 magnificent line illustrations. Galley, bark, caravel, longship, whaler, many more. Detailed, informative text on each vessel by noted naval historian. Introduction. 256pp. 5⅜ x 8½. 27332-6 Pa. $7.95

TEN BOOKS ON ARCHITECTURE, Vitruvius. The most important book ever written on architecture. Early Roman aesthetics, technology, classical orders, site selection, all other aspects. Morgan translation. 331pp. 5⅜ x 8½. 20645-9 Pa. $8.95

THE HUMAN FIGURE IN MOTION, Eadweard Muybridge. More than 4,500 stopped-action photos, in action series, showing undraped men, women, children jumping, lying down, throwing, sitting, wrestling, carrying, etc. 390pp. 7⅞ x 10⅝. 20204-6 Clothbd. $25.95

TREES OF THE EASTERN AND CENTRAL UNITED STATES AND CANADA, William M. Harlow. Best one-volume guide to 140 trees. Full descriptions, woodlore, range, etc. Over 600 illustrations. Handy size. 288pp. 4½ x 6⅜. 20395-6 Pa. $6.95

SONGS OF WESTERN BIRDS, Dr. Donald J. Borror. Complete song and call repertoire of 60 western species, including flycatchers, juncoes, cactus wrens, many more–includes fully illustrated booklet. Cassette and manual 99913-0 $8.95

GROWING AND USING HERBS AND SPICES, Milo Miloradovich. Versatile handbook provides all the information needed for cultivation and use of all the herbs and spices available in North America. 4 illustrations. Index. Glossary. 236pp. 5⅜ x 8½. 25058-X Pa. $6.95

BIG BOOK OF MAZES AND LABYRINTHS, Walter Shepherd. 50 mazes and labyrinths in all–classical, solid, ripple, and more–in one great volume. Perfect inexpensive puzzler for clever youngsters. Full solutions. 112pp. 8⅛ x 11. 22951-3 Pa. $4.95

PIANO TUNING, J. Cree Fischer. Clearest, best book for beginner, amateur. Simple repairs, raising dropped notes, tuning by easy method of flattened fifths. No previous skills needed. 4 illustrations. 201pp. 5⅜ x 8½. 23267-0 Pa. $6.95

A SOURCE BOOK IN THEATRICAL HISTORY, A. M. Nagler. Contemporary observers on acting, directing, make-up, costuming, stage props, machinery, scene design, from Ancient Greece to Chekhov. 611pp. 5⅜ x 8½. 20515-0 Pa. $12.95

THE COMPLETE NONSENSE OF EDWARD LEAR, Edward Lear. All nonsense limericks, zany alphabets, Owl and Pussycat, songs, nonsense botany, etc., illustrated by Lear. Total of 320pp. 5⅜ x 8½. (USO) 20167-8 Pa. $6.95

VICTORIAN PARLOUR POETRY: An Annotated Anthology, Michael R. Turner. 117 gems by Longfellow, Tennyson, Browning, many lesser-known poets. "The Village Blacksmith," "Curfew Must Not Ring Tonight," "Only a Baby Small," dozens more, often difficult to find elsewhere. Index of poets, titles, first lines. xxiii + 325pp. 5⅜ x 8¼. 27044-0 Pa. $8.95

DUBLINERS, James Joyce. Fifteen stories offer vivid, tightly focused observations of the lives of Dublin's poorer classes. At least one, "The Dead," is considered a masterpiece. Reprinted complete and unabridged from standard edition. 160pp. 5³⁄₁₆ x 8¼. 26870-5 Pa. $1.00

THE HAUNTED MONASTERY and THE CHINESE MAZE MURDERS, Robert van Gulik. Two full novels by van Gulik, set in 7th-century China, continue adventures of Judge Dee and his companions. An evil Taoist monastery, seemingly supernatural events; overgrown topiary maze hides strange crimes. 27 illustrations. 328pp. 5⅜ x 8½. 23502-5 Pa. $8.95

THE BOOK OF THE SACRED MAGIC OF ABRAMELIN THE MAGE, translated by S. MacGregor Mathers. Medieval manuscript of ceremonial magic. Basic document in Aleister Crowley, Golden Dawn groups. 268pp. 5⅜ x 8½. 23211-5 Pa. $8.95

NEW RUSSIAN-ENGLISH AND ENGLISH-RUSSIAN DICTIONARY, M. A. O'Brien. This is a remarkably handy Russian dictionary, containing a surprising amount of information, including over 70,000 entries. 366pp. 4½ x 6⅛. 20208-9 Pa. $9.95

HISTORIC HOMES OF THE AMERICAN PRESIDENTS, Second, Revised Edition, Irvin Haas. A traveler's guide to American Presidential homes, most open to the public, depicting and describing homes occupied by every American President from George Washington to George Bush. With visiting hours, admission charges, travel routes. 175 photographs. Index. 160pp. 8¼ x 11. 26751-2 Pa. $11.95

NEW YORK IN THE FORTIES, Andreas Feininger. 162 brilliant photographs by the well-known photographer, formerly with *Life* magazine. Commuters, shoppers, Times Square at night, much else from city at its peak. Captions by John von Hartz. 181pp. 9¼ x 10¾. 23585-8 Pa. $12.95

INDIAN SIGN LANGUAGE, William Tomkins. Over 525 signs developed by Sioux and other tribes. Written instructions and diagrams. Also 290 pictographs. 111pp. 6⅛ x 9¼. 22029-X Pa. $3.95

ANATOMY: A Complete Guide for Artists, Joseph Sheppard. A master of figure drawing shows artists how to render human anatomy convincingly. Over 460 illustrations. 224pp. 8⅜ x 11¼. 27279-6 Pa. $10.95

MEDIEVAL CALLIGRAPHY: Its History and Technique, Marc Drogin. Spirited history, comprehensive instruction manual covers 13 styles (ca. 4th century thru 15th). Excellent photographs; directions for duplicating medieval techniques with modern tools. 224pp. 8⅜ x 11¼. 26142-5 Pa. $12.95

DRIED FLOWERS: How to Prepare Them, Sarah Whitlock and Martha Rankin. Complete instructions on how to use silica gel, meal and borax, perlite aggregate, sand and borax, glycerine and water to create attractive permanent flower arrangements. 12 illustrations. 32pp. 5⅜ x 8½. 21802-3 Pa. $1.00

EASY-TO-MAKE BIRD FEEDERS FOR WOODWORKERS, Scott D. Campbell. Detailed, simple-to-use guide for designing, constructing, caring for and using feeders. Text, illustrations for 12 classic and contemporary designs. 96pp. 5⅜ x 8½. 25847-5 Pa. $2.95

SCOTTISH WONDER TALES FROM MYTH AND LEGEND, Donald A. Mackenzie. 16 lively tales tell of giants rumbling down mountainsides, of a magic wand that turns stone pillars into warriors, of gods and goddesses, evil hags, powerful forces and more. 240pp. 5⅜ x 8½. 29677-6 Pa. $6.95

THE HISTORY OF UNDERCLOTHES, C. Willett Cunnington and Phyllis Cunnington. Fascinating, well-documented survey covering six centuries of English undergarments, enhanced with over 100 illustrations: 12th-century laced-up bodice, footed long drawers (1795), 19th-century bustles, 19th-century corsets for men, Victorian "bust improvers," much more. 272pp. 5⅝ x 8¼. 27124-2 Pa. $9.95

ARTS AND CRAFTS FURNITURE: The Complete Brooks Catalog of 1912, Brooks Manufacturing Co. Photos and detailed descriptions of more than 150 now very collectible furniture designs from the Arts and Crafts movement depict davenports, settees, buffets, desks, tables, chairs, bedsteads, dressers and more, all built of solid, quarter-sawed oak. Invaluable for students and enthusiasts of antiques, Americana and the decorative arts. 80pp. 6½ x 9¼. 27471-3 Pa. $8.95

HOW WE INVENTED THE AIRPLANE: An Illustrated History, Orville Wright. Fascinating firsthand account covers early experiments, construction of planes and motors, first flights, much more. Introduction and commentary by Fred C. Kelly. 76 photographs. 96pp. 8¼ x 11. 25662-6 Pa. $8.95

THE ARTS OF THE SAILOR: Knotting, Splicing and Ropework, Hervey Garrett Smith. Indispensable shipboard reference covers tools, basic knots and useful hitches; handsewing and canvas work, more. Over 100 illustrations. Delightful reading for sea lovers. 256pp. 5⅜ x 8½. 26440-8 Pa. $7.95

FRANK LLOYD WRIGHT'S FALLINGWATER: The House and Its History, Second, Revised Edition, Donald Hoffmann. A total revision–both in text and illustrations–of the standard document on Fallingwater, the boldest, most personal architectural statement of Wright's mature years, updated with valuable new material from the recently opened Frank Lloyd Wright Archives. "Fascinating"–*The New York Times*. 116 illustrations. 128pp. 9¼ x 10¾. 27430-6 Pa. $11.95

PHOTOGRAPHIC SKETCHBOOK OF THE CIVIL WAR, Alexander Gardner. 100 photos taken on field during the Civil War. Famous shots of Manassas Harper's Ferry, Lincoln, Richmond, slave pens, etc. 244pp. 10⅝ x 8¼. 22731-6 Pa. $9.95

FIVE ACRES AND INDEPENDENCE, Maurice G. Kains. Great back-to-the-land classic explains basics of self-sufficient farming. The one book to get. 95 illustrations. 397pp. 5⅜ x 8½. 20974-1 Pa. $7.95

SONGS OF EASTERN BIRDS, Dr. Donald J. Borror. Songs and calls of 60 species most common to eastern U.S.: warblers, woodpeckers, flycatchers, thrushes, larks, many more in high-quality recording. Cassette and manual 99912-2 $9.95

A MODERN HERBAL, Margaret Grieve. Much the fullest, most exact, most useful compilation of herbal material. Gigantic alphabetical encyclopedia, from aconite to zedoary, gives botanical information, medical properties, folklore, economic uses, much else. Indispensable to serious reader. 161 illustrations. 888pp. 6½ x 9¼. 2-vol. set. (USO) Vol. I: 22798-7 Pa. $9.95
Vol. II: 22799-5 Pa. $9.95

HIDDEN TREASURE MAZE BOOK, Dave Phillips. Solve 34 challenging mazes accompanied by heroic tales of adventure. Evil dragons, people-eating plants, blood-thirsty giants, many more dangerous adversaries lurk at every twist and turn. 34 mazes, stories, solutions. 48pp. 8¼ x 11. 24566-7 Pa. $2.95

LETTERS OF W. A. MOZART, Wolfgang A. Mozart. Remarkable letters show bawdy wit, humor, imagination, musical insights, contemporary musical world; includes some letters from Leopold Mozart. 276pp. 5⅜ x 8½. 22859-2 Pa. $7.95

BASIC PRINCIPLES OF CLASSICAL BALLET, Agrippina Vaganova. Great Russian theoretician, teacher explains methods for teaching classical ballet. 118 illustrations. 175pp. 5⅜ x 8½. 22036-2 Pa. $5.95

THE JUMPING FROG, Mark Twain. Revenge edition. The original story of The Celebrated Jumping Frog of Calaveras County, a hapless French translation, and Twain's hilarious "retranslation" from the French. 12 illustrations. 66pp. 5⅜ x 8½. 22686-7 Pa. $3.95

BEST REMEMBERED POEMS, Martin Gardner (ed.). The 126 poems in this superb collection of 19th- and 20th-century British and American verse range from Shelley's "To a Skylark" to the impassioned "Renascence" of Edna St. Vincent Millay and to Edward Lear's whimsical "The Owl and the Pussycat." 224pp. 5⅜ x 8½. 27165-X Pa. $4.95

COMPLETE SONNETS, William Shakespeare. Over 150 exquisite poems deal with love, friendship, the tyranny of time, beauty's evanescence, death and other themes in language of remarkable power, precision and beauty. Glossary of archaic terms. 80pp. 5³⁄₁₆ x 8¼. 26686-9 Pa. $1.00

BODIES IN A BOOKSHOP, R. T. Campbell. Challenging mystery of blackmail and murder with ingenious plot and superbly drawn characters. In the best tradition of British suspense fiction. 192pp. 5⅜ x 8½. 24720-1 Pa. $6.95

THE WIT AND HUMOR OF OSCAR WILDE, Alvin Redman (ed.). More than 1,000 ripostes, paradoxes, wisecracks: Work is the curse of the drinking classes; I can resist everything except temptation; etc. 258pp. 5⅜ x 8½.   20602-5 Pa. $5.95

SHAKESPEARE LEXICON AND QUOTATION DICTIONARY, Alexander Schmidt. Full definitions, locations, shades of meaning in every word in plays and poems. More than 50,000 exact quotations. 1,485pp. 6½ x 9¼. 2-vol. set.
Vol. 1: 22726-X Pa. $16.95
Vol. 2: 22727-8 Pa. $16.95

SELECTED POEMS, Emily Dickinson. Over 100 best-known, best-loved poems by one of America's foremost poets, reprinted from authoritative early editions. No comparable edition at this price. Index of first lines. 64pp. 5³⁄₁₆ x 8¼.
26466-1 Pa. $1.00

CELEBRATED CASES OF JUDGE DEE (DEE GOONG AN), translated by Robert van Gulik. Authentic 18th-century Chinese detective novel; Dee and associates solve three interlocked cases. Led to van Gulik's own stories with same characters. Extensive introduction. 9 illustrations. 237pp. 5⅜ x 8½.   23337-5 Pa. $6.95

THE MALLEUS MALEFICARUM OF KRAMER AND SPRENGER, translated by Montague Summers. Full text of most important witchhunter's "bible," used by both Catholics and Protestants. 278pp. 6⅝ x 10.   22802-9 Pa. $12.95

SPANISH STORIES/CUENTOS ESPAÑOLES: A Dual-Language Book, Angel Flores (ed.). Unique format offers 13 great stories in Spanish by Cervantes, Borges, others. Faithful English translations on facing pages. 352pp. 5⅜ x 8½.
25399-6 Pa. $8.95

THE CHICAGO WORLD'S FAIR OF 1893: A Photographic Record, Stanley Appelbaum (ed.). 128 rare photos show 200 buildings, Beaux-Arts architecture, Midway, original Ferris Wheel, Edison's kinetoscope, more. Architectural emphasis; full text. 116pp. 8¼ x 11.   23990-X Pa. $9.95

OLD QUEENS, N.Y., IN EARLY PHOTOGRAPHS, Vincent F. Seyfried and William Asadorian. Over 160 rare photographs of Maspeth, Jamaica, Jackson Heights, and other areas. Vintage views of DeWitt Clinton mansion, 1939 World's Fair and more. Captions. 192pp. 8⅞ x 11.   26358-4 Pa. $12.95

CAPTURED BY THE INDIANS: 15 Firsthand Accounts, 1750-1870, Frederick Drimmer. Astounding true historical accounts of grisly torture, bloody conflicts, relentless pursuits, miraculous escapes and more, by people who lived to tell the tale. 384pp. 5⅜ x 8½.   24901-8 Pa. $8.95

THE WORLD'S GREAT SPEECHES, Lewis Copeland and Lawrence W. Lamm (eds.). Vast collection of 278 speeches of Greeks to 1970. Powerful and effective models; unique look at history. 842pp. 5⅜ x 8½.   20468-5 Pa. $14.95

THE BOOK OF THE SWORD, Sir Richard F. Burton. Great Victorian scholar/adventurer's eloquent, erudite history of the "queen of weapons"–from prehistory to early Roman Empire. Evolution and development of early swords, variations (sabre, broadsword, cutlass, scimitar, etc.), much more. 336pp. 6⅛ x 9¼.
25434-8 Pa. $9.95

AUTOBIOGRAPHY: The Story of My Experiments with Truth, Mohandas K. Gandhi. Boyhood, legal studies, purification, the growth of the Satyagraha (nonviolent protest) movement. Critical, inspiring work of the man responsible for the freedom of India. 480pp. 5⅜ x 8½. (USO) 24593-4 Pa. $8.95

CELTIC MYTHS AND LEGENDS, T. W. Rolleston. Masterful retelling of Irish and Welsh stories and tales. Cuchulain, King Arthur, Deirdre, the Grail, many more. First paperback edition. 58 full-page illustrations. 512pp. 5⅜ x 8½. 26507-2 Pa. $9.95

THE PRINCIPLES OF PSYCHOLOGY, William James. Famous long course complete, unabridged. Stream of thought, time perception, memory, experimental methods; great work decades ahead of its time. 94 figures. 1,391pp. 5⅜ x 8½. 2-vol. set.
Vol. I: 20381-6 Pa. $12.95
Vol. II: 20382-4 Pa. $12.95

THE WORLD AS WILL AND REPRESENTATION, Arthur Schopenhauer. Definitive English translation of Schopenhauer's life work, correcting more than 1,000 errors, omissions in earlier translations. Translated by E. F. J. Payne. Total of 1,269pp. 5⅜ x 8½. 2-vol. set.
Vol. 1: 21761-2 Pa. $11.95
Vol. 2: 21762-0 Pa. $12.95

MAGIC AND MYSTERY IN TIBET, Madame Alexandra David-Neel. Experiences among lamas, magicians, sages, sorcerers, Bonpa wizards. A true psychic discovery. 32 illustrations. 321pp. 5⅜ x 8½. (USO) 22682-4 Pa. $8.95

THE EGYPTIAN BOOK OF THE DEAD, E. A. Wallis Budge. Complete reproduction of Ani's papyrus, finest ever found. Full hieroglyphic text, interlinear transliteration, word-for-word translation, smooth translation. 533pp. 6½ x 9¼.
21866-X Pa. $10.95

MATHEMATICS FOR THE NONMATHEMATICIAN, Morris Kline. Detailed, college-level treatment of mathematics in cultural and historical context, with numerous exercises. Recommended Reading Lists. Tables. Numerous figures. 641pp. 5⅜ x 8½.
24823-2 Pa. $11.95

THEORY OF WING SECTIONS: Including a Summary of Airfoil Data, Ira H. Abbott and A. E. von Doenhoff. Concise compilation of subsonic aerodynamic characteristics of NACA wing sections, plus description of theory. 350pp. of tables. 693pp. 5⅜ x 8½. 60586-8 Pa. $14.95

THE RIME OF THE ANCIENT MARINER, Gustave Doré, S. T. Coleridge. Doré's finest work; 34 plates capture moods, subtleties of poem. Flawless full-size reproductions printed on facing pages with authoritative text of poem. "Beautiful. Simply beautiful."—*Publisher's Weekly*. 77pp. 9¼ x 12. 22305-1 Pa. $6.95

NORTH AMERICAN INDIAN DESIGNS FOR ARTISTS AND CRAFTSPEOPLE, Eva Wilson. Over 360 authentic copyright-free designs adapted from Navajo blankets, Hopi pottery, Sioux buffalo hides, more. Geometrics, symbolic figures, plant and animal motifs, etc. 128pp. 8⅜ x 11. (EUK) 25341-4 Pa. $8.95

SCULPTURE: Principles and Practice, Louis Slobodkin. Step-by-step approach to clay, plaster, metals, stone; classical and modern. 253 drawings, photos. 255pp. 8⅛ x 11.
22960-2 Pa. $11.95

THE INFLUENCE OF SEA POWER UPON HISTORY, 1660–1783, A. T. Mahan. Influential classic of naval history and tactics still used as text in war colleges. First paperback edition. 4 maps. 24 battle plans. 640pp. 5⅜ x 8½. 25509-3 Pa. $12.95

THE STORY OF THE TITANIC AS TOLD BY ITS SURVIVORS, Jack Winocour (ed.). What it was really like. Panic, despair, shocking inefficiency, and a little heroism. More thrilling than any fictional account. 26 illustrations. 320pp. 5⅜ x 8½. 20610-6 Pa. $8.95

FAIRY AND FOLK TALES OF THE IRISH PEASANTRY, William Butler Yeats (ed.). Treasury of 64 tales from the twilight world of Celtic myth and legend: "The Soul Cages," "The Kildare Pooka," "King O'Toole and his Goose," many more. Introduction and Notes by W. B. Yeats. 352pp. 5⅜ x 8½. 26941-8 Pa. $8.95

BUDDHIST MAHAYANA TEXTS, E. B. Cowell and Others (eds.). Superb, accurate translations of basic documents in Mahayana Buddhism, highly important in history of religions. The Buddha-karita of Asvaghosha, Larger Sukhavativyuha, more. 448pp. 5⅜ x 8½. 25552-2 Pa. $12.95

ONE TWO THREE . . . INFINITY: Facts and Speculations of Science, George Gamow. Great physicist's fascinating, readable overview of contemporary science: number theory, relativity, fourth dimension, entropy, genes, atomic structure, much more. 128 illustrations. Index. 352pp. 5⅜ x 8½. 25664-2 Pa. $8.95

ENGINEERING IN HISTORY, Richard Shelton Kirby, et al. Broad, nontechnical survey of history's major technological advances: birth of Greek science, industrial revolution, electricity and applied science, 20th-century automation, much more. 181 illustrations. ". . . excellent . . ."–*Isis*. Bibliography. vii + 530pp. 5⅜ x 8¼. 26412-2 Pa. $14.95

DALÍ ON MODERN ART: The Cuckolds of Antiquated Modern Art, Salvador Dalí. Influential painter skewers modern art and its practitioners. Outrageous evaluations of Picasso, Cézanne, Turner, more. 15 renderings of paintings discussed. 44 calligraphic decorations by Dalí. 96pp. 5⅜ x 8½. (USO) 29220-7 Pa. $4.95

ANTIQUE PLAYING CARDS: A Pictorial History, Henry René D'Allemagne. Over 900 elaborate, decorative images from rare playing cards (14th–20th centuries): Bacchus, death, dancing dogs, hunting scenes, royal coats of arms, players cheating, much more. 96pp. 9¼ x 12¼. 29265-7 Pa. $11.95

MAKING FURNITURE MASTERPIECES: 30 Projects with Measured Drawings, Franklin H. Gottshall. Step-by-step instructions, illustrations for constructing handsome, useful pieces, among them a Sheraton desk, Chippendale chair, Spanish desk, Queen Anne table and a William and Mary dressing mirror. 224pp. 8⅛ x 11¼. 29338-6 Pa. $13.95

THE FOSSIL BOOK: A Record of Prehistoric Life, Patricia V. Rich et al. Profusely illustrated definitive guide covers everything from single-celled organisms and dinosaurs to birds and mammals and the interplay between climate and man. Over 1,500 illustrations. 760pp. 7½ x 10⅛. 29371-8 Pa. $29.95

Prices subject to change without notice.

Available at your book dealer or write for free catalog to Dept. GI, Dover Publications, Inc., 31 East 2nd St., Mineola, N.Y. 11501. Dover publishes more than 500 books each year on science, elementary and advanced mathematics, biology, music, art, literary history, social sciences and other areas.